A PHILOSOPHER'S HARVEST

The Philosophical Papers of ISAAC FRANCK

A PHILOSOPHER'S HARVEST

The Philosophical Papers of Isaac Franck

William Gerber

EDITOR

GEORGETOWN UNIVERSITY PRESS

Washington, D.C.

Original sources of the papers in this volume are indicated in a box on the opening page of each chapter.

Printed in the United States of America

Library of Congress Cataloging-in-Publication Data

Franck, Isaac.
A philosopher's harvest : the philosophical papers of Isaac Franck / William Gerber, editor.
p. cm.
Bibliography: p.
ISBN 0-87840-459-7. ISBN 0-87840-460-0 (pbk.)
1. Philosophy, Jewish. 2. Philosophy. I. Gerber, William, 1908- . II. Title.
B945.F693P45 1988 88-4704
100—dc19 CIP

Contents

IV. Other Topics

Isaac Franck: As I Remember Him

Who can compare with the wise man?
Who else understands what things mean?
A Man's wisdom lights up his face, and
the hardness of his countenance is transformed.

Eccles. Viii, 1

I shall always remember my first and last meetings with Isaac Franck. In the first, I was introduced to the quality of his mind, and in the last to the quality of his person. In the years between, I came to appreciate the qualities of both, so familiar to his friends and colleagues, but so difficult to transmit even in his own essays.

A word or two about those meetings might not be remiss for those who will read this work but perhaps will not have had the pleasure of Isaac's presence among them. It is always important to know when a philosopher's teaching and thinking so closely conform to the way he lived his life.

My first meeting occurred during a seminar at The Catholic University of America when I was its President. An eminent scholar had just delivered a fine talk on a topic in medieval philosophy. He had handled several difficult questions faultlessly when Professor Franck, whom I had never met, raised his hand. In a quiet, precise, polite, yet pointed way, Franck went directly to the heart of the speaker's argument. Gracefully, but unequivocally, he uncovered each flaw in the line of reasoning and offered remedies drawn from his own considerable erudition in both the Jewish and Christian medieval philosophy.

Here was the philosopher in a classical mode—the man in pursuit of wisdom, the patient teacher, at one with the student in the quest for knowledge, the gifted scholar at home with both Maimonides and Aquinas. Franck made his points meticulously but without condescension and also without the mordant air that so frequently sours philosophic discourse. Logical analysis was at the service of a new synthesis, not the tool of intellectual hubris.

Isaac Franck took his philosophy full strength. Not for him the neurotic self-analysis of the post-foundational, post-analytic school. He tackled the recurrent problems: Who and what is man? What is his destiny? What kind of life should he lead? What kind of community should he forge? He would have found alien the humbler task of "underlaborer," i.e., the philosopher as maieutic assistant in the parturition of ideas conceived by the other disciplines.

Yet, even as Franck pursued wisdom with the tools of reason, he recognized the limitations of those tools. He philosophized from a Jewish perspective, conscious always of the Law and the Word, and the ineffable God behind it all. This is, I believe, why he was so fascinated with Maimonides and Spinoza, on whose work he throws such interesting light in these essays. He tackled, perhaps for the same reason, the questions of freedom and determinism generated by modern psychology, as well as the ethical implications of a misreading of some of its fundamental concepts. Perhaps most significant in this respect is his essay confronting what it is we can know about God. Drawing on both Aquinas and Maimonides, Franck argues convincingly for a distinction between a knowledge of God's existence and a knowledge of his nature.

But these essays can give only a glimpse of the range of Franck's speculative and practical intelligence. They do not, for example, convey the increasing depth of his interests in the problems of contemporary bioethics, particularly as they might be approached in the Judaic tradition. These interests were evident in his vigorous participation in our weekly discussions of bioethical papers at the Kennedy Institute of Ethics. In 1980, Dr. Franck edited one of the first series of papers on biomedical ethics from the standpoint of Jewish tradition and teaching. He was also responsible for a special issue of the *Journal of Medicine and Philosophy* on the same topic.

What is also not fully revealed in his writing is Isaac Franck's practical wisdom—his unusual ability to bring his philosophy into contact with the most difficult problems of the day. His leadership in the Jewish community in Washington, and in the reconciliation of the races during and after the Washington riots, has been widely acclaimed. To all of his "active" pursuits he brought the calm cogitation of the "contemplative" so that action was always tempered by thought, and thought by action.

During my years as Director of the Kennedy Institute of Ethics, I often took advantage of Isaac's wisdom and practical good sense. His office door was always open. He always suffered my intrusions into his reading and writing with graciousness. We often shared our mutual admiration for Aquinas and Maimonides. He gave me freely of his knowledge of the Hebrew Scriptures and the Judaic tradition. I profited immensely from the play of his mind over the problems I brought him. I always left better informed and better disposed to a solution than when I entered.

My last meeting with Isaac was on the day before he entered the hospital for surgery of a pancreatic carcinoma. He was already jaundiced to such a degree that it took little diagnostic acumen to discern that he was mortally ill. We had discussed several times the terrible implications of the diagnosis. He understood clearly what risks he ran and what poor chances lay before him. Nonetheless, there he was, two days before surgery attending the regular Tuesday luncheon seminar and taking full part in the discussion with undiminished enthusiasm and astuteness. As we parted that day I suspected—as I believe he did—that our goodbye was a final one. In his confrontation with death he was true to the dictum that the purpose of philosophy is to learn to die well.

Isaac Franck's family, friends and colleagues are indebted to William Gerber for selecting and editing these essays. It is fitting that they be published by the Georgetown University Press, to whose parent university he felt so close and to which he contributed so much.

Edmund D. Pellegrino, M.D.

Preface

Isaac Frank's contributions to humane letters were not only numerous but weighty. He directed the light of his learning on topics as varied as community relations and metaphysics. Moreover, in every area of interest that he undertook to write about he brought to light previously unnoticed facets and subjected them to sympathetic but thorough examination.

The present volume constitutes a selection of Franck's major philosophical essays. Most of the essays included here were previously published in professional journals or in cooperative, multi-author books. I heartily thank the editors of those journals, and the owners of the copyright of the books, for generously granting permission to reprint the essays.

In preparing these essays for publication in the present volume, I have aimed to make only such editorial adjustments as were required for consistency of printing style. For example, whereas citations in the essays as originally published appear in some cases at the bottoms of the proper pages and in other cases at the end of the study, here all citations and other footnotes are printed at the bottoms of the proper pages.

I have harmonized the style of citations, abbreviations, spelling, capitalization, etc., within each essay, but where one style was used in one essay and another style was used in another, I have not made them all conform to a single, Procrustean set of typographical rules.

In addition, the titles of sources cited have been harmonized within each essay, but not in all cases between essays. As an illustration, where Maimonides' *Guide* is called *The Guide of the Perplexed* more or less regularly in one essay and *The Guide for the Perplexed* in another essay, I have made the wording of the title consistent in this respect only within each essay.

A few misprints and other inadvertencies have been corrected or smoothed over.

Brackets in the text of an essay are Franck's. Occasionally in a footnote I have made an insertion and have so indicated by the bracketed words "Note by W.G."

It is a pleasure to record my appreciation of the help that I have received from Edmund Pellegrino and Pearl Franck in the work on this project. I trust that the volume will constitute a worthy memorial to a dedicated and creative scholar whom I am proud to have counted as a friend.

W.G.

I. Maimonides

1. *Maimonides and Aquinas on Man's Knowledge of God: A Twentieth-Century Perspective*

2. *Maimonides' Philosophy Today*

1. *Maimonides and Aquinas on Man's Knowledge of God: A Twentieth-Century Perspective*

In the opening chapter of his book, *Eclipse of God,* Martin Buber recalls the hesitant but passionate reaction of a friend, an elderly scholar, against the author's repeated use of the word "God" in one of his writings:

> "How can you bring yourself to say 'God' time after time?" the old scholar asked. "How can you expect that your readers will take the word in the sense in which you wish it to be taken? What you mean by the name of God is something above all human grasp and comprehension, but in speaking about it you have lowered it to human conceptualization. What word of human speech is so misused, so defiled, so desecrated as this!"[1]

A long backward leap in time is undertaken in this essay, from the idea of God as adumbrated in the words of Buber's aging friend to the "negative theology" of Moses Maimonides and Thomas Aquinas. On the question, "Can man have knowledge of God?" neither the simple statement by Buber's friend that "God is something above all human grasp and comprehension," nor the more complex views propounded by Maimonides and Aquinas, seem to have wide acceptance among philosophers and theologians today. Indeed, in the past two or three decades several sharp attacks have appeared against negative theology and its doctrine of the *unknowability of God.*

It would thus seem appropriate at this time to set forth some of the elements of a radical negative theology, the principal tenet of which is

[1]Martin Buber, *Eclipse of God* (New York: Harper, 1952), pp. 16–17.

The Review of Metaphysics, vol. 38, March 1985, pp. 591–615.

that while we do know *that God is,* on the other hand, *what* God is, i.e., God's *nature* or *essence,* in the words of Thomas Aquinas, "remains absolutely unknown" (*penitus manet ignotum*).[2] With some significant deviations or modifications, the doctrine outlined here of the utter unknowability of God is derived from Rabbi Moses ben Maimon, the towering 12th-century Jewish philosopher and theologian, more widely known as Moses Maimonides, and from Saint Thomas Aquinas, who was thoroughly familiar with Maimonides' major philosophical work, *The Guide of the Perplexed,* and was clearly influenced by it.

Before presenting an extended consideration of the views of Maimonides and Aquinas on man's knowledge of God, it will be of value to note that much of the contemporary criticism of negative theology and of the doctrine of the unknowability of God has concentrated, as we shall see below, on exposing alleged logical flaws in its reasoning. These criticisms require and deserve attention, and such comments as need to be made on some of them by way of rejoinder will be reserved for the second half of this paper. However, part of the analysis by one of these critics will be helpful at this point in the pursuit of the question of God's knowability.

In his acute and instructive essay entitled, "What We Can Say About God," Fred Sommers provides the reader with a distillation of essentially five views, or doctrines, classified according to their claims as to what attributes we may predicate of the divine being.[3]

1. That which Sommers calls "the naive, anthropomorphic view" according to which everything predicable of a human being is also predicable of the divine being
2. The "standard or sophisticated conception," rooted in Cartesian ontology and in the theology seemingly entailed by Descartes' ontology, namely, that no *material* predicates may be predicated of God
3. The view which rejects Descartes' dualistic ontology, but also rejects the naive anthropomorphic theology (referred to in doctrine 1 above), and therefore must, according to Sommers, end up with an animistic or panpsychistic metaphysics like that of Alfred North Whitehead, and a theology that speaks of God as a bodiless spirit

[2]Thomas Aquinas, *On the Truth of the Catholic Faith—Summa contra gentiles,* trans. Anton C. Pegis (New York: Image Books, Doubleday Doran, 1955), book 3, chapter 49, par. 9, p. 170. Cf. Anton C. Pegis, "*Penitus Manet Ignotum,*" in *Medieval Studies* 27 (1965): 212–26.

[3]Fred Sommers, "What We Can Say About God," *Judaism: A Quarterly Journal of Jewish Life and Thought* (Winter 1966): 61–73.

4. The view, which has been called "negative theology," but which falls short of being thoroughgoingly negative, namely, the view that nothing predicable of man is predicable of God
5. The doctrine that no affirmative or *positive attributes of any kind* are predicable of God, that God is completely unknown and unknowable, that we can meaningfully say about God only *what he is not* (to speak of Him in *negative attributes*); the doctrine that man's highest knowledge of God is to know that we are *unable to know Him*

We need be concerned here only with doctrines 4 and 5, since the views of both Maimonides and Aquinas are clearly at this end of Sommers's spectrum of possible positions. The differences between these two philosophers (albeit minimal on the main issue), and the apparent ambivalence discernible both in Aquinas and in Maimonides, make it perhaps a little risky to ascribe to them categorically doctrine 5 rather than 4, for fear of projecting on them the *extreme* view espoused in this paper. But at this point we had best let the two philosophers and some of their texts speak for themselves.

II

Maimonides' incisive and striking treatment of the problem of divine attributes, and of man's knowledge of God, is developed principally in Chapters 51 through 60 of Book 1 of *The Guide of the Perplexed*.[4] His conclusion is that no positive attributes may be predicated of God. The only affirmative attributes that may be employed in speaking about God are those that in fact refer to God's *actions* and their *effects* but "do not mean that He possesses qualities" or that such attributes are "notions subsisting within the essence of the agent"—meaning God—or are superadded to God's essence. (This modification of his negative theology is surely a Maimonidean equiv-

[4]Moses Maimonides, *The Guide of the Perplexed.* The standard Arabic edition is *Dalalat Al-ha'irin,* ed. Issachar Joel (Jerusalem: J. Jumovitch, 1930–31). The most authoritative English translation is by Shlomo Pines, with an introductory essay by Leo Strauss (Chicago: University of Chicago Press, 1963), pp. 112–47.

(Moses Maimonides was born in 1135 and died in 1204. His philosophic *magnum opus* was *The Guide of the Perplexed,* written in Arabic but in Hebrew characters, and completed about the year 1190. The first translation into Hebrew was completed in the year of the author's death. One or more translations into Latin were made from the Hebrew and were in circulation among Christian philosophers and theologians well before the middle of the 13th century.)

ocation. It is noted by Aquinas in his *De Potentia Dei* and is properly criticized by him.)

Moreover, the ascription of positive attributes to God either constitutes in fact a definition by genus and differentia which would function merely as a stipulative, nominal definition of a term, and would thus tell us nothing about God. On the other hand, it may be a *real* or *essential* definition. But this would entail the assumption of a higher genus than God, under which God could be subsumed, and would thus imply an assumed cause for the *definiendum.* But God, who has no causes anterior to Him, and for Whom there is no higher genus, cannot be thus defined. Another kind of predication of attributes would constitute a *partial* definition because it would offer only a partial *definiens*—for example, in the case of man, the assertion that man is a living thing. This kind of predication would suggest that if we could properly ascribe to God *part* of an essence, then His essence would have to be composite. This we must reject as we reject any notion of plurality within God. The rejection of plurality also requires the rejection of a multiplicity of all kinds of qualities, and thus also a rejection of quantity, as belonging to the nature or essence of God. Finally, any affirmative attributes that might be proposed as predicable of God are *human conceptions,* and it is an error to assume that there is a relation or a correlation between God and these human conceptions or the referents for which they stand. There cannot be any such correlation between God's existence and the existence of things and their qualities, since God

> has a necessary existence while that which is other than He has a possible or contingent existence. . . . There accordingly can be no correlation between them. . . . For it is impossible to represent to oneself that a relation subsists between the intellect and color . . . although both of them are comprised by the same "existence." How then can a relation be represented between Him and what is other than He when there is no notion comprising in any respect both of the two, inasmuch as existence is . . . affirmed of Him . . . and of what is other than He merely by way of absolute equivocation . . . How could there subsist a relation between Him . . . and any of the things created by Him, given the immense difference between them with regard to the true reality of their existence, than which there is no greater difference?[5]

This exclusive and absolute distinction between God and what is not God logically rules out for Maimonides even any analogical predication. Aquinas, however, does allow it, though apparently with some reservations. The logic of Maimonides' rejection of analogical

[5]Ibid., Chapter 52, pp. 117–18.

predication is clearly based on one or both of two considerations that are corollaries of his negative theology:

(1) For an attribute *X* (e.g., "good") to be predicated analogically of two entities, e.g., God and man, it would be necessary first to know that the attribute under discussion as it applies to one of the entities in the analogy is the same as, similar to, or overlaps with the attribute as it applies to the other entity in the analogy. There can be no analogy unless at least such similarity or overlapping exists. However, since we cannot possibly know what the attribute *X* would mean in its application to God, we have nothing on which to base an analogical ascription of attribute *X* to both God and man.

(2) The doctrine of the absolute and irreducible difference between God and what is not God means that any attribute *X* when predicated of God, if such predication were possible, would be completely and utterly different from the predicate carrying the same name when it is predicated of man, and therefore no analogy would be possible.

Predicating positive attributes of God would thus result in unavoidable equivocation, not because, as Aristotle maintained, things of different types can *never* have the same attributes. Indeed, as Sommers has shown, when *comparisons* are admissible between two things of different types with respect to a given attribute, that attribute *can* be predicated *univocally* of both things, as, for example, when it makes sense to say that the duration in time of the solar eclipse was less, or more, or about the same as the duration in time of my working out this algebraic equation.[6] Rather, the unavoidability of equivocation when positive attributes are predicated of God results precisely because the radical otherness of God makes all comparisons between God and other things utterly impossible, and any term used both about God and about other things therefore cannot be used univocally. There indeed is no middle ground here between univocity and equivocity.

What then can we know or say about the nature or essence of God? We can only speak in terms of *negative* predications. *We do not know what God is,* but we can and must only say *what God is not.* This is the doctrine of "negative attributes," or of the knowledge of God through the *via negativa.* When we say that God exists, the only meaning this can have is that non-existence is impossible for Him. When we say that God is living, the only possible meaning of the statement is that He is not dead or not mortal. When we say that He is eternal, what it means is that no cause has brought Him into existence. When we say "that He is powerful and knowing and willing" this is only to signify "that He is neither powerless, nor inattentive, nor negligent."[7] Or,

[6]Fred Sommers, "What We Can Say About God," pp. 63–65.

[7]Moses Maimonides, *The Guide of the Perplexed,* I, 58, p. 136.

to restate it once more in one of Rabbi Moses' own succinct formulations:

> Consequently, He exists, but not through an existence other than His essence; and similarly He lives, but not through life; He is powerful, but not through power; He knows, but not through knowledge.[8]

By way of anticipation of the next section, on Aquinas' negative theology, it is worth noting here that, whereas in other texts Aquinas states this Maimonidean doctrine as his own, in *De Potentia Dei* (q. 7, a. 2) he quotes in the name of Maimonides, giving an almost exact translation of the above:

> Rabbi Moses says that God is a being but not in an essence, is living but not with life, is powerful but not with power, wise but not with wisdom.

It is not the case, Maimonides insists, that God's existence, or knowledge, or life, or power, is more permanent, more durable, greater, or more perfect than ours. "The matter is not so in any respect," Maimonides emphasizes.[9]

God is utterly different. When we say that God is *one,* what is meant is not numerical oneness. "The meaning is that He has no equal and not that the notion of oneness attaches to His essence."[10] God is unique; He is *sui generis;* He is, to borrow a phrase from Rudolf Otto, *"wholly other."*[11] It is this doctrine of God's otherness, of His uniqueness, that dictates the doctrine of negative attributes. That human descriptions cannot express the essence of God, that the human mind cannot know what God's nature is, is only another way of saying that God is non-human. "We are only able to apprehend the fact that He is, and cannot apprehend his quiddity," says Maimonides.[12] Only God can apprehend or know His own essence. God's knowledge and man's knowledge are heterotypical, and in God, in Whom there is no plurality, His knowledge and His essence are one and the same. Accordingly, man cannot even desire or try to know God's essence.

For man to desire or endeavor to know God's essence would be as if man wished or endeavored to have *God's apprehension* or *God's*

[8]Ibid., I, 57, p. 132.
[9]Ibid., I, 56, p. 130.
[10]Ibid., I, 57, p. 133.
[11]Rudolf Otto, *The Idea of the Holy,* trans. John W. Harvey (Oxford: Oxford University Press, 1926), pp. 25ff.
[12]Moses Maimonides, *The Guide of the Perplexed,* I, 58, p. 135.

knowledge. But "we cannot comprehend God's knowledge . . . for He is His knowledge and His knowledge is He," hence our desire to know Him would be "as if we desired that we be He and our apprehension His apprehension."[13] What is known to man is necessarily known in terms of *human* knowledge. God's essence cannot be known to man because knowledge of God is available only to God himself—His knowledge and His essence being one and the same—and not to man. For man to try to *know* God would be as if man tried to *be* God. Thus, the formulation of this doctrine by some commentators in the form of the epigrammatic apothegm, "If I knew Him, I would be He" *(Ilu y'dativ, he'yitiv),*[14] is clearly in full consonance with the Maimonidean spirit.

Let us then conclude this less than fully adequate account of the negative theology of Moses ben Maimon by summarizing in his own words:

> [I]t is not possible, except through negation, to achieve even that [limited] apprehension of God which it is in our power to achieve, . . . on the other hand, negation does not give knowledge in any respect of the true reality of the thing with regard to which the particular matter in question has been negated. . . . God cannot be apprehended by the human intellect, and none but He himself can apprehend what He is, and our knowledge [of Him] consists in our knowledge that we are unable truly to apprehend Him.[15]

It is interesting to note the slight variations in the rendering of the concluding clause by various translators. However, the core meaning is unambiguously clear. Shlomo Pines's version is: ". . . our apprehension of Him consists in our inability to attain the ultimate term in apprehending Him."[16] Friedlander's rendition is "our knowledge of Him consists in knowing that we are unable truly to comprehend

[13]Ibid., III, 21, p. 485.

[14]See Simon Rawidowicz, *"Adam Ve'eloha: Prakim B'toldot Ha'elohut shel Harambam"* ("God and Man: Chapters in Maimonides' Theology"), in *I'yunim Bmakshevet Yisrael (Studies in Jewish Thought)* (Jerusalem: Rubin Mass) 1 (1969): 297–331, esp. pp. 297–303. There appears to be some confusion about the authorship of the apothegm, "If I knew Him, I would be He." Rawidowicz does not directly ascribe it to Maimonides, but says only that his formulated doctrine is Maimonides' version of the apothegm. However, Julius Guttmann does ascribe it to Maimonides, in his lecture *"Typussim shel Havayah Datit"* ("Types of Religious Experience"), in *D'Varim al Haphilosophia shel Hadat (Lectures on the Philosophy of Religion)* by Julius Guttmann (Jerusalem: The Hebrew University, 1958), p. 93. I have not been able to find this apothegm, *in his verbis,* in any Maimonidean text.

[15]Moses Maimonides, *The Guide of the Perplexed,* I, 59, p. 139.

[16]Ibid.

Him."[17] Jacob B. Agus's translation is: "We understand Him in the measure in which we grasp His final incomprehensibility."[18]

III

Let us now turn to the negative theology of Thomas Aquinas. We cannot be diverted for more than a paragraph or two to the interesting *historical* matter of Maimonides' influence on Aquinas. One need only refer to such scholars as Richard McKeon[19] and Etienne Gilson[20] for some of the evidence. However, the following should be noted here, in addition to what has already been said. The works of other medieval Christian philosophers and theologians immediately before and after Thomas contain numerous references to Maimonides' *Guide*. Among them, probably the most notable was Albertus Magnus (ca. 1200–1280). A German monograph on the relationship between Albert the Great and Maimonides, published in 1863, exhibits many extensive passages from Albert and Rabbi Moses, in parallel columns, which show them to be either completely or almost completely identical. The author of the monograph, M. Joel, stated:

[17]Moses Maimonides, *The Guide of the Perplexed,* trans. M. Friedlander (New York: Hebrew Publishing Company, 1881), p. 215.

[18]Jacob B. Agus, *The Evolution of Jewish Thought* (New York: Abelard-Schuman, 1959), p. 189.

[19]Richard McKeon, "Maimonides the Philosopher," in *Essays on Maimonides,* ed. Salo W. Baron (New York: Columbia University Press, 1941), pp. 2–8. See especially p. 7.

[20]Etienne Gilson, *The Philosophy of St. Thomas Aquinas: Authorized Translation . . . of Le Thomisme* (St. Louis: B. Herder Book Company, 1925). This book contains numerous references to Maimonides. However, one lengthy footnote on page 34 is worth quoting in full:

> Apart from Christian thought, a special place must be reserved, among the sources of St. Thomas, to the influence of Moses Maimonides. On a good many points the position of the "Rabbi Moses" prepares that adopted by Thomism and their respective interpretation of Aristotle is often analogous. Maimonides is opposed to the Arabic "motecalemin" (theologians) just as St. Thomas opposes the Augustinian traditionalists; their mental attitude, positive and full of common-sense, is singularly akin and the study of their relationship would be worthy of an exhaustive treatment.

Gilson's later book, *The Christian Philosophy of St. Thomas Aquinas* (New York: Random House, 1956) (which is a much expanded version of the earlier *Le Thomisme*), contains repeated references to Maimonides, with occasional identification of a Maimonidean idea as the source of a Thomistic passage.

> Es handelt sich nämlich nicht um einzelne Stellen, sondern um ganze Abhandlungen des Maimonidischen Werkes . . . die in den Schriften Alberts reproduziert sind.[21]

Albert was Aquinas's teacher. The very distinguished scholar in medieval philosophy, the late Anton C. Pegis, with whom it was this author's privilege to discuss the subject of this essay (and from whose insights and erudition he profited greatly), expressed the belief that the great influence of Albert on Aquinas has not been sufficiently researched, and is still far from being fully understood and appreciated. There is clearly good reason to suppose that it was Albert who introduced St. Thomas to Maimonides' *Guide.*

On numerous occasions Aquinas quotes directly from the *Guide.* Locutions and concepts from the *Guide* are often reflected in Aquinas' two *Summas.* In *De Potentia,* and in other works, he frequently refers to Maimonides by name, calling him Rabbi Moyses, or Moyses Egyptius, and on occasion voices disagreement with him. Without a doubt Aquinas was significantly influenced by Maimonides' ideas. As Emile Saisset, a Catholic professor of philosophy, said in 1862:

> Maimonide est le précurseur de Saint Thomas d'Aquin, et le *Moré Neboukhim* annonce et prépare la *Summa Theologiae.*[22]

Accordingly, the discovery that so much of Aquinas' negative theology bears a close resemblance to that of Maimonides should occasion no surprise.

What follows relies heavily on the work of Professor Anton C. Pegis, and especially on his definitive and instructive paper entitled *"Penitus Manet Ignotum,"* which appeared some 19 years ago, in *Medieval Studies.*[23] Aquinas shares with Maimonides the doctrine of negative attributes. Affirmative attributes cannot be predicated of God. We can talk about God only by negating any attributes ascribed to Him. It is interesting to note, however, that in some respects Aquinas is more thorough and more consistent than Maimonides on the matter of ascribing affirmative attributes to God, whereas in other re-

[21]M. Joel, *Verhältniss Albert des Grossen zu Moses Maimonides: Ein Beitrag zur Geschichte der Mittelalterischen Philosophie* (Breslau: Verlag der Schletter'sschen Buchhandlung, 1863), p. 2. "What is actually involved is not isolated passages, but rather entire discourses in Maimonides' writings . . . that are reproduced in Albert's writings."

[22]"Maimonides is the precursor of St. Thomas Aquinas, and *The Guide of the Perplexed* announces and paves the way for the *Summa Theologiae.*" Émile Saisset, "La Philosophie des Juifs: Maimonide et Spinoza," *Revue des Deux Mondes* 37 (1862): 296–325.

[23]Anton C. Pegis, *"Penitus Manet Ignotum."*

spects he is less consistent and less thorough in his rejection of them. The following discussion will provide some instructive examples.

On the one hand, as was pointed out earlier, in *De Potentia Dei* Aquinas disagrees with Maimonides' view that, in talking about God, it is proper to use *some* positive attributes, because they indicate only God's actions and their effects, rather than purporting to signify the divine essence. In his strictures against Maimonides here, Aquinas points out that if, because God's actions have produced *wisdom* in man, it were proper to speak of God as being *wise,* then, since God's action also produces, as one of its effects, *anger* in man, or *fire* in combustible things, why would it not be proper to say that God is *angry,* or that God is *fire?* He repeats this argument in the *Summa Theologiae,* again referring directly to Rabbi Moses, by saying that no reason could be assigned

> why some names more than others should be applied to God. For He is assuredly the cause of bodies in the same way as He is the cause of good things; therefore if *God is good* signified no more than *God is the cause of good things,* it might in like manner be said that God is a body, inasmuch as he is the cause of bodies.[24]

On the other hand, however, Aquinas is less than consistent and thoroughgoing in his rejection of positive attributes, when he allows that some names, or attributes, "signify the divine substance, but in an imperfect manner. . . . We cannot know the essence of God as He really is in Himself, but we know Him according as He is represented in the perfections of creatures."[25]

This is part of the evidence of the ambivalences referred to at the beginning, in the negative theology of both Maimonides and Aquinas. An additional comment on these ambivalences will appear later. However, it is, I think, quite clear that the main thrust of Aquinas' doctrine is that the essence, the nature, of God is unknowable. Early in the *Summa Theologiae* he asserts categorically that

> since we cannot know what God is, but rather what He is not, we cannot consider how He is but how He is not. . . . We can show how God is not, by denying of Him whatever is opposed to the idea of Him.[26]

[24]Thomas Aquinas, *The Summa Theologica,* trans. Fathers of the English Dominican Province (New York: Benzinger Brothers, 1947), q. 13, a. 2, vol. 1, p. 61.

[25]Ibid., p. 62.

[26]Ibid., q. 3 (preamble), p. 14.

We cannot know the nature of God from knowledge of creatures, because this would be claiming to have knowledge from effect to cause. But, says Aquinas, "it is not possible in any of these ways to know from the effect what the cause is, unless the effect be adequate to the cause, one in which the entire virtuality of the cause is expressed."[27] In Book I of the *Summa Contra Gentiles* Aquinas establishes that we must use the negative way in our investigations about God, because God surpasses anything that our intellect can know, and is completely and utterly different. Thus, "through negations, when we have a proper knowledge of a thing, we know that it is distinct from other things, yet what it is remains unknown."[28] Accordingly, to quote again, "while we know of God what He is not, what God is *penitus manet ignotum, remains completely unknown.*"[29]

This *via negativa,* as Professor Pegis pointed out, has momentous consequences. Nothing positive can be said about God's quiddity. Everything positive that *is* said about God is a distortion; it is a reduction of God to human terms. We can achieve the highest knowledge about God when we realize that we do not and cannot know Him.

> Then only do we know God truly when we believe Him to be above everything that is possible for men to think about God; . . . for the divine substance transcends the natural knowledge of men. Hence, by the fact that some truths are proposed to man about God that exceed his reason, the opinion that God is something above that which he can think is strengthened in man.[30]

And, to quote once more:

> It is because human intelligence is not equal to the divine essence that this same divine essence surpasses our intelligence and is unknown to us; wherefore man reaches the highest point in his knowledge about God when he knows that he knows Him not, inasmuch as he knows that that which is God transcends whatever he conceives of Him.[31]

And finally these words of Thomas:

> To know God consists in this for us here and now: that we do not know what God is.[32]

[27]*Summa Contra Gentiles,* Book III, Chapter 49, par. 3, p. 168.

[28]Ibid., Book III, Chapter 39, par. 1, p. 127.

[29]Ibid., Chapter 49, par. 9, p. 170.

[30]Ibid., Book I, Chapter 5, no. 3, p. 70.

[31]Thomas Aquinas, *De Potentia Dei,* q. 7, a. 5, *ad* 14, concluding paragraph.

[32]Thomas Aquinas, *In Librum B. Dionysii Nominibus Expositio,* ed. C. Pera (Rome-Turin, 1950), VII, Lectio 4, no. 731. (Quoted by Anton C. Pegis, *Basic Writings of Thomas Aquinas,* p. 225.)

Can we possibly be in error when we hear in this significant statement by Aquinas a direct echo of the words of Maimonides quoted earlier: "[O]ur knowledge of God consists in knowing that we are unable truly to comprehend Him"?

Anton C. Pegis distilled out of the Thomistic negative theology consequences which seem most faithful to Thomas, theologically and philosophically sound, and very moving in emotional impact. He called the Thomistic doctrine "a radical doctrine . . . that has not escaped controversy."[33] (Let me say parenthetically that Maimonides' doctrine, too, was radical, and that it too has not escaped controversy.) Aquinas' doctrine requires us, according to Professor Pegis, to insist that in fact nothing can be said affirmatively about the nature of God. "Man must come to *unsay* the whole universe in order to say *God exists* properly."[34] Nothing in the universe is in any way God or like God, and man must *unsay* and *unknow* everything with reference to any God-talk. Pegis's closing paragraph says it better than any summary possibly could:

> God transcends anything and everything that we can think about Him. But to be true to Him we must unknow Him rather than simply be ignorant of Him. We must seek Him in all His creation, we must unsay everything that His creatures are, in order thereby to stand nearer and nearer to His transcendence. When St. Thomas said that God was utterly unknown, what was he saying but that man should seek the divine transcendence by a total unknowing?[35]

IV

The doctrine of the utter unknowability of God, or of radical negative theology, has encountered much criticism and resistance. This is not surprising. A relationship of congeniality between this doctrine and many of the traditional assumptions of popular religion, or even of the more sophisticated theologies that are based on the assumption of a personal God, is hardly to be expected. Numerous objectionable or even pernicious implications and consequences have been imputed to the negative theology of Maimonides and Aquinas in the controversies triggered by this doctrine both recently and in earlier days. I single out six such critical imputations for brief analysis, discussion, and attempted rejoinder:

[33]Anton C. Pegis, *"Penitus Manet Ignotum,"* p. 225.
[34]Ibid., p. 219.
[35]Ibid., p. 226.

1. God, the unknown and unknowable subject in such a theology, is "no subject at all," and therefore negative theology cannot even claim to have knowledge that He exists.
2. This negative theology leads to and entails *mysticism.*
3. This negative theology leads to and entails *agnosticism.*
4. This negative theology is subversive of *religious doctrine,* of "The Law."
5. This doctrine leads "directly to the theology of silence."
6. This negative theology is a *reductio ad absurdum* of rational theology.

(1) *If God is unknowable, then there cannot even be knowledge that He exists.* The first of these animadversions has received various formulations. For example, the question is asked, "If God is unknowable, then how could Maimonides and Aquinas know that God exists?" In an article on "The Logic of Negative Theology," George Englebretsen said:

> If all we ever know of a subject is that certain attributes are denied of it . . . we will never know anything about that subject (an uncircumscribed subject is an unknown subject and thus no subject at all).[36]

And in the same journal, two years later, Joseph A. Buijs concluded his "Comments on Maimonides' Negative Theology" with the assertion,

> How we can know the fact that God exists without thereby knowing anything positive about His nature is an epistemic and metaphysical issue.[37]

In its extreme form, this criticism alleges that one of the consequences entailed by negative theology is the denial of God's existence:

> But if we finally succeed in negating every attribute, we may well ask, what have we left at all. Not only can we not describe what God is, but we must define Him by the very negation of description. The conclusion of the whole matter would seem to be that God is pure negation, not only non-describable, but non-existent.[38]

In rejoinder to this last version of the allegation, the late Leon Roth, who had formulated it in these words more than half a century be-

[36]*The New Scholasticism* 47 (1973): 231.
[37]*The New Scholasticism* 49 (1975): 93.
[38]Leon Roth, *Spinoza, Descartes, and Maimonides* (Oxford: Clarendon, 1924), p. 77.

fore, hastened to point to "the characteristic view of Maimonides that this consequence does not follow."[39] However, before reviewing Roth's reading of Maimonides on this matter, it seems proper to go back and note the contrast between Buijs's moderate contention that there is "an epistemic and metaphysical issue" in the doctrine (a cautious admonition from which one can hardly dissent), and Englebretsen's assertion that an uncircumscribed or unknown subject is "no subject at all." It is of course less than axiomatic that "an uncircumscribed subject," or an "unknown subject," is synonymous with "no subject at all." The claim that only the known, or only the knowable, exists, or even that only the knowable can be a subject of discourse, seems far from self-evident.

Leon Roth's explication of Maimonides on the ascription of attributes to God properly emphasized the frequently neglected point that the doctrine does not deny that God has a "nature."

> That human descriptions are inadequate to express the nature of God does not mean that God has no nature . . . each negation of inadequate conceptions of God's being reaffirms the fact that He exists. Existence in the case of God is not an accident; it is identical with His essence. The more we negate the attributes the more we affirm the essence, and we are left finally with the idea of God as absolute existence.[40]

Without knowing the nature or essence of God, we know that God exists because we know from our experience that things, contingent things, exist. If *anything* exists, and obviously finite, contingent things, such as you and I, do exist, then it cannot be the case that *everything* that exists is *contingent*. To be contingent means that the existence of the contingent thing is *contingent upon, depends upon,* some *other thing* or being. But *not everything* can be dependent on something else, i.e., *not everything* can have been *caused by,* or brought into being by, something else. At least *one entity* must be in existence *by itself, independent of anything else,* must have come into being (if it did not exist eternally) by itself, must be *its own cause,* i.e., must *exist necessarily not contingently,* and its non-existence is inconceivable. This *necessarily existent being* is what we call God. Some may call it *existence itself* (whatever this may mean), or *the totality of existence.* What we call God is thus the non-contingent, that which is *causa sui.* God is the absolute existent, to Whom existence is so essential as to be His very essence. Accordingly, His very existence is different from the existence of contingent things. The very term "existence" "can only be applied equivocally to His existence and to the existence of things

[39]Ibid.
[40]Ibid.

other than He."[41] We *know that* God exists, that His absolute, essential existence is radically different from our existence, and our knowledge *that He exists* is utterly independent of any affirmative attributes we may be tempted to ascribe to Him.

(2) *Negative theology leads to and entails mysticism.* To say that God is unknowable is not to propound or imply a doctrine of *mysticism.* Admittedly, as Shlomo Pines points out, an approach similar to Maimonides' emphasis on the importance of negative attributes in discourse about God "may be found in mystical writings." However, Pines says categorically, "Maimonides is no mystic," and his negative theology does not recommend any mystical or obscurantist detachment from the knowledge of things that are not God. Its intention and effect is rather the pursuit of the kind of knowledge of things that avoids "misplaced references to God's essence."[42]

The label "mystic" hardly befits Maimonides or Aquinas. Mysticism is a doctrine or a range of doctrines that espouse a variety of notions about the nature of God and assert that there are modes of apprehending God, such as direct intuition or other "mystical experiences." These mystical methods are putatively different from and more reliable than the "normal" empirical and rational methods of apprehending other entities. To assert that God is unknowable in no way entails the espousal of mysticism or the acceptance of its claims; in fact, the two are mutually exclusive. To say that God is unknowable to the human intellect is, indeed, to say, using the word in its narrow, lexical sense, that God is a "mystery." But this is only to say that we do not know or apprehend or understand the nature of God, and that we know only that He exists; and it is not to suggest or propound a doctrine of mysticism with all the claims that it would entail.

(3) *Negative theology leads to and entails agnosticism.* In the article referred to above, George Englebretsen concluded that "the way of negation is no new way to God," and that this negative theology is "indiscernible from agnosticism."[43] The charge of agnosticism is also made several times by F. C. Copleston, in his book on Thomas Aquinas: "Exclusive adherence to the negative way would lead to agnosticism about the divine nature."[44] "In Aquinas' account of our natural knowledge of the divine nature there is, then, a certain agnosticism."[45] "As Aquinas saw clearly, a certain measure of 'agnosticism' is inevitable."[46] However, Copleston appears to be equivocating here

[41]Moses Maimonides, *The Guide of the Perplexed,* p. 80.
[42]Shlomo Pines, Introduction to *The Guide of the Perplexed,* p. xcvi.
[43]George Engelbretsen, p. 232.
[44]F. C. Copleston, *Aquinas* (New York: Penguin Books, 1955), p. 128.
[45]Ibid., p. 131.
[46]Ibid., p. 134.

in two ways. On the one hand he seems to be shuttling back and forth between the interpretation of Aquinas as saying that man can have *no* knowledge at all of God's nature, and the interpretation of Aquinas as saying that man can have *some* knowledge of the divine nature. Admittedly, there is evidence of such equivocation in both Aquinas and Maimonides—a subject to which we shall return. On the other hand, Copleston also appears to be equivocating in *his own* use of the term "agnosticism," using it at times as a disparaging name for an erroneous doctrine, but at other times as a label for a perhaps regrettable but unavoidable doctrine, the alternatives to which are beset by difficulties.

Clearly, Copleston acknowledges, affirming positive predicates of God inescapably leads either to anthropomorphism, or to the reduction of statements about God to myths. But, "Aquinas was not prepared to accept either an anthropomorphic view of God or an interpretation of theological propositions as so many myths."[47] Copleston ends up with a question-begging declaration to the effect that

> Aquinas' agnosticism, then, is not agnosticism in the modern sense. He has no doubt about the existence of God, and he is far from saying that we can know nothing about the divine nature or that we can make only negative statements about it.[48]

This conclusion here is question-begging because, first, as was shown earlier, the logic of radical negative theology does not entail doubts about the *existence* of God. Secondly, it is question-begging because the full, authentic doctrine of Aquinas and of Maimonides (except for the equivocations to which we shall return) says clearly and precisely what Copleston cavalierly claims Aquinas did not say, namely, that "we know nothing about the divine nature," and "that we can make only negative statements about it." The two distinct issues, namely, *whether man can know that God exists* and *whether man can know God's nature or essence,* must be kept distinct from each other. To the former question the answer is clearly affirmative. To the latter, the answer is clearly negative: the nature of God is *unknowable,* and to call this doctrine "agnosticism" is not to refute it or to disparage it, but only to describe it. It is of some use, in this context, to rehabilitate the terms "agnostic" and "agnosticism" and restore them to respectable company in the philosophical lexicon. In their unadulterated, etymological sense these terms betoken an acknowledgement of *not knowing.* An agnostic position with reference to any issue is a position which says that the subject in question is unknown or unknowable. And

[47]Ibid.
[48]Ibid.

this, *simpliciter*, is what the adherent of negative theology says about the nature of God.

(4) *Negative theology is subversive of religious doctrine, of "The Law."* The charge that negative theology is subversive of religion has been lodged principally against Maimonides, and was repeated most recently by the late Leo Strauss, who stated that "the teaching that positive attributes of God are impossible . . . clearly contradicts the teaching of the law."[49] In this charge we hear reverberations of nearly eight centuries of anti-Maimonidean argument and polemic by some of the teachers and thinkers in the mainstream of Jewish religious and philosophical literature. In elaborating his charge, Strauss averred that:

> Maimonides' doctrine of attributes would be entirely negative and even subversive. For the doctrine culminates in the assertion that we grasp of God only that he is and not what he is.[50]

But this is very puzzling, coming as it does from Strauss, since the latter view, namely, "that we grasp of God only *that He is* and *not what He is,*" is precisely what was held by both Maimonides and Aquinas, as we tried to show above. Moreover, as Strauss surely knew, Maimonides anticipated these attacks, and took the offensive himself, as it were. For he in fact warned that, on the contrary, it is the ascription of affirmative attributes to God that is subversive of religion. In the *Guide* he stated categorically that "he who affirms that God has affirmative attributes . . . has abolished his belief in the existence of the Deity without being aware of it."[51] Baldly stated, then, the paradox is that on the one hand Maimonides clearly rejected the ascription of positive attributes to God and characterized such predication as equivalent to the denial of God's existence, whereas Strauss, on the other hand, alleged that the teaching which denies affirmative attributes to God contradicts the teaching of the Law and is subversive.

It appears to me that what is involved here is a puzzling neglect or circumvention by Strauss, in this relatively recent work of his on Maimonides, of a fundamental, all-important aspect of Maimonides' thought that has eluded very many of his readers throughout the centuries since the publication of his *Guide;* but in systematically explicating this aspect Leo Strauss himself has generally been among

[49]Leo Strauss, "How to Begin to Study *The Guide of the Perplexed,*" in Moses Maimonides, *The Guide of the Perplexed*, pp. xlviii–xlix.

[50]Ibid., p. xlviii.

[51]Ibid., I, 60, p. 143.

the very few and among the most diligent and incisive readers in recent years.[52] In the passages quoted above from his "Introduction to the *Guide*," Strauss explains that Maimonides' doctrine of the attributes "is a secret doctrine."[53] Though a number of other scholars and commentators have made the same observation, including some contemporaries of Maimonides, this aspect of his philosophical theology is neither widely known nor well understood. Regrettably, the limitations of this paper do not make possible an adequate exposition of it, and a brief and much simplified sketch will have to suffice here.

An understanding of this matter can be helped by noting, first, that throughout the text of the *Guide* there are scattered numerous admonitions by its author not to disclose certain truths to the masses, and second, that these admonitions are not limited only to his doctrine of attributes. Among the locutions conveying Rabbi Moses' wish for secrecy we find the following: "my purpose is that the truths be glimpsed and then again concealed"; "If we explained what ought to be explained, it would be unsuitable for the masses among the people"; "I adjure every reader of this Treatise of mine . . . not to explain to another anything in it"; "in speaking about very obscure matters it is necessary to conceal some parts and disclose others"; "these matters are only for a few solitary individuals of a very special sort, and not for the multitude"; "it is not permitted to divulge these matters to all people"; "these are obscure matters . . . they are truly the mystery of the Torah . . . matters that ought not to be spoken of except in chapter headings."[54] Specifically with reference to his doctrine of the attributes, Maimonides cautions that "this notion concerning them also should not be divulged to the masses."[55]

The important fact about Maimonides to which these caveats draw the attention of the careful student is that, under a variety of disguises and deliberate obfuscations, he propounded in the *Guide* two distinguishable though related and overlapping doctrines about God, a *manifest doctrine* and a *secret doctrine;* or a "double faith" theory consisting respectively, to use Maimonides' own terminology, of (*a*) *"necessary beliefs"* and (*b*) *"true beliefs."*[56] "Necessary beliefs" embrace a wide range of religious observances and rituals, as well as ethical prescriptions and imperatives that in the aggregate make possible an

[52]Leo Strauss, *Persecution and the Art of Writing* (Glencoe, Ill.: The Free Press, 1952). (See especially "The Literary Character of *The Guide of the Perplexed,*" pp. 38–94.) Cf. also Yaacov Becker, *Mishnato Haphilosophit shel Rabbenu Moshe ben Maimon (The Philosophical Doctrine of Moses ben Maimon)* (Tel Aviv: J. Simoni Publishing House, 1955).

[53]Moses Maimonides, *The Guide of the Perplexed,* p. xlviii.

[54]Ibid., pp. 7, 9, 15, 18; I, 34, p. 79; I, 71, p. 175; pp. 80–81.

[55]Ibid., I, 59, p. 142.

[56]Ibid., III, 28, pp. 512–14.

orderly, civilized, tranquil, and just society and that presuppose belief in the traditional doctrine of a personal God who commands, gets angry, punishes and rewards, and responds to our actions and prayers. "True beliefs," on the other hand, include the de-anthropomorphization and even the de-personalization of God, recognition that the nature and essence of God are unknowable, that God is "wholly other," wholly unlike the things of the world, and is imperturbable and unaffected by human expressions. God, therefore, is an object of pure, disinterested love and contemplation, and man's most exalted worship and piety is this kind of disinterested, contemplative love. Few humans are capable of achieving this purely intellectual love and contemplation. Certainly the masses are not. For the masses it is the system of "necessary beliefs" that is important, and only if these beliefs are followed will there be a civilized society that will make possible the rise of the small number of rare individuals who will be capable of understanding and living by the "true beliefs."

"Necessary beliefs" therefore concern actions, behavior, societal interrelations and imperatives, and the system of "practical commandments" in the written *Torah* and in the transmitted Oral Tradition of Rabbinic teaching and codes. "True beliefs," on the other hand, concern what Maimonides calls "opinions" or "correct opinions," i.e., philosophical beliefs concerning the nature of the universe, creation *ex nihilo,* the meaning of words that purport to refer to God, etc. Maimonides explains this succinctly:

> Sum up what we have said concerning beliefs as follows: In some cases a *commandment* communicates a *correct* belief, which is the one and only thing aimed at—as, for instance the belief in the unity and eternity of the deity and in His not being a body. In other cases the belief is *necessary* for the abolition of reciprocal wrongdoing or for the acquisition of a noble moral quality—as, for instance, the belief that He, may He be exalted, has a violent anger against those who do injustice . . . and as the belief that He, may He be exalted, responds instantaneously to the prayer of someone wronged or deceived.[57]

In numerous instances the "true beliefs" or "correct opinions" clearly coincide with the "necessary beliefs" which have as their goal the establishment of morality and social justice. One of the examples given by Maimonides is the statute of the Sabbath, the "first intention" of which is "the belief in correct opinions, namely, in the creation of the world in time," and "its contribution in fortifying this principle." However, "the intention also included the abolition of mutual wrongdoing among men."[58]

[57]Ibid., pp. 513–14.
[58]Ibid., III, 32, p. 531.

Now, it is belief in the unknowability of God, God's being "wholly other," imperturbable, depersonalized, not characterized by anthropomorphic attributes, etc., that is among the "true beliefs" to which philosophical thought and analysis will lead the religiously committed Jew who is able to engage in such inquiries. But the masses are unable to comprehend many of these beliefs. Indeed the exposure of the masses to such beliefs may weaken their faith in and jeopardize their adherence to the imperatives that are part of the system of "necessary beliefs." *True beliefs* may be taught only to very special, singular individuals, and must not be disclosed to the masses. Such beliefs form a secret doctrine, limited to the intellectual elite who form the hypothetical audience to whom much of the *Guide* is addressed. For this elite group, the secret doctrine, including the denial of affirmative attributes in relation to God and the doctrine that we can know only *that* God is and not *what* God is, far from being subversive of their faith, is its very strength and its firm foundation, and the ground for their true contemplative love and worship of God.

The secret doctrine does indeed contradict some of the traditional, popular "teaching of the Law" that is part of the system of "necessary beliefs" and is ordained by divine decree in order to reduce mutual wrongdoing among humans and assure a moral society. It is precisely for this reason that the doctrine should not be disclosed to the multitudes who are unable to understand it and are likely to draw erroneous conclusions from it. Leo Strauss was among those who understood and explicated most acutely this obscure aspect of Maimonidean thought;[59] hence the perplexity evoked by his comments quoted above.

Now, two questions arise here in connection with Thomas Aquinas. First, was his negative theology among the elements in his thought that triggered controversy and opposition to him in his own day? Second, did Thomas feel or ever say that some philosophico-theological teachings should be considered secret doctrine and not be divulged to the masses? These are interesting historical questions, but I am not familiar with any of the published systematic research on them. However, one Aquinas text seems to indicate that the subject of secret truths to be concealed from the masses did receive some attention in Christian theological literature, and that St. Thomas leaned toward the view that some divine truths ought to be concealed from the masses to whom they might do harm. The discussion occurs in Thomas's *Commentary on the De Trinitate of Boethius,* in the article entitled "Whether Divine Truths Ought To Be Concealed By New and

[59]See n. 52 above.

Obscure Words." After raising the question, and quoting Biblical and other texts on both sides, Aquinas concluded

> But . . . there are other [truths] . . . which, if openly presented, cause harm to those hearing them. . . . If any subtleties are proposed to uncultivated people, these folk may find in the imperfect comprehension of them matter for error.[60]

Then, after quoting concurring views from Gregory and Augustine, Aquinas reiterates his view that "there is no denial of the fact that there are mysteries which ought to be concealed by obscuring words."[61] I leave this matter without further comment.

(5) *Negative theology leads directly to the theology of silence.* This charge, in these very words, was made by George Englebretsen, whom we quoted earlier,[62] and the same charge was also made, but more dramatically and forcefully, by the logician Fred Sommers, in his essay entitled "What We Can Say About God."[63] In that essay Sommers claimed that, to the question "'what can we say about God?' the negative theologian answers, 'nothing!'"[64] There is a deceptive appearance of plausibility in this claim by Sommers, deceptive, I venture to suggest, for the author himself as well as the reader, because of the tacit, uncritical, and question-begging assumption that underlies it, namely, that rational discourse about God is possible *only* in terms of *affirmative divine attributes.* Naturally, therefore, on this assumption, since negative theology insists that affirmative attributes cannot be predicated of God, the negative theologian appears self-condemned, strictly speaking, to saying nothing about God. The seeming plausibility of Sommers's charge can be further unmasked if we exhibit the unarticulated tautological syllogism into which he seems to have trapped himself, while trapping the negative theologian as well as the reader:

> Whatever we can say nothing affirmative
> about, we can say nothing about.
> We can say nothing affirmative about God.
>
> ---
>
> Therefore, we can say nothing about God.

[60]Thomas Aquinas, "Commentary on the De Trinitate of Boethius," q. 2, a. 4. According to the standard edition, *Sancti Thomae De Aquino Expositio Super Librum Boethii De Trinitate,* 2nd ed., ed. B. Decker (Leiden: E. J. Brill, 1959), p. 99. I am grateful to John Wippel of Catholic University for bringing this Aquinas text to my attention.

[61]Ibid.

[62]George Englebretsen, p. 232 (see n. 36).

[63]Fred Sommers, "What We Can Say About God," (see n. 3 above).

[64]Ibid., p. 66.

But manifestly, the question-begging, tautological reasoning here is Sommers's, and is not to be charged to the negative theologian. For the latter, discourse about God is not only possible (though of course not via the ascription to Him of affirmative attributes), but is indeed mandatory (see below), and it is *negative discourse* about God that is mandatory. To the question "What can we say about God?" the negative theologian responds as follows:

> We have an inexhaustibly large number of things to say about God, namely, to say *what God is not!* Because erring mankind has for so long in the past been saying and repeating an infinitely large number of things about God in ascribing affirmative attributes to Him, and because mankind will continue in its erring future to make an infinitely great number of attributions of affirmative characteristics to Him, it is the task of negative theologians, and of those who have been persuaded by them, to "unknow" and "unsay" what has been claimed to be known about God, and what has been said about God, and to continue saying and repeating in an infinitely great number of ways *what God is not!*

Now, this can hardly be called a theology of silence!

And thus, by this path, we arrive finally at "rational theology" and its place within negative theology.

(6) *Negative theology is a* reductio ad absurdum *of rational theology.* This imputation also comes from the pen of Fred Sommers, in the same essay in which charge number 5 appeared.[65] The rejoinder here is essentially the same as the rejoinder above. For a long time, "rational theology" was taken to mean largely the systematic setting forth, analysis, and explication of *affirmative attributes* of God. This seems to be also Sommers's assumed definition, and, as explained earlier, understood in this way the enterprise is misguided and also idolatrous. If, however, the discipline of theology were understood to be the systematic pursuit of the countless ways of saying *what God is not,* then what can possibly be more *rational* in that pursuit than to continue with relentless perseverance to deny and unsay the affirmative statements about God, and thus to spread understanding of God's utter differentness and ultimate incomprehensibility? To teach that every positive attribution that is predicated of God is distortion, is a reduction of God to human terms, and thus is idolatrous, this is the task of "rational theology." Let no one be under any illusion that this task is an easy one.

[65]Ibid.

2. *Maimonides' Philosophy Today*

Maimonides is often referred to as a philosopher, and *The Guide of the Perplexed* is generally regarded as his principal philosophical work. The present paper will be limited exclusively to a consideration of Maimonides *as a philosopher,* and will pursue two questions: (1) What original contribution, if any, did Maimonides make to philosophy? (2) What in the philosophy of Maimonides is still alive and worthy of our attention today? However, when we thus resolve to ignore the vast encyclopedic range of Maimonides' interests and achievements, and concentrate on a pursuit of these two questions with respect to his philosophic work, serious difficulties arise, and the results threaten to be disappointing.

To confront directly some of these difficulties, it may be useful to pass over all subsidiary matters, and begin with the most radical question of all: Is *The Guide of the Perplexed* really a philosophic work? Two recent commentators answer this question categorically in the negative. The late Isaac Husik stated that, in the *Guide,* Maimonides' "purpose is deliberately apologetic and concordistic. The work is not a treatise of science or philosophy."[1] Leo Strauss expresses the same view, with even greater emphasis. He states that ". . . the *Guide* is not a philosophic book,"[2] and that Maimonides "cannot possibly be a philosopher, and consequently a book of his in which he explains his views concerning all important topics cannot possibly be a philosophic book."[3] "Thus we are led," continues Strauss, "to the conclusion

[1]Husik, Isaac, *A History of Medieval Jewish Philosophy,* Jewish Publication Society, 1941, p. 239.

[2]Strauss, Leo, *Persecution and the Art of Writing,* The Free Press, 1952, p. 42 (in Chapter III, entitled "The Literary Character of the Guide for the Perplexed").

[3]Ibid., p. 43.

Judaism: A Quarterly Journal of Jewish Life and Thought, vol. 4, Spring 1955, pp. 99–109.

that no philosophic topic of any kind is, as such, the subject matter of the *Guide*."[4] Moreover, if we go back almost three hundred years to Spinoza, we may perhaps find it significant that Spinoza, who certainly knew the work of Maimonides intimately,[5] passed down to us a broad generalization to the effect that ". . . the Jews, despisers of philosophy, . . . preached a religion free from all philosophical speculation,"[6] and that he did not deem it necessary to exempt Maimonides from this judgment.

Nor do we find any encouragement in Maimonides himself with respect to classifying the *Guide* as a philosophic work. In his introduction to the *Guide*, Maimonides says:

> My primary object in this work is to explain certain words occurring in the prophetic books . . . The object of this treatise is to enlighten a religious man who has been trained to believe in the truth of our holy law . . . and at the same time has been successful in his philosophical studies . . . This work also has a second object in view. It seeks to explain certain obscure figures which occur in the prophets . . .[7]

To be sure, Maimonides emphasizes that "It is not here intended to explain all these expressions to the unlettered or to mere tyros, a previous knowledge of Logic and Natural Philosophy being indispensable . . .,"[8] and that his book is addressed to those "who have studied philosophy and have acquired sound knowledge." But he characterizes the audience for whom the *Guide* was written as those "who while firm in religious matters are perplexed and bewildered on account of the ambiguous and figurative expressions employed in the holy writings."[9] Thus, while philosophical training is one of the qualifications of those to whom the *Guide* is addressed, the accent is on

[4]Ibid., p. 45.

[5]Harry Austryn Wolfson refers to Maimonides as one of the three dominant influences on the philosophy of Spinoza. Cf. Wolfson, H. A., *The Philosophy of Spinoza*, Harvard University Press, 1948, Vol. I, pp. 14, 19. A Hebrew translation of *The Guide of the Perplexed* was among Spinoza's books; cf. Serouya, Henri, *Spinoza: Sa Vie, Sa Philosophie*, Editions Albin Michel, Paris, 1947, p. 31. There are several specific references to Maimonides in the *Tractatus Theologico-Politicus*.

[6]Spinoza, Benedict de, *Tractatus Theologico-Politicus*, Chapter XI, near end. Cf. Benedicti de Spinoza *Opera*, edited by Van Vloten and Land, Nijhoff, The Hague, 1913, Vol. II, p. 229. The phrase "*philosophiae scilicet contemtoribus*" is often mistranslated "who despised philosophy," introducing into it a *past* tense which is not in the Latin. Cf. *The Chief Works of Spinoza*, translated by R. H. N. Elwes, Dover Publications, 1951, Vol. I, p. 164.

[7]*The Guide for the Perplexed*, translated by M. Friedlander, E. F. Dutton & Co., 1928, p. 2.

[8]Ibid.

[9]Ibid., p. 5.

firmness in religious belief, and bewilderment caused by the language of the Torah. The stated purpose of the *Guide* is therefore clearly *not* philosophical.

If we turn, in our quest, to an examination of the *texts* themselves, the results threaten to be no less disappointing. In considering Maimonides as a philosopher, no violence will be done to our subject if we limit our texts to the *Guide* and to the early treatise on logic, *Millot Ha-Higgayon.*[10] In these two works, as in the works of Spinoza as Prof. H. A. Wolfson sees them,[11] we may discern two distinct and in a sense conflicting personalities. On the one hand we discover the traditionalist Jew, the enormously erudite and profound Biblical and Talmudic scholar, the religious man who was born into an intensely religious age, the man whose religion was as natural to him as the air he breathed, but who found it a subject for serious reflection since he was a thoughtful and analytic person. This man, whom I shall call by the name assigned to him in Jewish tradition, the Rambam, was manifestly engaged in Jewish religious apologetics. He wrote the *Guide* not for the purpose of converting the unbeliever, but to justify Judaism to the believing and philosophically sophisticated Jew. Of course, such religious apologetics, involving as they must some philosophical considerations, have an obvious tangency with the field of philosophy. This is evident in the *Guide*, and in such works of Christian apologetics as Thomas Aquinas' *Summa Theologica*, or the more recent and undeservedly neglected *Grammar of Assent* by Cardinal Newman. However, since this paper is not concerned with Jewish religious apologetics *as such*, this man, the Rambam, must remain outside the scope of the present discussion.

But one or two of the points of tangency with philosophy might perhaps be mentioned here, as a matter of historical interest, without further comment or elucidation. As a theologian the Rambam devised one original proof for the existence of God. It is known as the proof based on the idea of *"necessary existence,"*[12] and it was adopted by later theologians, Jewish, Christian, and Arabic alike, and used extensively. It may be further recorded that the Rambam departed radically from his Jewish and Arabic predecessors, who customarily had proceeded to demonstrate the existence of God only *after* having attempted to prove that the universe had a beginning, i.e., that it was created *ex nihilo*. The Rambam rejected this method

[10]*Maimonides' Treatise on Logic*, critically edited and translated by Israel Efros, American Academy for Jewish Research, 1928 (published as Volume VIII of the *Proceedings of the American Academy for Jewish Research*).

[11]Wolfson, op. cit., p. 326.

[12]*Guide*, op. cit., Book II, Chap. 1, p. 152.

> because all the proofs for the Creation have weak points, and cannot be considered as convincing except by those who do not know the difference between a proof, a dialectical argument, and a sophism.[13]

"The true method," says the Rambam,

> which is based on logical and indubitable proof, consists, according to my opinion, in demonstrating the existence of God, His unity, and His incorporeality, by such philosophical arguments as are founded on the theory of the *eternity* of the universe. I do not propose this method as though I believed in the eternity of the universe, for I do not follow the philosophers on this point, but by the aid of this method these three principles, viz., the existence of God, His unity and His incorporeality, can be fully proved and verified, irrespective of the question whether the universe had a beginning or not.[14]

Further examination of the two works mentioned above brings us face to face with another and strikingly different person. This man is the careful student of Greek and Arabic philosophy, of logic, of mathematics, of physics, and the other sciences of his day. Him it is more proper to call Maimonides, keeping in mind the Greek form of this name. He was frankly a follower, and perhaps a slavish follower, of Aristotle. In spite of his disparaging comment about those who "consider it wrong to differ from Aristotle,"[15] Maimonides by and large adopted Aristotle's doctrines in metaphysics, physics, and ethics, but systematized them in a manner suited to his own needs. Thus, for example, he laid the groundwork for Book II of the *Guide* by assembling twenty-six propositions based on Aristotle's *Physics* and *Metaphysics* and Aristotle's Arabic commentators. On the basis of these twenty-six propositions he developed his proofs for the existence of God. To do justice to this aspect of the man, that is, to Maimonides, a detailed exposition and analysis of some of the major doctrines of Aristotle would be required. However, since one of the objectives of our inquiry was to try to discover Maimonides' *original* contributions to philosophy, and since an extensive exposition of Aristotle would be beyond the scope of the present paper, we are again compelled to dismiss the man whom we have here called *Maimonides* as also outside the sphere of this discussion as originally defined.

Here too, however, we might mention, again merely as a matter of historical record, and without further amplification, some of the points at which Maimonides deviated from Aristotle. While in the

[13]Ibid., Book I, Chap. 71, p. 110.
[14]Ibid., Book I, Chap. 71, p. 111.
[15]Ibid., Book II, Chap. 15, p. 176.

Natural Sciences, or, to use the terminology of Maimonides, in matters of *Natural Law,* and in such metaphysical doctrines as Matter and Form, Potentiality and Actuality, etc., he followed Aristotle slavishly, in matters of *cosmology* and *cosmogony,* i.e., in the branches of knowledge dealing with the structure and origin of the universe, he often departed from Aristotle, either reinterpreting him, or completely abandoning him, so that he, Maimonides, would not be in conflict with Jewish theology. For example, the *Intelligences* which Aristotle assumes as explanations for the movements of the sun, the moon, the planets, and the stars, in the treatment of Maimonides are equated with the angels of the Bible and Jewish tradition,[16] and it is they that move the sun and all the stars.

Or, let us use as another example the problem of the origin of the universe. It is one of the fundamental propositions in all Greek science and philosophy, and particularly in Aristotle, that *ex nihilo fit nihil,* i.e., that out of nothing nothing can be created. It was, furthermore, generally recognized among philosophers that Aristotle's philosophical system, his doctrine of Matter and Form and its implied Prime Matter, as well as the nature of the circular motion of the heavenly bodies, made it a necessary consequence that the universe was *eternal,* uncreated. However, it is of course a fundamental principle in Jewish theology that the world is *not* eternal, that it was *created* by God. In this conflict Maimonides bowed before the Rambam and declared that the universe *was created by God, ex nihilo,* out of nothing.

To this deviation from Aristotle Maimonides devoted a good half of Book II of the *Guide.* Two of his arguments are worth restating here. In the first place, Maimonides claimed that the Aristotelian belief in the eternity of the universe is based on the erroneous assumption that the universe as a whole must have come into existence in the same way as its parts continue to come into being now that the whole universe exists. Obviously these parts come into being at present in accordance with Natural Law. Therefore, since the assumption is that the *whole universe* came into existence according to Natural Law, it is presupposed that Natural Law is *prior* to, and existed or prevailed before, the whole universe. This Maimonides held to be false. Natural Law, Maimonides maintained, is *part of this world,* and is therefore itself *a creation,* having been produced by God in the process of creation *ex nihilo.*[17]

The second argument carries this deviation from Aristotle's view still further. Maimonides believed the difference between an Aristotelian eternal universe subject to Natural Law, and a universe created

[16]Ibid., Book II, Chap. 2, pp. 258 ff.
[17]Ibid., Book II, Chaps. 13 ff., pp. 281 ff.

by God, to be much more fundamental than might appear on a superficial reading of the text. Basically it resolves itself into a difference between a world that is a mechanical engine, operating purposelessly and meaninglessly in accordance with impersonal Natural Law, and on the other hand a world created by God, with an intelligence involved in its creation and therefore some design, some purpose, some meaning in the existence of the universe and of man. The mechanical world excludes freedom of the will, divine miracles, and the efficacy of prayer, and as such this conception, were it to be accepted, would invalidate some of the most fundamental doctrines in a religious view of the world. The created world, on the other hand, is the world of the religious man, and the Rambam again relegated Maimonides into the background, and proclaimed the view of the world as *created* to be the true view.[18]

That these arguments are inconclusive was as obvious to Maimonides as it is to us today. At best these arguments may only raise doubts about the Aristotelian position, and render it unacceptable to the person who is unwavering in his religious beliefs. They do nothing toward *demonstrating the truth* of the doctrine of creation. Maimonides never failed to see this. His contention was that

> . . . it is well known to all clear and correct thinkers who do not wish to deceive themselves, that this question, namely, whether the universe has been created or is eternal, cannot be answered with mathematical certainty; here human intellect must pause.[19]

Since all Maimonides was able to do was to point out the weaknesses in the doctrine of the eternity of the universe, and since he could produce no cogent *proofs* for the doctrine of creation, he faced the situation honestly, and stated his position with admirable candor:

> Since I am convinced of the correctness of my method, and consider *either of these theories*—viz., the Eternity of the universe, and the Creation—*as admissible, I accept the latter on the authority of Prophecy,* which can teach things beyond the reach of philosophic speculation.[20]

With this triumph of the Rambam over Maimonides we seem to have exhausted most of what is important about Maimonides as a philosopher. A few theological contributions to Judaism, some developments of and deviations from Aristotle, interesting points in his attempt to achieve the mutual translatability of Jewish theology and

[18]Ibid., Book II, Chaps. 19–25.
[19]Ibid., Book I, Chap. 71, p. 111.
[20]Ibid., Book II, Chap. 16, p. 178. Italics mine.

Aristotelianism, and that seems to be all. Moreover, even in his adherence to and deviations from Aristotle, Maimonides follows in the footsteps of a predecessor, Abraham Ibn Daud, author of *Emunah Ramah*. Ibn Daud, born a quarter of a century before Maimonides, was the first to attempt specifically a harmonization of Judaism with the doctrines of Aristotle. Maimonides was a more profound thinker, and the more systematic of the two, and his achievement in this undertaking is far more impressive than that of Ibn Daud. He follows Ibn Daud in his identification of the Aristotelian Intelligences with the Biblical angels, but with greater thoroughness and systematic arrangement. In the allegorical interpretations of Biblical passages Maimonides is once again a follower of the method developed by Philo some twelve hundred years earlier.[21]

Strange and disappointing results indeed! And the question as to what was original and is still alive today in the philosophy of Maimonides remains unanswered.

Have we perhaps overlooked something? Is there anything that has escaped us in this brief and inadequate account of the relationship of the Rambam to Maimonides? I think there is. The relationship between these two aspects of the man cannot be dismissed by simply listing the individual instances in which one is suppressed by the other. Behind this problematic relationship one perceives a more profound and more universal problem; a problem more fundamental than the historical question of the relationship between Jewish theology and the philosophy of Aristotle, or the attempt to harmonize the two: ultimately it is the basic philosophical problem of the relationship of *two ways of knowledge*, the way of *Reason* and the way of *Faith.*

I shall now attempt to present this problem at some length, avoiding technical terms, and deliberately ignoring some of the refinements that a strictly technical treatment would require. Superficially it might appear as if the problem of the relation of Reason to Faith is of importance only as it touches the alleged conflict between Science and Religion. Most frequently, in popular discussion, the question takes some such form as, "How can both the account of creation in Genesis and the theory of evolution be true?", or the guise of many other such problems that may be found in the 19th century writings of a T. H. Huxley. To those who profess to be non-religious, and take a "tough-minded," strictly "scientific" point of view, the problem thus simply stated seems to be of little, if any, importance.

However, the problem is not as simple as just suggested. It is the problem of the relation of two ways of knowledge. In the realms of

[21]Cf. Wolfson, H. A., *Philo*, Harvard University Press, 1948, Vol. I, Chap. II, pp. 87–163, especially pp. 155–163.

reason, in logic, in mathematics, in the sciences, in philosophy, we presumably start from simple propositions that require no demonstration, either because they state what is given to us by the senses, such as, for example, the proposition that paper burns; or because the propositions are such that the mind grasps them immediately and intuitively; of this latter kind, the proposition that a thing cannot both be and not be at the same time is an example. From such propositions we proceed logically to make inferences, give our demonstrations, and erect our structures of knowledge.

In religious matters the situation is radically different. What *defines* the *religious* realm, what differentiates it from any other realm of human activity, is *faith,* faith in entities or propositions the truth of which is apprehended and adhered to neither because they tell us what is given to us by the senses, nor because they are self-evident axioms or logical laws implicitly fundamental to the very processes of all rational thought. The propositions or entities apprehended by faith are apprehended in a manner apart from and *prior to* the activities of the senses or of reason. How this problem of the relation of faith to reason arose for Maimonides is not difficult to perceive, and we shall return to it presently.

However, this problem arises not only in connection with religion. It is because it arises also in situations which are much more familiar and of everyday consequence that the problem is so urgent. A simple illustration which a teacher of mine was fond of using will help to explain this. Suppose that you have a friend. You have known him for many years. You cherish a profound affection for him. If anyone should ask you whether your friend is honest you would unhesitatingly say that he is. If some one asked you *why* you believe him to be honest, you could probably, after some thought, produce what you would consider evidence to establish his honesty. But what is important in the present context is that you had believed your friend to be honest *long before* you began seeking evidence for your belief. You believed that he is honest *not because* you knew the evidence that you subsequently marshalled to establish the fact of his honesty. It was *pure belief,* completely apart from reason, from demonstration, from sense perception, or axiomatic self-evidence.

Such is the nature of belief or faith. It arises in all aspects of life. The most universal example of its occurrence is the belief, or assumption, on the part of all men, including scientists and philosophers, that this universe of ours is in some sense ordered and reasonable, that it displays some constant natural laws. This is believed long before and completely apart from any attempt to *reason* about the world. If we did not possess this faith we would not venture beyond our doorstep, because there would be nothing to assure us that the earth or the pavement beyond our doorstep still exists. This very explanation of what the absence of such belief would mean is a *consequence* of the belief, and not a *premise* from which it is inferred. The belief is never inferred; it is an *a priori* conviction, a matter of pure *faith.*

Under certain circumstances a conflict arises between our faith and our reason. What would happen to your conviction about the honesty of your friend, to whom we referred above, if you were told that he was caught stealing? Here your belief would conflict with the evidence of the senses, which is one of the starting points in the process of reasoning. There is a strong possibility that even under these circumstances you would not readily give up your faith in your friend's honesty. You might attempt to explain it away by saying that he was probably in dire need, or that it may have been a case of yielding to momentary temptation, or of temporary derangement, but your friend's honesty might still remain unimpeached in your eyes.

In the case of religion we are confronted with the assertion that reason and the senses do not exhaust the knowledge of all reality. There is the belief in the realm of the supernatural, in a supernatural being. We experience awe and exaltation in the presence of a Reality greater, more powerful, and more enduring than anything observed by the senses or comprehended by reason. There is the experience of what Rudolf Otto called *Das Heilige.*[22] Experiencing the presence of that Reality—of the Holy—gives us a sense of meaning, of value, of purpose in our lives. This is the *subjective* aspect of the phenomenon, which has its *objective* counterpart. To borrow a pair of terms from I. A. Richards, our "belief-state" has a "belief-object."[23] The belief-object is God, who, we say, exists "out there," *ontologically,* and gives meaning to the world and to our existence.

This is another example of *faith.* It is of the same kind as our belief in the reality of the honesty of our friend, or of the ordered character of the universe. It is *apart* from and *prior* to any considerations of evidence. Only *after* we ask ourselves or are asked *why* we believe that these things really are so, do we begin searching for reasons to justify or support our belief. Some of the beliefs arise in individual experience; others are handed down to us by tradition. In connection with the inevitable formalization of the belief in the existence of God and in a supernatural realm, some beliefs arise that appear to be, from the point of view of reason, absurd. Thus a conflict is engendered.

Such was the problem as it arose for Maimonides. He was a religious Jew. He wrote the *Guide* in order to help solve the perplexities of other religious Jews who found themselves faced with the task of

[22]Cf. Otto, Rudolf, *The Idea of the Holy,* Oxford University Press, 1926.

[23]Richards, I. A., "Belief," in *The Symposium* (a quarterly), October 1930, Vol. I, No. 4, pp. 423–439.

defending their faith against the attack of Reason. He was not the first to deal with the problem in these terms. Some interesting answers are recorded in Christian theology. Tertullian, at the end of the 2nd century and the beginning of the 3rd, threw Reason overboard completely and answered: "*Credo quia impossibile est*"—"I believe *because* it is impossible." St. Augustine, at the end of the 4th century, and St. Anselm after him in the 11th century, said "*Credo ut intelligam*"—"I believe *in order to* understand"; in other words, without belief it is impossible to know, to understand.

This may sound absurd to some modern ears. However, in a real sense every starting point for reasoning, whether it be propositions based on what is given us by the senses, or so-called self-evident axioms, is a matter of faith, of revelation, since these are not *demonstrated* propositions arrived at by rational processes. We, of today, with our scientific or pseudo-scientific bias, might hastily claim, if we spoke Latin, "*Intelligo ergo credo*"—"I understand, *therefore* I believe." We would wish to flatter ourselves that we believe only because and only after we understand with our Reason. But in fact even the faith of the ordinary man in the powers and claims of science is on the whole a matter of pure belief; and, on a more sophisticated intellectual level, the assumption about the reasonableness and ordered character of the universe is in a real sense a matter of Faith, beyond the possibility of rational proof.

It is in his solution of this problem, of the relationship of Reason to Faith, that Maimonides' contribution to philosophy appears to me to be of genuine and permanent importance. Viewed in its broad context, this problem is one of the perennial and fundamental problems of philosophy. It is among the problems which distinguish the philosophical enterprise from other intellectual pursuits. What is unique about philosophy is its analytic and critical role in examining the concepts, methods and presuppositions of all human knowledge. This is reflected in statements by contemporary thinkers of widely varying views. Alfred North Whitehead said:

> I hold that philosophy is the critic of abstractions. Its function is the double one, first of harmonizing them by assigning them their right relative status as abstractions, and secondly of completing them by direct comparison with more concrete intuitions of the universe, and thereby promoting the formation of more complete schemes of thought.[24]

John Dewey's view was that

[24]Whitehead, A. N., *Science and the Modern World,* Macmillan Co., 1925, p. 126.

> . . . philosophy is inherently criticism, having its distinctive position among various modes of criticism in its generality; a criticism of criticisms, as it were.[25]

> . . . philosophy is and can be nothing but this critical operation and function become aware of itself and its implications, pursued deliberately and systematically.[26]

In a recent introductory textbook in philosophy we find the following:

> . . . philosophic thinking . . . is confronted with the task of clarifying and criticising the fundamental methods, rules, procedures, and standards or norms of all theoretical enterprises, including those of scientific inquiry itself . . . The methods and tests of knowing have always occupied a central place in philosophical thinking.[27]

In another textbook, William Ernest Hocking states:

> The especial responsibility of philosophy is to bring the care for literal truth, sound evidence, and accurate thinking into the larger aspects of the world . . . philosophy must reason as far as reason will go. It must know what can be proved and what cannot; it must know what is myth and what is literal. If there is a sphere of truth which must be left to probability or to faith, it must indicate that sphere. If there are limits to reason, it must furnish a reasoned chart of those limits. It must everywhere keep faith with the scientific spirit and, seeking for certainty, make clear the area in which certitude has given way to conjecture.[28]

The philosophical enterprise is thus basically a methodological one, and Maimonides' solution of the problem of the relation of Reason and Faith is a methodological solution. It is important to point out that in this case also he had predecessors on whom to draw. Saadia, in the first half of the 10th century, was explicitly concerned with this problem in his work *Emunot V'Deot.* Here Saadia distinguished between four sources of knowledge: 1) Direct observation (sense perception); 2) Intuition of the intellect (self-evident knowledge); 3) Logical inference; 4) Authentic tradition.[29] However, by saying that knowledge "which is furnished by authentic tradition and the books

[25]Dewey, John, *Experience and Nature,* Open Court, 1925, p. 398.

[26]Ibid., p. 403.

[27]Randall, John Herman Jr., and Buchler, Justus, *Philosophy: An Introduction,* Barnes and Noble, 1942, pp. 9–10.

[28]Hocking, Blanshard, Hendel, and Randall, Preface to *Philosophy: A Textbook,* Macmillan Co., 1946, p. 420.

[29]Saadia Gaon, *The Book of Beliefs and Opinions,* translated by Samuel Rosenblatt, Yale University Press, 1948, pp. 16–18.

of prophetic revelation" is based on the other three sources of knowledge, Saadia really evaded the problem. He held that an investigation of the beliefs and teachings of religious or prophetic authority, "even if it should take a long time," will reveal a complete and unquestionable translatability of these beliefs into terms of "rational knowledge and logical inference."[30] Saadia thus merely equated knowledge on the basis of reason with revelation and tradition. He explained that knowledge by tradition and revelation is needed only because: a) it would take too long for man to discover the truths of revelation through the process of reasoning, and "we would have remained without religious guidance whatever, for a while, until the process of reasoning was completed by us"; and b) those who are held back from rational investigation, or "women and young people and those who have no aptitude for speculation, can thus also have a perfect and accessible faith."[31]

Maimonides' solution was altogether different. In his early treatise on logical terminology, Maimonides distinguished substantially the same four sources of knowledge that we find listed by Saadia. The fourth source, "traditions" *(m'kubalot)*, he describes as "whatever is accepted on the authority of one or more of the chosen few."[32] In the *Guide* he describes the fourth type of knowledge, which he here calls "belief" (*emunah* or *ha'amanah*—Ibn Tibbon's version) as

> . . . not merely that which is uttered by the lips, but also that which is apprehended by the soul, the conviction that the object (of belief) is exactly as it is apprehended.[33]

Further on, Maimonides says:

> . . . belief is only possible after the apprehension of a thing; it consists in the conviction that the thing apprehended has its existence beyond the mind (in reality) exactly as it is conceived in the mind.[34]

He then proceeds to state his view on the relation between Reason and Faith in what, from a philosophico-methodological point of view, I am inclined to consider the most important passage in the *Guide:*

> If in addition to this we are convinced that the thing cannot be different in any way from what we believe it to be, and that *no reasonable argument*

[30]Ibid., pp. 26–33.
[31]Ibid., pp. 31–32.
[32]*Millot HaHiggayon*, Chap. VIII; cf. Efros' translation, in *Proceedings of the American Academy for Jewish Research*, Vol. VIII, 1938, p. 47.
[33]*The Guide of the Perplexed*, Book I, Chapter 50, p. 67.
[34]Ibid., Book I, Chap. 50, p. 68.

can be found for the rejection of this belief or for the admission of any deviation from it, then the belief is true.[35] (Italics supplied)

In other words, among the mental activities of human beings is the activity we call *Belief*. Through this activity we apprehend certain data. We are convinced that corresponding to our *belief-state* there is a *belief-object* which has its existence in reality exactly as it is apprehended by us. In addition to this knowledge through Belief there is knowledge through Reason. It is incumbent upon us to examine all our beliefs thoroughly in the light of Reason, and *if we find them to be in conflict with Reason*, i.e., to be absurd, *we must discard them.*

Maimonides had no patience with those who start with their beliefs and then attempt to *justify* these beliefs. The task as he saw it was almost the opposite. We must examine our beliefs in the light of Reason, and we must honestly attempt almost to disprove them. In the course of this process of critical examination, we may find that our beliefs are supported by Reason, or by Natural Law, as in the case of the existence of God. When such support or verification is found, we of course accept it; but then the emphasis must be on *Natural Law*, and on the *scientific validity* of the proof and of the ground for our belief. When Reason disproves our beliefs, *we must discard them* as superstition.

If, in the course of our thoroughgoing examinations *we can find no reasonable argument for rejecting our belief*, if we find that logic and science break down and cease to be relevant to the belief under consideration, *only then may we hold on to our belief* with a clear conscience, even though we cannot supply any logical proof of its truth.

If Maimonides had written in Latin he is likely to have said something like *"Credo et intelligo"*—"I believe *and* understand." Reason and Faith are on an equal footing as sources or methods of knowledge. *Genetically*, in the sequence of the process of acquiring knowledge, Faith comes first, both in religious and in non-religious matters. However, Faith must be checked by Reason, since it may and often does lead us into absurdities and superstitions.

The fact that beliefs through revelation and prophecy are attained *prior to and apart from* Reason in no way renders the revealed truths irrational. That some of these revealed truths, like the existence of God, can subsequently be *demonstrated* by *Reason* is evidence that at least some of these truths are rational, and that both the way of Reason and the way of Faith are ways to the truth. But faith, revelation, prophecy, or authoritative tradition are not given to man merely because some men's reasoning powers are inferior; they are given to

[35]Ibid., p. 68.

man because they sometimes lead us to the discovery of truths which Reason is altogether impotent to discover by its own procedures. We may never be able to prove some of these revealed truths logically, but if we cannot find any logical reason for rejecting them they are valid.

What is most striking about this position is the relentless honesty of the man who formulated it. Here was a religious Jew who believed, and an analytic man, a first-rate logician and philosopher, who reasoned. When he was confronted with the problem of Creation versus the Eternity of the universe, and found that he could only show the inconclusiveness of Aristotle's doctrine of the Eternity of the universe but could not conclusively prove its Creation, he faced the situation squarely, as pointed out earlier in this paper, and said explicitly that he *accepts Creation on authority,* since "the theory of Creation, as taught in Scripture, contains nothing that is impossible."[36] And so we find him on the one hand banishing superstition with the zeal of the Rationalist, but declaring in his "Thirteen Principles of Faith" his belief in the coming of the Messiah and in the Resurrection. Obviously neither of these two beliefs can be established scientifically, nor can they be disproved, and Maimonides' own position required him to accept them as a matter of Faith.

Maimonides has frequently been called a Rationalist, and with some degree of justification. In a religious age dominated by Faith, he insisted on systematizing what is given by Faith and checking it by the merciless scalpel of Reason. Maimonides, however, was more than that. Against blind irrationalism he was a Rationalist, insisting on the supremacy of Reason both as a tool to check blind impulse and control superstitious belief, and as a noble, distinguished end in itself. Against extreme Rationalism he pointed out the limitations of Reason, and maintained the autonomy of Faith as a way of knowing so long as it does not conflict with Reason where Reason is supreme.

[36]Ibid., Book II, Chap. 16, p. 178.

II. Spinoza

3. *Spinoza's Logic of Inquiry: Rationalist or Experientialist?*

4. *Spinoza's Onslaught on Judaism*

5. *Was Spinoza a "Jewish" Philosopher?*

3. *Spinoza's Logic of Inquiry: Rationalist or Experientialist?*

Readers whose approach to Spinoza's philosophy reflects widely held, traditional assumptions concerning Spinoza and Rationalism, frequently espouse two fashionable stereotypes. The first is that, in the title of this paper, the "or" between "Rationalist" and "Experientialist" is necessarily an exclusive "or," and that there can be no intermingling between these two modes of philosophical inquiry. The second stereotype is that Spinoza was a rigid, uncompromising *Rationalist* who ". . . completely separated . . . rational thought and . . . empirical observation [with] no way of getting from one to the other."[1] In this paper I propose to discuss these two still fashionable assumptions.

I

Many years ago, in a lecture on Spinoza, the late Professor Frederick J. E. Woodbridge of Columbia University said that Spinoza's *Ethics* "does not represent the way he arrived at his conclusions, but the way he expressed them."[2] This distinction between the "Geometric

[1] W. T. Jones, *A History of Western Philosophy*, 2d ed. (New York: Harcourt, Brace & World, 1969), Vol. III, 217–218.

[2] Frederick J. E. Woodbridge, *Spinoza*, lecture delivered at Columbia University, January 26, 1933, published as a separate brochure (New York: Columbia University Press [no date]), 9.

Richard Kennington (ed.), *The Philosophy of Baruch Spinoza* (Washington: The Catholic University of America Press, 1980), pp. 247–272.

Order" in which the *Ethics* is presented, with its formidable deductive apparatus, and on the other hand the putatively different way in which the doctrines of the *Ethics* were arrived at, or could be arrived at, is reinforced by a passage in a powerful but sadly neglected book, published at about the same time as Woodbridge's lecture. I refer to H. F. Hallett's *Aeternitas: A Spinozistic Study*. On page 4 Hallett pointed out that

> It is because it has not always been remembered that the order of discovery often reverses the logical order, i.e., the real order of nature, that Spinoza's doctrine has commonly been misinterpreted . . . And the position is not rendered more safe for the unwary by Spinoza's attempt to identify the order of nature and the order of exposition by the use of the . . . geometric form in his chief metaphysical work, the *Ethics*.[3]

The exposition or presentation in the *Ethics* is *ordine geometrico*. From Definitions and Axioms it proceeds deductively to generate theorems, called Propositions by Spinoza, each of which ostensibly claims the right to be part of the deductive system by virtue of a demonstration that shows it to follow logically from: (a) these initial Axioms and Definitions; or from (b) additional Axioms, Definitions, and also a number of Postulates, that are later introduced at various points in the *Ethics;* or from (c) other theorems or Propositions the logical dependence of which upon prior Axioms, Definitions, Postulates, or theorems has already been demonstrated; or from combinations of these. What has occasioned voluminous comment is the fact that these Axioms, Postulates, and Definitions are, like those in Euclid's *Elements,* themselves undemonstrated. This fact, in turn, has inevitably led to the question, whence, for Spinoza, do these Axioms, Postulates, as well as the Definitions derive their truth?

From among the several interpretations to be found in the extensive Spinoza literature, I focus on what appear to me to be three prototypical biases with respect to this question. I shall call them a) The Euclidean Bias; b) The Rationalist Bias; c) The Historicist Bias.

a) *The Euclidean Bias.* Because of its geometric form, and consequently the inevitable comparison that is drawn between Spinoza's *Ethics* and Euclid's *Elements,* the attempt has often been made to approach this question by way of the traditional interpretation of Euclid, according to which his Axioms have been accepted as self-evident, and his Definitions either as necessarily true, or as nominal explanations of the use of terms and thus neither false nor true. The theorems deduced from these axioms, definitions, and postulates are

[3]H. F. Hallett, *Aeternitas, A Spinozistic Study* (Oxford: Clarendon Press, 1930), 4.

therefore said to gain their truth from the self-evident certainty of the presuppositions. For a long time Spinoza's *Ethics* was interpreted as having tried to do the same thing, or something similar to it. From allegedly self-evident axioms and definitions he was said to have deduced, or drawn out, his entire system; and on the *self-evident* truth of these presuppositions his system supposedly rests.

This interpretation has persisted at least since the year 1661 when Spinoza's contemporary, Henry Oldenburg, criticized his early experiments with the geometric order. Oldenburg wrote to Spinoza as follows:

> The third question is, whether you hold those axioms, which you communicated to me, as indemonstrable principles, recognized by the light of nature, and standing in no need of proof? It may be that the first axiom is of such a kind; but I don't see how the remaining three can be included in the number of such principles . . . Since, then, these axioms do not seem to me to be placed beyond all risk of doubt, you will easily conjecture that your propositions which are based on them cannot but be shaky. And the more I consider them, the more I am overwhelmed with doubts about them.[4]

It is interesting to note that, while Spinoza obviously held that his axioms were true, there is no evidence that he placed them at the beginning of the *Ethics* with any illusions that they would be accepted as self-evident. As a matter of fact, in his reply to Oldenburg's letter Spinoza made no attempt to persuade him that the axioms are self-evident. His reply amounts almost to an acquiescence in Oldenburg's contention. These are Spinoza's words:

> You proceed . . . to object to my assertions, [and state] that [my] axioms are not to be reckoned among Common Notions. Over this, however, I will not dispute.[5]

It is important also to note that, if self-evidence had been Spinoza's criterion for placing any proposition among the axioms, and if his system were purely a deduction from these self-evident axioms, the beginning portions of the first part of the *Ethics* should hardly have undergone the drastic changes they did undergo from earlier versions[6] to their final form. It would have been inconceivable for propo-

[4]A. Wolf (ed. and transl.), *The Correspondence of Spinoza* (London: George Allen & Unwin, 1928), Ep. 3, 79. Hereafter cited as Wolf (a).

[5]Wolf (a), Ep. 4, 82.

[6]*Spinoza's Short Treatise on God, Man, and His Well-Being*, transl. A. Wolf (London: Russell & Russell, 1963), Appendix I, 153–156; Wolf (a), 371–373. *Spinoza's Short Treatise* is hereafter cited as Wolf (b).

sitions that were originally classed as (self-evident) Axioms to have migrated later, as they in fact did, into the bulk of *demonstrated* theorems in the text of the *Ethics.* As a result of such migration, we find the system endeavoring to *prove* some of the propositions that presumably had been, at least at one time, considered by Spinoza to be among its putatively self-evident axioms or presuppositions. Such behavior is hardly what one expects from a respectable deductive system whose starting point is a group of self-evident Axioms.

But Spinoza had no illusions about self-evidence. In his work we find a keen awareness of the fact that what may be self-evident to one person is only too frequently quite obscure to another. We sometimes find him doing what a logically competent person, who is constructing a strict *a priori,* deductive system logically drawn out of self-evident axioms, would be expected never to do, namely, yielding to human frailty, and quite consciously placing, among the theorems to be proved, a proposition which he considered axiomatic. Such is proposition 7 of Part I of the *Ethics:* "It pertains to the nature of substance to exist." In the Scholium to the very next Proposition Spinoza remarks that

> . . . if men would attend to the nature of substance, they would not entertain a single doubt of the truth of proposition 7; indeed this Proposition would be considered by all to be axiomatic, and reckoned among the common notions.[7]

b) *The Rationalist Bias.* Spinoza has been almost universally denominated a Rationalist. In the recent *Encyclopedia of Philosophy* Alasdair MacIntyre refers to him as "rationalist metaphysician," and identifies him, in accord with the traditional, received classification in most histories and textbooks of philosophy, as one of the three "Continental Rationalists."[8] As to the meaning of Rationalism, Bernard Williams, writing in the same *Encyclopedia of Philosophy,* singles out among the "several different outlooks and movements of ideas" included under the label "rationalism," as "by far the most important . . . the philosophical outlook or program which stresses the power of *a priori* reason to grasp truths about the world."[9]

Spinoza's *Ethics* is generally taken to be an example *par excellence* of Rationalist thought, a product of such *a priori* reasoning, which proceeds deductively from certain "innate ideas," or "clear and distinct ideas," perceived by man's *lumen naturale,* or "natural light" of rea-

[7]*Ethics,* Part I, Proposition 8, Scholium.

[8]Alasdair MacIntyre, "Spinoza," in *The Encyclopedia of Philosophy* (New York: Macmillan, 1967), Vol. 7, 530–541.

[9]Bernard Williams, "Rationalism," ibid., Vol. 7, 69.

son. Such ideas include God, Thought, Extension. They are verbalized in and represented by the Axioms and Definitions in the *Ethics*. The Geometric Order is deemed the most congenial to this kind of methodology, and indeed, the "Geometric *Method*" (a locution repeatedly used by many commentators as if it were Spinoza's own, though in fact this locution was never used by Spinoza himself)[9a] is deemed *the* philosophical method for the discovery of new ideas and facts about the universe. The Axioms and Definitions are thus versions of our autonomous, self-validating innate ideas, uncontaminated by experience, and grasped *a priori* by the *natural light*, through the exercise of *scientia intuitiva*. From these ideas, employing the rational technique of logical deduction, Spinoza spun the logically coherent, rational diagram of the rationally structured universe, bringing forth in the *Ethics* what to W. T. Jones "seems a dream philosophy—a magnificent, even inspiring edifice, but still a dream."[10]

In the face of this prevalent bias it was, for many years, considered ill-mannered and intellectually disreputable to suggest that Spinoza did not resemble quite perfectly the stereotypical portrait of the rigid Rationalist, or that his alleged disparagement of and contempt for experience as a source of knowledge was not as thoroughly immaculate or consistent as believed or claimed. Those who, beginning two or three decades ago, thought they discovered significant empirical or experientialist elements in Spinoza's philosophical methodology, and flirted with the idea that some of the Axioms and Definitions of the *Ethics* may be based on *experience*, and may have been seen as so based by Spinoza himself, therefore constituted a kind of unorganized underground in Spinoza scholarship that began to surface only in the past two decades. Such books as H. G. Hubbeling's *Spinoza's Methodology*[11] and C. de Deugd's *The Significance of Spinoza's First Kind of Knowledge*[12] are examples, as well as more recent individual essays by G. H. Parkinson and E. M. Curley, to which reference will be made later.

c) *The Historicist Bias*. Under this rubric are included those who approach the *Ethics* almost exclusively from an historical point of view, and are engaged largely in tracing its intellectual antecedents to

[9a]Referring to this statement by Dr. Franck to the effect that Spinoza did not use the locution "Geometric Method," Herman de Dijn, of the Catholic University of Louvain, declared, in *The Review of Metaphysics*, vol. 40 (September 1986), p. 64, that "Spinoza himself talks about the geometrical *way* as being a *method*." Professor de Dijn gave the following citations in support of his declaration: *Ethics*, Part II, Proposition 40, and *Ethics*, Part III, preface. [Note by W. G.]

[10]W. T. Jones, op. cit., Vol. III, 217.

[11]H. G. Hubbeling, *Spinoza's Methodology* (Assen: Van Gorcum, 1964).

[12]Cornelius de Deugd, *The Significance of Spinoza's First Kind of Knowledge* (Assen: Van Gorcum, 1964).

the writings of his predecessors. The most distinguished of these Spinoza scholars was, of course, the late Professor H. A. Wolfson of Harvard. His great and irreplaceable work, *The Philosophy of Spinoza,* throws a powerful new light on Spinoza's work in general and on the *Ethics* in particular. However, so overwhelming is the cumulative massing of the historical evidence that questions about the logical, methodological, and epistemological status and sources of the Axioms and Definitions and other central ideas in the *Ethics* are almost lost sight of. It would seem almost as if Spinoza's philosophical ideas propounded in the *Ethics* were not at all based on any processes of philosophical or logical analysis or speculation. It would seem rather as if they were woven altogether out of the ideas of his predecessors and his critical responses to them—from Plato through Aristotle, the Neo-Platonists, the Stoics, the Arabic philosophers, the Scholastics and Descartes, as well as the thinkers in the mainstream of Jewish philosophy: the rabbis of the Talmudic period, Philo, Isaac Israeli, Saadia, Solomon ibn Gabirol, Bahya ibn Pakuda, Yehudah Halevi, Abraham ibn Ezra, Moses Maimonides, Gersonides, Hasdai Crescas, Joseph Albo, etc.

II

However, such interpretations are far removed from the spirit, the intentions, and the convictions incorporated in the *Ethics*. Spinoza's chief concern in this work is exactly what the title of his book is, namely, *ethics*. It is a concern with striving for a way of life that will attain the highest good that man is capable of, namely the life of freedom; freedom, in the words of Prof. Woodbridge, "from our unruly wills and emotions that are the causes of our misery,"[13] freedom from *perturbationes mentis*. "Everything in the sciences that does not promote this endeavor must be rejected as useless,"[14] says Spinoza. The only way this goal can be attained, according to Spinoza, is through "the knowledge of the union which the mind has with the whole of nature,"[15] and this entails the study of nature. Spinoza wrote the *Ethics* in order to exhibit this very union. He wanted to exhibit the structure of things, and to show man's place in this structure. He did not write the *Ethics* as an exercise in logic, or in *a priori* reasoning, or in the synthesizing or criticizing of the ideas of his predecessors.

[13]Woodbridge, op. cit., 3.

[14]*Tractatus de Intellectus Emendatione* (hereafter cited as TdIE), Para. 16.

[15]TdIE, Para. 13.

The procedure of the *Ethics* is accurately described in its subtitle as *Ordine Geometrico Demonstrata.* The *Ethics* is a *demonstration,* an ἀπόδειξις, but it is a demonstration in *geometrical* order. Every demonstration proceeds deductively from certain premisses, first principles, or ἀρχαί; in the case of Spinoza's *Ethics,* these premisses are furnished by the definitions, axioms, and postulates. Therefore, the question of the truth of the definitions and axioms of the *Ethics* is not only relevant but of crucial importance. However, in the *Ethics,* as in any demonstration, the truth of the premisses is taken for granted or assumed *in the course of the demonstration,* and may be inquired into and discovered only *outside* of the framework or procedure of the particular demonstration itself. To put it succinctly: the order or logic of demonstration is distinct from any order or logic of inquiry or discovery, and questions of the *order* or *logic of inquiry and discovery* are improper to the process of the demonstration itself. The axioms and definitions of the *Ethics* perform the function of putatively true premisses in a demonstration, and these may be discovered, and their truth grasped, *not as a consequence* of the demonstrations of the *Ethics,* but outside of their framework and their procedure.[16]

The *Ethics* is not an *Inquiry;* it is not a *Critique;* it is not a *Discourse;* it is not a set of *Meditations;* it is not a *Summa;* it is not a *Tractatus.* The *Ethics* is a *Demonstration,* or a series of demonstrations, of an elaborate group of doctrines concerning nature, man, man's body and mind, his emotions, his slavery to his emotions, and his liberation from this slavery. This demonstration, or group of demonstrations, is in the nature of an attempt to show that these doctrines propounded by Spinoza are related as conclusions to the premisses (in this case the definitions, axioms, and postulates) that stand at the head of the various parts of the demonstration; and the discovery of which occurs outside and apart from its order. This approach to the *Ethics* as a demonstration has, as I shall attempt to show, important consequences in its interpretation.

If we ask whether or not the premisses of an *apodeixis* or demonstration are themselves true, we are told that, while the question is legitimate and even imperative, nevertheless the answer to it cannot be given in terms of, or within the framework of, the apodeixis itself. The answer to this question must be sought in an inquiry outside the confines of the demonstration proper. The truth of the premisses has its foundation in knowledge that is prior to the deductive procedure and the conclusions of the demonstration. This, of course, is the

[16]This and what follows immediately below of course reflect Aristotle's analysis of "demonstrative knowledge" in the *Posterior Analytics* I, 1–4, 71a 1–73a 23; and II, 18–19, 99b 15–100b 17.

Aristotelian analysis, according to which "all instruction given or received by way of argument proceeds from pre-existent knowledge," and demonstrative or apodeictic reasoning is such that by its very nature it assumes an audience that accepts its premisses.[17]

If we now proceed to inquire, outside of the framework of the demonstration, in what manner this previous knowledge, or what is the same thing, the putatively true premisses, were obtained, it may be answered, of course, that they themselves are in turn conclusions of demonstrations; but this tracing back cannot continue, because, either it will involve an infinite regress, which amounts to a denial of the possibility of demonstrative knowledge; or, if no infinite regress is allowed, it will amount to an admission that all knowledge is circular.[18] But since demonstrative knowledge *is* in fact possible, we must assume the existence of another kind of knowledge, which is "independent of demonstration,"[19] and by means of which it is possible to obtain the "basic truths," the premisses, the first principles, on which demonstrated knowledge is based.

The concluding pages of Aristotle's analysis in the *Posterior Analytics* contain the account of how by ἐπαγογή (*epagoge,* generally translated "induction"), by a leading on, knowledge is built up from sense perception into memory, thence into experience, and thence into scientific knowledge; how νοῦς (*nous,* translated "intuition" in the Oxford Press translation) grasps the universal; and how the universal is then given as premiss for demonstrative knowledge.[20] It can be shown, and has been shown quite clearly by H. A. Wolfson,[21] that Spinoza's explication of the *origin* of knowledge is not as different from that of Aristotle as it has frequently been assumed to be.

Clearly also Spinoza followed Aristotle in his conception of what constitutes scientific knowledge. The premisses from which a scientific conclusion is demonstrated are the logical causes, the principles, the *archai,* on which the conclusion depends and through which it is known. Spinoza's principle that "true science proceeds from cause to effect"[22] is only a paraphrase of Aristotle's statement that "we have scientific knowledge . . . when we think we know the cause on which the thing depends."[23] Indeed, Spinoza makes it axiomatic that "the knowledge of an effect depends upon and involves the knowledge of

[17]Ibid., I, 1, 71a 1–7.

[18]Ibid., I, 3, 72b 5–17.

[19]Ibid., I, 3, 72b 18–20.

[20]Ibid., II, 19, 99b 18–100b 17.

[21]H. A. Wolfson, *The Philosophy of Spinoza,* 2 vols. (Cambridge, Mass.: Harvard University Press, 1934), II, 151–154.

[22]TdIE, Para. 85.

[23]Aristotle, *Posterior Analytics,* I, 2, 71b 20–22.

the cause."[24] Ernst Cassirer, in his classic (and still untranslated) history of the problem of knowledge in the philosophy and science of the modern era, summed up neatly Spinoza's relationship to Aristotle on this issue, in the following sentence:

> So bleibt hier die Aristotelische Definition der Wissenschaft, dass sie die Erkenntnis der Wirkungen aus den Ursachen sei, im Kraft.[25] (Thus the Aristotelian definition of science as the knowledge of effects through their causes remains in force here.)

To sum up then, the truth of the premisses is not demonstrable within the particular demonstration itself. Their truth is assumed in the demonstration, and questions of their origin and ground are irrelevant and improper to the course of the demonstration. How the premisses were arrived at, or may be arrived at, is a subject for a separate inquiry. And it is to be noted that the order and logic of inquiry into and discovery of such basic truths, or premisses, or axioms, that are employed in the structure of any given apodeictic system, are different and distinct from the order and logic of demonstration of that system.

III

There is an abundance of evidence that Spinoza was keenly aware of this distinction between the proper order and logic of inquiry and the order of demonstration. His decision to write a special treatise, the *Tractatus de Intellectus Emendatione,* for the purpose of showing how the intellect "may be directed towards a true knowledge of things,"[26] testifies cogently that he did not consider the enterprise of this treatise, namely, the enterprise of "directing the intellect," to be part of the task of the *Ethics.* Neither did his correspondents. In one of his letters to Spinoza, Tschirnhaus inquires, "when are we to have your method of controlling reason rightly in acquiring knowledge of unknown truths?"[27] Tschirnhaus was obviously not referring to the *Ethics,* since most of *Ethics* I was already in his hands. The TdIE was never completed, and therefore there are serious lacunae in Spinoza's theory of the correct order and logic of inquiry. The fact remains,

[24]*Ethics,* Part I, Axiom 4.

[25]Ernst Cassirer, *Das Erkenntnisproblem in der Philosophie und Wissenschaft der neueren Zeit,* II, 16.

[26]From the subtitle of the TdIE.

[27]Wolf (a), Ep. 59, 298.

however, that this treatise was begun for the purpose of explaining just what such an order should be, and of thus leading up to some of the premisses and first principles on which the demonstration, or group of demonstrations, that the *Ethics* is, logically rests.

It will be instructive to digress here in order to note how this approach to the *Ethics*, as a demonstration the premisses of which are discovered outside of the demonstration itself, eliminates some alleged difficulties that seemingly present themselves on other interpretations. The nineteenth-century Spinoza scholar, James Martineau, interpreted the TdIE correctly as "laying down the principles of knowledge and the order of discovery," but in the very next breath he proceeded to claim that to this order of discovery "the order of the [*Ethics*] should conform."[28] He thus conceived it to be part of the task of the *Ethics* to *discover* the "substantive truth." Consequently, it seemed paradoxical to him that in the TdIE we find Spinoza's "exposition of the rules of knowing already bespeaking the things known; so that if he had completed his theory of method, he would have told, in the process, the substantive truth which was professedly waiting to take shape from it."[29] This alleged paradox is only a result, first, of erroneously assigning to the *Ethics* the task of *discovering* "the substantive truth"; and, second, of being blinded, by virtue of having reserved this assignment for the *Ethics*, to the possibility of achieving this discovery in the course of the inquiry of the TdIE.

It would have been logically impossible, and methodologically inconceivable, to discover this "substantive truth" (meaning of course *God*) in the course of the argument of the *Ethics*, since this truth is itself one of the ἀρχαί, or more properly, the one major fundamental principle that is presupposed by the subject matter of the *Ethics*, and from which this work logically proceeds. The discovery of this substantive truth in the TdIE is not at all paradoxical. In Spinoza's view, the mere exposition of the correct order of inquiry and discovery inevitably leads to some of what this correct order is designed to discover, namely, some of the premisses of the basic truths from which the demonstration of scientific knowledge must proceed. It would have been strange, in the context of Spinoza's thought, if the TdIE, even in its unfinished state, did not lead us to the two major ἀρχαί, God and the human understanding, the first of which is the major principle involved in the demonstrations of Part I of the *Ethics*, and the second in the demonstrations of Part II.

There is also evidence within the *Ethics* itself that Spinoza did *not* consider it among the tasks of that work to inquire into the sources of

[28]James Martineau, *A Study of Spinoza* (London: Macmillan, 1895), 48.
[29]Ibid., 48–49.

its axioms or to expound the proper order or logic of such an inquiry. In Part II of the *Ethics,* after having demonstrated that the *notiones communes* are to be included among adequate ideas (Prop. 37–39), Spinoza appends a scholium to the next proposition, in which he says that it would also be advantageous to discuss further other *causes of other axioms and notions;* such a discussion would enable us to distinguish *useful notions* from *useless* or *partially useful ones,* and to distinguish further those which are *common* and those which are clear and distinct, and those which are ill-founded. Moreover, he says, such an inquiry would tell us "whence those notions called secondary, and consequently whence *the axioms which are founded on them,* derive their origin." But, Spinoza continues, "I have set apart this subject for *another treatise.*"[30] The reference here to the TdIE is unmistakable.[31] First of all, there is evidence that Spinoza worked on the TdIE at the time of the composition of the *Ethics.* Secondly, the description of the subject matter of such a treatise fits fairly accurately the discussions in the TdIE.

This internal evidence, taken from the *Ethics,* is of utmost importance. It points conclusively to the TdIE as the treatise in which matters proper to a method and logic of inquiry are properly discussed. It does away, once and for all, with the assumption that axioms were, for Spinoza, self-evident propositions, concerning the genesis and the truth of which no questions need be asked. Indeed, Spinoza states unequivocally that he has just explained, first *"the causes of those notions which are called common,"* second, that *"of some axioms or notions other causes exist"* (*"cause,"* of course, in the sense of ἀρχή, principle of explanation), and, third, he points to *the problem of whence certain* "axioms . . . derive their origin" as a problem that will be treated in the TdIE. Now, a phrase in the passage just quoted from the first scholium to Proposition 40 of Part II of the *Ethics* will require some attention. It will show that the prejudice concerning the self-evidence of Spinoza's axioms has even resulted in unnecessary and unwarranted tampering with the Latin text of the *Ethics.* The full passage reads as follows in the Latin:

> Praeterea constaret, unde notiones illae, quas *Secundas* vocant, et consequenter axiomata, quae in iisdem fundantur suam duxerunt originem . . .

The ordinary and correct translation of the passage should read:

[30] *Ethics,* Part II, Proposition 40, Scholium 1.

[31] Cf. Charles Appuhn's translation of Spinoza's *Ethics* (Paris: Librairie Garnier, n.d.), I, 422, note b to *Ethics,* Part II, Proposition 40, Scholium 1.

> Moreover, it should be manifest whence these notions which are called *Second*, and consequently *the axioms founded upon them*, have taken their origin . . .

This is the translation given by W. H. White, and that of Fullerton is substantially the same. The French translation by Charles Appuhn follows the same reading.

However, two widely used English translations, that of Elwes and that of Boyle (Everyman's Library), find it necessary to alter the passage and render it thus:

> . . . Whence these notions which are called secondary, and consequently whence *the axioms on which they are founded*, derive their origin . . .[32]

The difference between the two translations is that one says that *the axioms are founded on the second notions* (which is clearly what the Latin says), and the other says that *the second notions are founded on the axioms* (which requires that the Latin text be read "*in quibus eaedem fundantur*" instead of the universally accepted "*quae in iisdem fundantur*"[33]).

That this is not merely another quibble about an unimportant textual difference becomes obvious when we consider that no scholar has suggested any reason for questioning the authenticity of the text, and when we observe carefully the nature of the difference between the two interpretations. The assumption behind the Elwes and Boyle translations seems to be that the reading ". . . these notions . . . and consequently *the axioms founded upon them* . . ." must be wrong because, they would maintain, axioms cannot be founded upon any other notions, since again, as in Euclid, axioms are self-evident. The translator, in changing the text, seems to be saying that if there is any relation of dependence between *axioms* and *second notions*, the second notions must be founded on the axioms, and not *vice versa*, and any text which asserts the contrary is *ipso facto* corrupt.

Professor H. A. Wolfson follows Elwes and Boyle in their interpretation of this disputed passage.[34] A reading of his book suggests that Wolfson shares the preconception concerning axioms which seems to lurk behind Boyle's and Elwes' translation of the passage. Wolfson treats the doctrine of the *Ethics* as if it were a logically and metaphysically autonomous, self-dependent, self-complete system, based not on an examination of reality, but stitched together out of an examination of the doctrines of previous thinkers. The axioms, therefore, are

[32]Spinoza's *Ethics*, Everyman ed., trans. Boyle, 67; also Elwes II, 111.
[33]This textual problem is extensively discussed in Wolfson, op. cit., II, 122–123.
[34]Ibid.

for Wolfson not statements concerning the world and experience, but rather summaries or critiques of ideas encountered in Spinoza's reading. Accordingly, in Wolfson's interpretation, the axioms of the *Ethics* are not derived from other logical foundations or sources or evidence, since they must have been modelled on Euclid, and are identical with the *common notions.*[35] Furthermore, Wolfson finds that Maimonides used the term *second notions* as identical with the theorems in Euclid,[36] and suggests that therefore Spinoza must have meant by *second notions* "the conclusions in demonstrative syllogisms."[37] This, of course, would make it impossible for axioms (if they were *common notions*) to be founded upon *second notions,* since these latter are themselves derived from the common notions.

However, there is no reason to believe that Spinoza equated axioms, i.e., his axioms in the *Ethics,* with the *notiones communes;* nor is there reason to believe that Spinoza could not think that some axioms were founded upon, or had their origin in, what he called *second notions.* What Spinoza meant by common notions we know quite clearly. These common notions are the ideas of those things "in which all bodies agree,"[38] and the things in which all bodies agree are first, that they involve the same attribute, i.e., extension, and second, that "they are capable of motion and rest, and of motion at one time quicker and at one time slower."[39] It is these common notions that are "the foundations of our reasoning."[40] Certainly these notions are not the axioms at the beginning of each of the five parts of the *Ethics.* They are among the first elements in the different steps which the mind, in the pursuit of the logic of inquiry and discovery, follows in building up knowledge. On the other hand Wolfson[41] is correct when he relates these notions to Aristotle's description of the procedure by which the mind builds up knowledge from sense perception, in the closing pages of the *Posterior Analytics.*

Whatever Spinoza may have meant by *second notions,* and this appears to be a matter of dispute among philologists and historians of philosophy,[42] it seems obvious that the tampering with the text of the *scholium* under discussion is motivated only by the wrong assumption that Spinoza's axioms are self-evident propositions in the structure of an *a priori* deductive system. However, if we look upon the *Ethics* as a

[35]Ibid., II, 120–121.
[36]Ibid.
[37]Ibid., II, 122.
[38]*Ethics,* Part II, Proposition 38, Scholium.
[39]*Ethics,* Part II, Lemma 2, Demonstration.
[40]*Ethics,* Part II, Proposition 40, Scholium 1.
[41]Wolfson, op. cit., II, 151–154 (cf. supra, note 21).
[42]Cf. Wolfson II, op. cit., II, 120–123.

demonstration, or a *systematic exposition* of doctrine, the starting points of which are arrived at as a result of a process of philosophical inquiry, the text in which axioms are spoken of as "founded" on other notions is not only above suspicion, but is fully consistent with the philosophical enterprise as it is exemplified in Spinoza's *Ethics*.

There is an additional body of evidence, out of the history of 16th and 17th century thought, that supports the distinction between the order or logic of inquiry and the order or logic of demonstration, and its application to Spinoza's *Ethics* as shown above, namely, the distinction between the method of *analysis* and the method of *synthesis*. It was well-recognized logical doctrine in the 17th century; it is summed up by Descartes in his reply to the Second Objections to his *Meditations;* and is explained by Ludwig Meyer in his Preface to Spinoza's earliest work, *Principia Philosophiae Cartesianae,* significantly characterized in its subtitle as *"Demonstratio More Geometrico."* Descartes (in a text that seems somewhat confusing) differentiates between the methods of *synthesis,* which "does indeed clearly demonstrate its conclusions, and . . . employs a long series of definitions, postulates, axioms, theorems" but "does not show the way in which the matter taught was discovered," and, on the other hand, *analysis,* the method he used in the *Meditations,* that "shows the way in which a thing was methodically discovered."[43]

Ludwig Meyer's Preface to Spinoza's *Principles of Descartes' Philosophy* paraphrases Descartes. Meyer says he had long hoped that someone would take what Descartes "had put in Analytic form" and "remold it in Synthetic order and demonstrate it in the more familiar forms of Geometry." Analysis, says Meyer, "is the method by which . . . truth is discovered," whereas synthesis is "the method by which it is set in order."[44]

IV

Spinoza's *Ethics* begins with a definition of that which is *causa sui,* that whose "essence involves existence,"[45] namely, God. His *Tractatus de Intellectus Emendatione* opens its discussion of method with an analysis of the different modes of perception.[46] The subject matter which in the order of demonstration, i.e., in the procedure followed

[43]*The Philosophical Works of Descartes,* trans. Haldane and Ross (Cambridge: Cambridge University Press, 1934), II, 48–49.

[44]Descartes, *Principia Philosophiae,* Ludwig Meyer's Preface, 3.

[45]*Ethics,* Part I, Definition 1.

[46]TdIE, Paras. 18–24.

by the *Ethics,* occurs in the latter pages of Part II, comes first in the treatise the task of which is to give an account of the nature, instruments, and order of philosophical inquiry. This is as it should be. *In the order of nature,* God is prior to modes; therefore things, and the human mind with its ideas of things, come fairly late in the course of the exposition that reflects this order. *In the order of inquiry,* we begin with the ideas we have of ourselves and of things, and, following the interconnections among these ideas, we proceed to the discovery of *the order of nature,* and of that which is first in this order, namely, God.

Spinoza's first steps in the order of inquiry are far removed from the rationalistic method that is usually attributed to him. His procedure is surprisingly experientialist, or empirical. He begins with the data of experience and out of these proceeds to build systematic knowledge. After enumerating the different modes of perception and posing the question as to which of *these modes is the best,* he tells us that the means necessary for making this choice are the following:

> I. To have an exact knowledge of our nature which we desire to perfect, and *to know as much of the nature of things as is necessary.*
> II. To gather from these the differences, agreements and oppositions of things.
> III. To learn thus exactly how far they can or cannot be modified.
> IV. To compare this result with the nature and power of man.[47]

This hardly sounds like deducing a world of things out of *a priori* innate ideas, or like spinning existence out of logic. To examine the different modes of perception, we go to experience, and "recapitulate all the modes of perception which I have hitherto employed for affirming or denying anything with certainty."[48] To discover the best of the different modes of perception, we again go to experience and compare what we have been able to learn of the nature and power of man with what we can learn concerning things as a result of gathering their "differences, agreements, and oppositions."[49] Things here are not deduced from something which is antecedent to things and which is accepted as the first datum. A world of things, and man as one among such things, are taken as givens, as data, and the enterprise of philosophical inquiry is the enterprise of pursuing the implications of the fact of our experience that there are things, and that there are observable differences and agreements among them.

His crucial reliance on the brute facts of experience in connection with some of the most important elements in Spinoza's doctrine is

[47]TdIE, Para. 25.
[48]TdIE, Para. 18.
[49]TdIE, Para. 25 (cf. No. II of the four "means" listed above).

consistently overlooked by interpreters with a doctrinaire rationalist bias about Spinoza's thought.[50] For example, they fail to take note of the fact that the existence of "finite modes," i.e., of the finite, contingent objects of everyday experience, is never *deduced* in the *Ethics.* Indeed, Spinoza says explicitly in his letter to Simon de Vries that "experience" is needed for our knowledge of the finite modes since, unlike the attributes of God, they "cannot be deduced from the definition of a thing."[51] With the exception of God, whose essence involves existence and who therefore necessarily exists, the existence of no individual object can be positively deduced from the idea of the object—no matter how comprehensible the idea—because, as Leon Roth pointed out more than half a century ago, of "our ignorance of the complete detail of the structure of things." The "*naturae ordo,*" Roth continues, in a footnote, "is therefore a problem to be worked out and the way is left open to the purest empiricism."[52] "For knowledge of particular things," says Spinoza, "experiments will need to be made,"[53] and H. G. Hubbeling comments here: "Spinoza does not deny the great value of experience for the finding of facts . . ."[54]

Moreover, it is significant that Spinoza found it necessary to include, among his proofs for the existence of God, one *a posteriori* proof, that takes as its first datum an observable experiential fact, namely, the existence of each of us as a finite human being.[55] *Premiss:* We, finite, contingent human beings, exist. Conclusion: (omitting the steps in the proof) *Therefore,* there is *something that necessarily exists;* that necessary existent is God. The procedure here is "analytic," in that it begins with sense perception and experience of the existence of things generally, and goes on to discover the truth that *something* must necessarily exist. This is the way knowledge is often built up. In the scholium Spinoza displays a full understanding of this when he explains that he "wished to prove the existence of God *a posteriori,* in order that the demonstration be more clearly understood."[56]

[50]Cf. E. M. Curley: "The view that Spinoza was a rationalist . . . is not only mildly inaccurate, it is wildly inaccurate. Experience has a much greater role to play in Spinoza's theory of knowledge than this view allows for" ("Experience in Spinoza's Theory of Knowledge," in *Spinoza: A Collection of Critical Essays,* ed. M. Grene [New York: Anchor Books, 1973], 26). Cf. also de Deugd: "Spinoza now and then speaks unhesitatingly of experience as valuable knowledge, and as dependable knowledge at that" (op. cit., 150).

[51]Wolf (a), Ep. 10, 109.

[52]Leon Roth, *Spinoza, Descartes and Maimonides* (New York: Russell and Russell, 1963), 57 and note 3.

[53]TdIE, Para. 103.

[54]Hubbeling, op. cit., 10.

[55]*Ethics,* Part I, Proposition 11, Demonstration (3d proof) and Scholium.

[56]*Ethics,* Part I, Proposition 11, Scholium.

Thus, we go to experience for our data. But, we must not rest there. Analysis of the data of experience and their implications must in turn lead to the order, the system of reality, that will comprehend the very data we begin with, assign them to their proper place in the system, and thus render them fully intelligible; for the truest knowledge is knowledge within the structure of such a system. If the system we arrive at, as a result of analyzing our data, is to be a system of the real, the reality of the data we start with must be guaranteed. The data must be known to be not illusory, not mere products of the human imagination. Things must be shown to be part of the productivity of nature, part of the whole which nature is. "*Nature* must in the end be both *dator* and *datum*."[57] Philosophical *inquiry* begins with the data of experience, analyzes them, and proceeds to the discovery of the system that will provide the epistemological and metaphysical intelligibility that these and all other data, or parts of the whole, fit into. *Demonstration*, or systematic exposition, or *deduction*, from the appropriate premisses, is the critical ordering of the system so that it may best exhibit this intelligibility.

Philosophical *inquiry* begins with the data of experience, and proceeds to discover axioms and postulates, i.e., the materials out of which a system may be deductively constructed. *A geometric system* starts with such definitions, axioms, and postulates, to which the first data in the *order of inquiry*, and other data, are in turn shown to be related as consequents to ground, or as conclusions to premisses. *Philosophical inquiry* begins with experienced things, traces the relations of these things to the ultimately real, and discovers their place in the scheme of the ultimately real. On the other hand, *geometric systematization*, in Spinoza's sense, begins with the ultimately real, and exhibits its structure, and the place of things in this structure.

This is the nexus between Spinoza's experientialist or empirical logic of inquiry and his rationalism. Neither is complete without the other. A sound naturalism, such as Spinoza's appears to be, embraces both as two complementary and equally indispensable approaches to the problem of securing knowledge and systematizing it. The geometrical logic of demonstration is *synthetic*, and the logic of inquiry is *analytic*. The *Ethics* follows the logic of synthesis. Spinoza's *Tractatus de Intellectus Emendatione* follows the logic of analysis. This treatise is, in Sir Frederick Pollock's words, "the analytical preface to Spinoza's latest work."[58] Method, the principal subject matter of the TdIE, is the unfolding of the order or logic of the search for knowledge that

[57]Hallett, op. cit., 150.

[58]Frederick Pollock, *Spinoza: His Life and Philosophy*, 2d ed. (New York: American Scholar, 1966), 115.

will lead us to the postulates of the system. Or, since for Spinoza true knowledge of anything is knowledge of its cause, method is the order that will direct us to the causes of things, and ultimately to the cause of all things. This cause of all things will, in turn, serve as the starting point for the systematic exposition of nature, *in accordance with nature's true order*.

But a search for knowledge implies a search somewhere, among some entities. A method must have a starting point. As Spinoza puts it: "If we wish to investigate the first thing of all, there must necessarily be some *basis* which must direct our thoughts toward it."[59] This sentence seems to contain Spinoza's own refutation of those who view the *Ethics* as an autonomous, *a priori*, intuitively revealed system, which starts with an intuitive apprehension of God, and proceeds to deduce the rest of the universe from the idea of God. Philosophical inquiry must begin somewhere, and its most natural beginning is our immediate, experienced world of extended and thinking beings. We have ideas, of our bodies, of other bodies, of our own ideas, and the *basis* from which our exposition of a method of inquiry begins is discovered through an examination of our ideas, and through research among them.

One of the things that Spinoza tells us repeatedly about method is that method is "*cognitio reflexiva*," or "*idea ideae*";[60] "it is the way in which truth itself, or the objective essences, or ideas of things (which are all the same) must be sought in their proper order."[61] Method starts with thinking about thinking, thinking about the fact of thought. Superficially, this methodological starting point might seem not to be far removed from the putative epistemology of pure rationalism. However, Spinoza's methodology is wedded to metaphysical convictions which, as we shall see below, transform this seeming rationalism into a concern with things and facts as we discover them in experience. It is our everyday ideas, the facts of accumulated knowledge, that are the first data from which our inquiry must proceed. For Spinoza, a mind without ideas cannot even be assumed: it would be a contradiction in terms. For the mind *is* itself the idea of the body, and the human body is such that its idea, which is "the first part that constitutes the actual being of the human mind,"[62] is capable of having ideas of itself, of the body, and of other bodies as they affect its own body.

But true ideas are ideas of things. When they are true, the ideas are the counterparts in thought of what exist also as extended, as bodies.

[59]TdIE, Para. 105.
[60]TdIE, Para. 38.
[61]TdIE, Para. 36.
[62]*Ethics*, Part II, Proposition 11.

This metaphysical confidence is basic to all of Spinoza's thinking. A true idea is, axiomatically, an idea which "must agree with its ideatum,"[63] and the proposition that "the order and connection of ideas is the same as the order and connections of things"[64] is central in the *Ethics*. Ideas are not abstract universals, in some detached, Platonic realm. Spinoza's rejection of such "ideas" is complete: his nominalism here is uncompromising. It is not such ideas that serve as the starting point for his method of inquiry. Each idea, for Spinoza, is a judgment concerning some part of the world of things: "An idea, in so far as it is an idea, involves affirmation or negation."[65] In this sense, a true idea is not a *disembodied* existence; on the contrary, it is *literally "embodied,"* for it is the counterpart in the realm of thought, of what also exists in the realm of extension, and it is an affirmation of that existence. In the case of man, his mind is the idea of his body. By virtue of its being that idea, the mind is also an affirmation of the existence of its own body.[66] "From the fact that I know the essence of the mind, I know it to be united to a body."[67] The very meaning of mind is that it is the objective essence of a body.

This relation between man's body and his mind is also the relation between all other things and their ideas. Spinoza states this quite clearly. Although "like objects, ideas differ from one another," nevertheless, "whatever we say concerning the idea of the human body must necessarily be said concerning the idea of any other thing."[68] All extended things have the ideas of them in the attribute of thought. Individual material objects are "all, though in various degrees, *animate*,"[69] i.e., there are in God, under the attribute of thought, *ideas* of all extended things. The ideas of such extended things are affirmations of the existence of the things. Ideas, in this sense, must be distinguished from the mere "*images* of things which we imagine."[70]

Research among ideas, which is the starting point of Spinoza's method of inquiry, involves and implicates the world of extended things. Research among *true* ideas will be in every sense equivalent to research among extended things. A methodology which starts on such terms is, to repeat, far from a procedure that can be accused of eliciting things out of abstract ideas, or existence out of logic. It is firmly anchored in a concern with things, and the fact that the exist-

[63]*Ethics*, Part I, Axiom 6.

[64]*Ethics*, Part II, Proposition 7.

[65]*Ethics*, Part II, Proposition 49, Scholium.

[66]*Ethics*, Part II, Propositions 11–13, especially 13 ("The object of the idea constituting the human mind is the body . . .").

[67]TdIE, Para. 22.

[68]*Ethics*, Part II, Proposition 13, Scholium.

[69]Ibid.

[70]*Ethics*, Part II, Proposition 49, Scholium.

ence of man's mind entails the existence of his body is the most striking illustration of the foundations of such a methodology.

V

This unity of mind and body is the fundamental beginning in an account of the nature, logic, and instruments of philosophical inquiry. But the human mind's first knowledge of its body and of its relation to its own body is confused and inadequate. All we know at first, *as a matter of experience,* is that we think (*"Homo cogitat," Ethics* II, Axiom 2),[71] that "we are aware *(sentimus)* that a certain body is affected in many ways,"[72] and that somehow this fact of thinking and this body are united, "but what is this feeling and union we cannot absolutely understand."[73] However, our mind cannot remain restricted to this confused and tentative knowledge:

> . . . this Idea (which the mind has of its body) can by no means find rest in the knowledge of the body without passing to the knowledge of that without which the body and Idea could neither be nor be understood . . .[74]

Our body is obviously not an isolated fact. Our experience, our ideas of the modifications of our body, tell us that we are in continuous intercourse with other bodies. If our body had no relations or commerce with other things *(commercium habere cum aliis rebus),* then our mind, which is the *essentia objectiva* of the body, would "also have no relation or dealings with other ideas, that is, we could conclude nothing concerning it."[75] But our body does have relations or commerce with other things. Therefore, the *objective essence* of our body (i.e., our mind), since it must agree in all respects with its *"formal essence"*[76] (i.e., its body), and, on the other hand, the ideas it has of the things with which our body is in commerce, "will have the same relations" or commerce with each other as our body has with other bodies.[77] Such relations can be traced and studied, and by means of such study "the instruments of our investigation are increased."[78]

[71] *Ethics,* Part II, Axiom 2.

[72] *Ethics,* Part II, Axiom 4. "We are aware" as translation of *"sentimus"* seems to me preferable to both Boyle's "we feel" and White's and Elwes' "we perceive."

[73] TdIE, Para. 21.

[74] Wolf (b) II, ch. 22, 134.

[75] TdIE, Para. 41.

[76] Ibid.

[77] Ibid.

[78] Ibid.

The commerce that our body has with other bodies is of a variety of descriptions. We observe in our experience that our body produces other bodies, and is produced by them.[79] Furthermore, our experience tells us that "the human body needs for its preservation many other bodies from which it is, so to speak, continuously regenerated,"[80] since "the human body is composed of many parts of different nature which need continuous and varied nourishment so that the whole body may be equally fit to discharge all the duties which can flow from its nature . . ."[81]

The mind, in experiencing and perceiving the many modifications that take place in its body as a result of its contact with other bodies, must necessarily be able to "perceive the nature of many bodies at the same time as the nature of its own body,"[82] for "the idea of every mode in which the human body is affected by external bodies must involve the nature of the human body and at the same time the nature of the external body."[83]

It is in this manner that the mind, as a result of its determination to study the agreements and differences among things, is able to discover through experience that its body has many things in common with all the other things with which it has commerce. If it had nothing in common with these external bodies it could in no way have commerce with them. The mind then discovers what those things are which its body *has in common with all other bodies,* namely, the observed facts that they are capable of motion and rest, that they may move more quickly or more slowly, and most of the other information that Spinoza gives us in the lemmas that follow Proposition 13 in Part II of the *Ethics,* as coming from experience.

This is the origin of the *notiones communes* which are "the foundations *(fundamenta)* of our reasoning."[84] They arise from experience, from the mind's originally confused knowledge of its body, and from the ideas, again at first confused and inadequate, which the mind has of other bodies as they affect ours. They are traceable back to our perceptions of "individual things, represented by the senses to us in a mutilated and confused manner, and without order."[85] Their origin is therefore in our knowledge of *the first kind,* "knowledge from vague experience *(cognitio ab experientia vaga).*"[86] Nevertheless, though they

[79]TdIE, Para. 41, Note.
[80]*Ethics,* Part II, Postulate IV following the Lemmas.
[81]*Ethics,* Part IV, Appendix, 27.
[82]*Ethics,* Part II, Proposition 16, Corollary 2.
[83]*Ethics,* Part II, Proposition 16.
[84]*Ethics,* Part II, Proposition 40, Scholium 1.
[85]*Ethics,* Part II, Proposition 40, Scholium 2; cf. Wolfson, op. cit., II, 125–127.
[86]*Ethics,* Part II, Proposition 40, Scholium 2.

arise from experience, these *common notions* "must be adequately, or clearly and distinctly, perceived by all."[87] The genesis and ground of their adequacy is in the circumstance that they are notions, or ideas, of invariant, common properties of all bodies, and that they are discovered by the mind in its empirical search for the "agreements among things," a search that by its very nature transcends the limited and therefore mutilated individuality of perceived individual things. "Things which we clearly and distinctly understand are either *common properties* of things or what we deduce from them."[88] It is by experience that we come to know them to be *common,* indeed, by a kind of *induction.*

The same position is outlined in Letter 37, where it is made clear by Spinoza once and for all that he was not committed to what has been interpreted stereotypically as a purely rationalist procedure, and that his comprehensive method of philosophical inquiry was such that the Baconian inductive procedure found a necessary place in it. Here Spinoza states that

> . . . as far as the method requires, there is no need to know the nature of the mind through its first cause; it is sufficient to put together a short history of the mind, or of perception, in the manner taught by Verulam.[89]

At this point it begins to be clear that *ratio,* Spinoza's *second* kind of knowledge, cannot function without the materials given by *imaginatio* or *experientia vaga,* i.e., the *first* kind of knowledge in his classification; and, as will be briefly maintained below, that *scientia intuitiva,* the highest kind, must have for its functioning the materials given by *ratio* if it is to give us significant knowledge.

That reason cannot operate without the materials given by the senses is quite evident. The common notions have their origin in the confused perceptions of the imagination, and all knowledge of the kind given by common notions is the result of the mind's search for the differences and agreements among those things which it first perceives in a confused manner through the senses. But the understanding, Spinoza tells us repeatedly, forms clear and distinct concep-

[87]*Ethics,* Part II, Proposition 38, Corollary.

[88]*Ethics,* Part V, Proposition 12, Demonstration.

[89]Wolf (a), Ep. 37, 228. We find the same methodological procedure described by Spinoza in the *Tractatus Theologico-Politicus:* "As in the examination of natural phenomena we try first to investigate what is most universal and common to all nature—such, for instance, as motion and rest, and their laws and rules, which nature always observes, and through which she continually works . . ." (Elwes I, 104). I am grateful to Richard Kennington for directing my attention to this passage.

tions which "depend solely on our nature . . . on our absolute power; . . . nor do they acknowledge any cause external to us . . ."[90] This has led commentators to assume that Spinoza believed that the understanding (or *scientia intuitiva*) forms its true ideas *in vacuo,* in an *a priori* manner, in total independence of experience.

Spinoza meant nothing of the sort. Rather, he insisted that while *imagination,* or vague experience, the perceptions of which came from the senses, was *passive,* and had little control over what impinged on its attention, clear and distinct ideas were the result of a conscious, deliberate, critical effort of the mind. It is in this sense that the perceptions of the understanding "depend solely on our nature," "on the power of the mind,"[91] and not on "fortuitous and unconnected sensations" which arise "from external causes."[92] But this critical activity of the mind can result in the clear and certain perceptions of the understanding only because it is a critical activity among ideas which the mind had previously formed in the course of its empirical inquiries, and which arose first from *imaginatio,* and only subsequently from *ratio.*

Of course, Spinoza continually endeavors to keep clear and sharp the distinction between *imaginatio* and *intellectus* (or *scientia intuitiva,* i.e., the third kind of knowledge). He says, for example, that "the effort or desire to know things by the third kind of knowledge cannot arise from the first kind . . ."[93] Nevertheless, this very same proposition, in Spinoza's own words, makes it abundantly clear that there is a link between *ratio,* the second kind of knowledge that depends on experience, and on the other hand *scientia intuitiva:* "The effort or desire to know things by the third kind of knowledge . . . may arise from the second kind of knowledge."[94] Indeed, the connection between reason and intuition is affirmed in Spinoza's thought in the early *Short Treatise.* Here of course the terminology is not the same as that of the *Ethics,* but the meaning is unmistakable. "True belief," says Spinoza, and by *true belief* he means the same as is meant by *reason* in the *Ethics,*[95] is good only because it is the way to "true knowledge [meaning knowledge of the highest kind—*intuition*], and awakens us to things which are truly lovable."[96]

[90]Wolf (a), Ep. 37, 227.

[91]TdIE, Para. 84.

[92]Ibid.

[93]*Ethics,* Part V, Proposition 28.

[94]Ibid.

[95]In fact, Spinoza equates the two terms "true belief" and "reason" even in the early *Short Treatise* (Ch. 14 of Part II): "True belief or reason . . . leads us to the knowledge of good and evil . . ." (Wolf [b], 99).

[96]Wolf (b), II, ch. 4, 76.

In some of the very recent Spinoza literature there is a reversal of the traditional, stereotypical assessment of the respective roles and importance of experience and intuition, the first kind of knowledge and the third kind of knowledge, in Spinoza's epistemology. Note is taken of Spinoza's puzzling candor when he said in the TdIE that "The things which I have been able to know by this kind of knowledge [i.e., *scientia intuitiva*] so far have been very few."[97] In fact, *what* it is precisely Spinoza claimed we knew through the third kind of knowledge is still an unresolved and controversial question. On the other hand we are also reminded that two paragraphs earlier in the TdIE Spinoza stated that by experience, or the first kind of knowledge, "I know nearly all things that are useful in life."[98]

De Deugd is an example of this recent reexamination of Spinoza's theory of knowledge, and he has gone further than others. A major conclusion of his is that ". . . untraditional though it may be (and to many even paradoxical) it seems that in Spinoza's system imagination [i.e., the first kind of knowledge] is of more actual value than intuitive science."[99] Among his reasons for this conclusion are: a) his view that the second kind of knowledge, i.e., *ratio*, would be impossible without the first kind, i.e., experience; "without sense data, it seems there can be no knowledge of the second kind";[100] b) his view that for Spinoza the distinctions between the three kinds of knowledge "are of a relative rather than absolute character";[101] and c) the abundance of evidence he finds in Spinoza's texts that "Spinoza does not hold empirical reality in low esteem and that in his system the first kind of knowledge is, in the ultimate sense at least, not considered inferior."[102] Similarly, G. H. R. Parkinson, in a recent essay, quotes numerous passages in which Spinoza appeals to experience in support of various doctrines or conclusions or postulates.[103] For example, when postulates which are not self-evident can be seen to agree with experience, Spinoza considers this fact as confirmation of their truth; he deems the testimony of experience acceptable when it is not contradicted by deductive reason; and he notes pointedly that men can understand and be more easily persuaded by a doctrine when it is proven by experience even when it has previously been proven deductively. These are among Parkinson's examples of Spinoza's reli-

[97]TdIE, Para. 22. Cf. E. M. Curley's interesting comment, op. cit., 54–55.

[98]TdIE, Para. 20.

[99]de Deugd, op. cit., 185, repeated on 188 and 262.

[100]de Deugd, 153.

[101]de Deugd, 188.

[102]de Deugd, 253.

[103]G. H. R. Parkinson, "Language and Knowledge in Spinoza," in *Spinoza: A Collection of Critical Essays*, op. cit., 96–97.

ance on and appeals to experience in the *Ethics*. There are others in the TdIE as well.

These recent reassessments appear to throw additional light on the logic of philosophical inquiry that I have tried to distill here out of what is explicitly present and is implicit in Spinoza's *oeuvre*. The received rigid rationalist paradigm in the traditional interpretations of Spinoza must be discarded, or, at the very least, radically modified. The paradigm of philosophical inquiry that emerges out of our analysis in the preceding pages may be crudely restated as follows.

Inquiry begins from knowledge based on *experience* (inadequate knowledge of the first kind) which is critically examined and refined. It proceeds to the formation of the second kind of knowledge, scientific knowledge, through the exercise of reason, for which the common notions derived from sense observation are fundamental materials. From the disclosures of reason, *scientia intuitiva*, the third and highest kind of knowledge, may arise, knowledge that will be completely adequate, and will glimpse something of the total, systematic character and structure of reality, or *natura*, and understand the interrelationships of things in their true order of nature *(ordo naturae)*. While some of the axioms, definitions, and postulates in the *Ethics* are in the nature of generalizations from empirical observation (e.g., Axioms 2 and 4 of Part II, and Axioms 1 and 2 and Lemmas 1 and 2 following Proposition 13 in Part II), most of them are the end product of the progression from experience to reason, and some (especially those that stand at the beginning of Part I) are products of the progression from reason to *scientia intuitiva*, and are grasped intuitively as a result of this progression. These, for Spinoza, are known to be true, and known with certainty, not because they are self-evident, nor as products of the apodeictic demonstrations in the *Ethics*, but as products of the mind's search for the implications of the human experiences and their disclosures, with which the mind begins its systematic search for knowledge.

4. *Spinoza's Onslaught on Judaism*

What this paper deals with is not a philosophical problem, but, rather, a socio-psychological one in the history of philosophy. It will be useful to begin by noting that whether a given philosopher may be properly denominated a *Jewish* one is a question that is neither of recent vintage nor uniquely limited to Spinoza. So far as Spinoza is concerned, apart from the judgment rendered against him in 1656 by Amsterdam's Jewish community in its excommunication decree, the controversy triggered by his philosophical ideas in the world of recorded Jewish thought had its beginnings at least as far back as 1703, only twenty-six years after his death. In that year David Nieto, the Sefardic Rabbi of the London Jewish congregation, was accused, by congregation members, of "Spinozism" on the basis of a philosophical sermon that he had preached.[1]

The controversy has continued from that time, through the 19th century and to our own day, in an undiminished crescendo of polarized opinion. As a brief sampling of those who reject Spinoza from the mainstream of "Jewish" thought, we might mention, first, Samuel David Luzzato (1800–1865), who said:

> Spinoza's books pour contempt on every good belief and every virtue, and everyone who reads them on the assumption that the author was a wise and honest scholar comes close to having his own beliefs and virtuous conduct damaged. Is there anyone pure of heart who will not rise up against all those who exalt, bless, and praise such a man?[2]

[1]Z. H. Ashkenazi, "David Nieto and Pantheism," in *A Treasury of Responsa*, ed. S. B. Freehof (Philadelphia: Jewish Publication Society, 1963), pp. 176–181.

[2]Samuel David Luzzato, *Mehkrei Hayahadut* (Studies in Judaism) (Warsaw: Hazfirah, 1913), Vol. I, part 2, p. 220 (my translation).

Judaism: A Quarterly Journal of Jewish Life and Thought, vol. 28, Spring 1979, pp. 177–193.

Second is Hermann Cohen (1842–1918), who asserted that Spinoza fully deserved the excommunication; that in the *Theological-Political Treatise* he wrote like the enemy of the Jews before an anti-Jewish world, and that in doing so he committed a "humanly incomprehensible act of treason."[3] Third is a contemporary traditionalist historian of Jewish thought, Avraham Korman, who in his book, "*Mussagim B'Mahshevet Yisrael*" (1972), refers twice to "the apostate, Spinoza" ("*Ham'shumad* Barukh Spinoza," and "Spinoza *hamumar*").[4]

And as a sampling of those who see Spinoza decidedly *within* the broad spectrum of "Jewish" thought, I single out, first, David Ben-Gurion, a diligent student of philosophy, who numerous times vociferously urged that the Jewish people rescind Spinoza's excommunication; second, the late Professor Leon Roth, who, in a Jerusalem Lecture in 1932, on the occasion of the 300th anniversary of Spinoza's birth, said that "the only way in this matter," i.e., in the understanding of authentic Judaism, "is via Spinoza's understanding of it," for "Spinoza saw clearly that what is characteristic of Judaism are the practical commandments *(mizvot ma'assiyot)*" and that this, as well as its character as a social or collective religion, rather than a religion of the individual, is what distinguishes Judaism from other religions, for example, from Christianity;[5] and third, the late Professor Joseph Klausner, who concluded his Hebrew University lecture in 1927, at the observance of the 250th anniversary of Spinoza's death, with the dramatic proclamation addressed to Spinoza:

> The excommunication has been lifted! The sin of Judaism against you has been wiped out, and *your* sin against Judaism is forgiven! *Ahinu atah, ahinu atah, ahinu atah!*—You are our brother, you are our brother, you are our brother![6]

And, finally, our contemporary, the distinguished scholar, Rabbi Jacob B. Agus, who in his book, *The Evolution of Jewish Thought*, declares, in much more measured tones: "Spinoza belongs in the total panorama of Judaism."[7]

[3]Hermann Cohen, *Jüdische Schriften*, ed. Bruno Strauss, Vol. III, pp. 333, 361, 363–364, 368, 371. Quoted by Leo Strauss, *Spinoza's Critique of Religion* (New York: Schocken Books, 1965), Preface, p. 19.

[4]Avraham Korman, *Mussagim B'Mahshevet Yisrael: Ba'aspaklariyah shel Hehagut Haklalit* (Concepts in Jewish Thought in the Light of General Ideas) (Tel Aviv: Sifriyati, 1972), pp. 84 and 112.

[5]Leon Roth, "Mishnato shel Spinoza Bayahadut" (Spinoza's Doctrine in Judaism), *Moznayim* (Tel Aviv), IV, 26 (June 1932): 7 and 6 (my translation).

[6]Joseph Klausner, "Haofi Hayehudi shel Torat Spinoza" (The Jewish Character of Spinoza's Doctrine), in *Philosophim V'hogai Deot* (Philosophers and Thinkers) (Tel Aviv—Jerusalem: 1934), p. 242 (my translation).

[7]Jacob B. Agus, *The Evolution of Jewish Thought* (New York: Abelard–Schuman, 1959), p. 300.

However, as was suggested above, this question is not limited to Spinoza. With varying degrees of acrimony, similar controversies have punctuated the unfolding of Jewish thought throughout the centuries and have characterized the reception accorded to the doctrines of various individual philosophers or of intellectual movements. In the millennial spiritual odyssey of the Jewish people there have often appeared dialectical tensions between philosophy and traditional religious belief; between the philosopher and the religious teacher; between the advocates of the primacy of reason and the advocates of the primacy of faith; between the rationalists and the mystics; between those who maintained that God was transcendent and those who argued that God was immanent; between those who espoused the doctrine of God's unknowability and those who held that man can know God; between *Hasidim* and *Mitnagdim;* etc., etc.

Not surprisingly, Judaism has often had problems with its philosophers. The "philosophical" God of the Jewish philosophers often was not the God of tradition to whom one prays, of whom one asks forgiveness, to whom one gives thanks and sings praises. Often, the God of the philosophers was remote, imperturbable, infinite, and fundamentally altogether different. Were such controversial or rejected doctrines or thinkers to be considered indigenous parts of Jewish thought? One need make only perfunctory reference to the bitterness of the controversy that raged around the philosophical doctrines of Maimonides, the burning of his books at the behest of rabbis in southern France, the proscription of the *Guide of the Perplexed* from study in many *yeshivot* in Eastern Europe, to indicate that the controversy around Spinoza and the questions who is, and whether Spinoza was, a "Jewish" philosopher are neither new nor unique. But the fact is that serious attention to such thinkers and doctrines hardly ever fails to be given in major works on the history of Jewish philosophy, and their legitimate place in the landscape of Jewish thought seems to be a matter of general acceptance. What about Spinoza?

We need waste no time on the frivolous suggestion that a philosopher's *Jewish birth* be the definitional criterion for determining who is a "Jewish" philosopher. Manifestly, the Jewish birth of Samuel Alexander, Henri Bergson, Emile Meyerson, Edmund Husserl, or Ernst Cassirer neither justifies nor assures for them inclusion among the representatives of Jewish thought, nor does it lead historians of philosophy, in general, or authors of textbooks on the history of philosophy to refer to these men as "Jewish philosophers." But hardly any textbooks, histories, or "dictionaries" of philosophy in the English language fail to include the adjective "Jewish" in front of Spinoza's name when they introduce his works.[8] These considerations, and the

[8]As representative examples see: Samuel Enoch Stumpf, *Philosophy: History and Problems,* second edition (New York: McGraw-Hill Book Co., 1977), p. 256: "Spinoza was

long controversy around him in Jewish intellectual history, make it necessary to try to formulate explicitly, or to bring to the surface, tacitly assumed answers to the question of definitional criteria. What do we mean by "Jewish" philosophy? What essential elements must be displayed in a man's work to justify our identifying him as a "Jewish" philosopher? These are not easy questions, and I am not aware of any satisfactory answers to them in the available literature. For the purpose of this paper, therefore, I propose, tentatively, as working suggestions, the following criteria for determining who is a *Jewish* philosopher:

1. Did the philosopher's inquiries, analyses, speculations, and doctrines arise out of the matrix of the collective experience, history, thought, and religion of the Jewish people, and were they a response to these collective experiences, doctrines, and traditions (even if the response was, in the last analysis, a critical, negative one that rejected some, much, or even all of the tradition)?

2. Was it the philosopher's intent to contribute to the advancement of Jewish thought, affirmatively or through criticism; were his philosophical ideas and doctrines, thus, addressed principally to an audience of committed Jews, either thoughtful and scholarly in the religious and philosophical life of Judaism, or a mass audience, or both?

3. Have the philosopher's inquiries, analyses, theories, and doctrines, in fact, contributed to the advancement, deepening, clarification, enrichment, reassessment, or revision of essential concepts, ideas, doctrines, and traditions of the Jewish people?

Trying to apply these admittedly crude and gropingly exploratory criteria to Spinoza's thought, within the compass of a brief paper, is a formidable enough task. Such an application is made even more so by an aspect of the contents of Spinoza's *Theological-Political Treatise* (henceforth referred to as *The Treatise*) that is adverted to by S. D. Luzzato and by Hermann Cohen in their assessments of Spinoza quoted earlier. This requires explication. As is well known, a dominant element in *The Treatise* is Spinoza's radical and severe critique of religion. In the service of his advocacy of a socio-political system characterized by freedom of thought, ideas, philosophizing, and religious belief, he wanted the State to be liberated from control by religious authorities and from their utilization of the State to coerce its citizens into religious and philosophical conformity. This necessitated, Spinoza believed, a sharp critique and polemic against Theocracy. And, since the model *par excellence* of Theocracy is contained paradig-

the greatest Jewish Philosopher." Also: A. R. Lacy, *A Dictionary of Philosophy* (New York: Charles Scribner's Sons, 1976), p. 207: "Spinoza, Jewish philosopher who was born and lived in Holland . . ."

matically in the Biblical accounts and in the history of the Jewish people until the Roman conquest and destruction of the Jewish commonwealth, this required, Spinoza thought, a critique of Biblical ideas, of Judaism, and, to some degree, also of Christianity. Moreover, since Maimonides held that the best society would be a *Torah-society,* this fact, for Spinoza, required also an attack on Maimonides.

Another objective of Spinoza's critique of religion was to strip religion of any *philosophical* pretentions. Philosophy is concerned with knowledge, with understanding—of the world, of man, of God, of man's relation to God—and seeks through such understanding to achieve man's highest goal, namely, the intellectual love of God. Such knowledge, *sub specie aeternitatis,* eliminates all temporal and transitory elements. This achievement, to be possible, requires man to liberate himself from bondage to his emotions and passions, through individual discipline, and through the discipline and obedience required by a proper social order. The job of religion is to teach and inculcate discipline and obedience to moral and social norms of conduct. The Bible is, and should be seen as, a manual of moral and societal obedience, and not as a *divinely revealed* book that teaches philosophical truths. The prophets are moral teachers, guides to social obedience, and not oracles of philosophic knowledge. The Hebrew Bible, or the Old Testament, is, thus, a socio-political document, the doctrine of which enabled Moses to forge into a people the masses of Jews liberated from Egyptian slavery, and to provide for them a civilizing code of obedience that was to make possible an orderly and viable commonwealth. Not only is the Pentateuch not a divinely revealed book; it was not even written by Moses, as Orthodox Jewish tradition claims, but was written and put together by different people, at different times, in later years, Ezra having perhaps been a principal author. Since it is a human document, the Bible must be studied critically by means of the methods and tools of empirical investigation, rather than accepted dogmatically as the revealed word of God.

There are numerous other elements in the critique of religion contained in *The Treatise* that are equally important and equally, and perhaps even more, at variance with Orthodox Judaism. But in trying to apply to his philosophy the three criteria suggested earlier, what creates difficulties is not Spinoza's heterodoxy, but an altogether different and puzzling element. It is his repeated and persistent singling out of Judaism, Jewish ideas and teachings, Jewish ideals and values, as well as Jewish personalities, for disparagement, downgrading, biting and almost sarcastic hostility; his employment of a *double standard* of evaluation as between Judaism and Christianity; and his reiteration of some of the stereotyped distortions of Judaism that are found in Christian writings and in popular Christian traditions and attitudes over the centuries. What is especially startling and intellectually repugnant about the multiple instances of such slanderous observations and comparisons, a number of which will be reviewed here, is that *none* of them is logically necessary for the support of the principal objectives of *The Treatise*. The deletion of any or all of them would in no way impair the strength of the book's argument and thesis, and, in fact, some of them flatly contradict other and major ideas propounded in *The Treatise* and in the *Ethics*.

However, before reviewing some of Spinoza's "Syllabus of Errors" against Jews and Judaism in *The Treatise*, it would be well to clear up an oft-repeated historical inaccuracy that is not without some significance. As noted earlier, Avraham Korman, in his 1972 book, twice refers to Spinoza as an "apostate." But the fact is that Spinoza never became a *m'shumad*.

He never formally left the faith of Judaism (he was, of course, expelled from Amsterdam's Jewish community), and he never became converted to any form or denomination of Christianity. On several occasions he was urged, importuned and pressured by friends and correspondents to convert, but he refused to do so. In letters in which he replied negatively to those who urged him to accept Christianity, Spinoza asserted, among other ideas, that there are good and just principles in all religions; that the claim of Christianity to truth as evidenced by its long history, its many adherents, and the many who have suffered martyrdom for it, is matched by other religions; that if the criterion of superiority is martyrdom, Judaism has had many more martyrs; and, in fact, he knows of one Jew who only recently had been burned at the stake for his religious faith, and died in the flames after exclaiming loudly: "Into Thy hands I commit my soul, O God!"[9]—a verse attributed to Jesus before his death on the cross. To another correspondent Spinoza said that the claim that God has assumed human nature is on a par with the claim that a square had assumed the nature of a circle.[10] In *The Treatise* he stated: "I must at this juncture declare that those doctrines which certain churches put forward concerning Christ, I neither affirm nor deny, for I freely confess that I do not understand them."[11] It should be quite clear, therefore, that Spinoza's denigrations of Judaism, in general, and the disparaging comparisons with Christianity, in partic-

[9]Barukh Spinoza, *The Correspondence of Spinoza*, translated and edited by A. Wolf (London: George Allen & Unwin, 1928), Letter #76, pp. 353–354.

[10]Ibid., Letter #74, p. 344.

[11]Barukh Spinoza, *A Theologico-Political Treatise*, in *The Chief Works of Benedict de Spinoza*, translated by R. H. M. Elwes [Volumes I and II bound as one] (New York: Dover Publications, 1951), Chapter I, p. 19. (All notes below will use the shortened title *Treatise* in references to this work.)

ular, whatever the explanation for them may be, cannot be interpreted as expressions of a newly embraced Christianity on his part, because he never did embrace it.

II

Before attempting to explain these animadversions, let us look at capsulated versions of some of this "Syllabus of Errors":

1. Judaism is *carnal*, its laws being designed to provide only for physical or material needs and values;[12] Christianity is spiritual and teaches laws designed to care for people's spiritual and moral values.[13]

2. Judaism is particularist and exclusivist, its laws having been taught only for the Jews;[14] Christianity is universalist and teaches laws for mankind generally.[15]

[12]Ibid., Chap. III, p. 47: "[I]n the law no other reward is offered for obedience than the continual happiness of an independent commonwealth and other goods of this life . . . security and its attendant advantages." P. 48: "[I]t is enough for my purpose to have shown that the election of the Jews had regard to nothing but temporal physical happiness and freedom." P. 56: "[T]his choice [of the Jews] . . . has no regard, in so far as it is peculiar to the Jews, to aught but dominion and physical advantage." Chap. V, p. 70: "In all the five books commonly attributed to Moses nothing is promised, as I have said, beyond temporal benefits, such as honors, fame, victories, riches, enjoyments, and health."

[13]Ibid., Chap. V, p. 70: "Christ . . . taught only universal moral precepts and for this cause promises a spiritual instead of a temporal reward. Christ was sent into the world . . . solely to teach the universal moral law." P. 71: "His sole care was to teach moral doctrines." P. 72: "The New Testament also confirms this view, for only moral doctrines are therein taught, and the Kingdom of God is promised as a reward." Cf. also Spinoza's *Correspondence*, Letter #75: "[A]ll that the Jews interpreted according to the flesh the Christians interpreted spiritually" (p. 349).

[14]*Treatise*, Preface, p. 8: "[T]he law revealed by God to Moses was merely the law of the individual Hebrew State." Chap. II, p. 41: "The reasonings" [which God presented to Job] "for the purpose of convincing him . . . are not universal, or for convincing all men." Chap. III, p. 47: "[T]he laws of the Old Testament were revealed and ordained to the Jews only." Chap. V, p. 70: The "many moral precepts besides ceremonies contained in [the five books of Moses] appear not as moral doctrines universal to all men, but as commands especially adapted to . . . the Hebrew people."

[15]Ibid., Chap. III, p. 53: "Paul especially desired to teach . . . his doctrine 'that God is the God of the Jews and of the Gentiles.' . . . [T]o all men absolutely was revealed the law . . . which has regard only to true virtue. . . . Paul concludes that . . . God is the God of all nations." Chap. IV, 64: Unlike Moses "Christ was sent to teach not only the Jews but the whole human race"; accordingly, "His mind [was] accommodated . . . to the opinion and fundamental teaching common to the whole human race—in other words, to ideas universal and true." Cf. also Chap. V, p. 70 as quoted above in note 13, and Chap. XII, p. 170: "The Apostles who came after Christ preached [religion] to all men as a universal religion solely in virtue of Christ's Passion."

3. The laws of Judaism were given as coercive laws to enslave the people; they were even cruel, evil laws given by an angry, vindictive God for the purpose of punishing the people, "laws whereby they should not live" (reflecting Ezekiel 20:25);[16] Christianity teaches a doctrine of worship of, and obedience to, God through love and in freedom.[17]

4. Moses was only a *legislator,* who legislated solely for the political purpose of bringing about obedience and social control;[18] Jesus (whom he always calls "Christ") was a *teacher*[19] (a classification higher than legislator) who taught spiritual values and ideals, and, in some sense, a *philosopher* because he *recognized truth as truth,* and taught universal moral principles.[20]

5. Moses communicated with God "mouth to mouth" and "face to face," a mode of communication in which the body was involved;[21] Jesus communicated with God "mind to mind."[22]

Spinoza's arbitrary upgrading of Jesus and downgrading of Moses, *without adducing any kind of evidence for these judgments or any attempt at rational justification,* may be worth quoting at some length:

> . . . a man who can by pure intuition comprehend ideas which are neither contained in nor deducible from the foundations of our natural knowledge, must necessarily possess a mind far superior to those of his fellow men, nor do I believe that any have been so endowed save

[16]Ibid., Chap. II, p. 39: "[T]he rule of right living, . . . was to [the Hebrews] rather a bondage than true liberty . . ." (Moses bid them keep the law and) "terrified them with threats if they transgressed." Chap. V, p. 76: "This, then, was the object of the ceremonial law, that men should . . . always act under external authority." Chap. XVII, p. 233: "[T]he celestial mind was so inflamed with anger that it ordained laws . . . with the purpose of vengeance, for the sake of punishment; so that the laws do not seem so much laws—that is, the safeguard of the people—as pains and penalties."

[17]Ibid., Chap. III, p. 53: "Paul concludes that . . . to all nations God did send His Christ to free all men equally from the bondage of the law, that they should no more do right by the command of the law, but by the constant determination of their hearts." Chap. IV, p. 65: Jesus "taught His doctrines as eternal truths, and he did not lay them down as laws, thus freeing the minds of his hearers from the bondage of that law . . ."

[18]Ibid., Chap. II, p. 39: "Moses taught [the Israelites] . . . like a lawgiver compelling them to be moved by legal authority." Chap. V, p. 70: "Moses does not teach the Jews as a prophet not to kill or steal, but gives them these commandments solely as a lawgiver and judge; he does not reason out the doctrine, but affixes for its non-observance a penalty . . ."

[19]Ibid., pp. 70–71: "Christ . . . was sent into the world not . . . to lay down laws, but solely to teach the universal moral law. . . . His sole care was to teach moral doctrines."

[20]Ibid., p. 70: Christ taught the moral doctrine "with reference . . . also to the tranquility and blessedness of the individual" and his "mental acquiescence." Cf. also Chap. IV, p. 64: "Christ perceived (truly and adequately) what was revealed . . ." See also above, footnote 17.

[21]Ibid., Chap. I, p. 19.

[22]Ibid.

> Christ. To Him the ordinances of God leading men to salvation were revealed directly without words or visions . . . the voice of Christ, like the voice which Moses heard, may be called the voice of God, and it may be said that the wisdom of God (i.e., wisdom more than human) took upon itself in Christ human nature, and that Christ was the way of salvation . . . What I have just stated I gather from Scripture (i.e., New Testament) that Christ was the Way of Life, and that the old law was given through an angel, and not immediately by God; whence it follows that if Moses spoke with God face to face as a man speaks to a friend (i.e., by means of two bodies) Christ communed with God mind to mind.[23]

There is an equivocation here, "What I have just stated I gather from Scripture," but the total impact is *not* equivocal.

6. Moses did not perceive God's teachings as eternal truths, nor were they revealed to him as such, but, rather, as

> precepts and ordinances, and he ordained them as laws of God, and thus it came to be that he conceived God as a ruler, a legislator, a king, as merciful, just, etc. but such qualities are simply attributes of human nature, and utterly alien from the nature of the Deity;[24] (whereas) *this must not be affirmed of Christ.* Christ, although he too seems to have written laws in the name of God, must be taken to have had a clear and adequate perception, for Christ was not so much a prophet as the mouthpiece of God. For God made revelations to mankind through Christ as He had before done through angels.[25]

7. God had revealed Himself to the (Hebrew) prophets through their imagination,

> through words and symbols;[26] (but God revealed Himself) to Christ, or to Christ's mind, immediately . . . and we must need suppose that Christ perceived truly what was revealed, in other words. He *understood* it, for a matter is *understood* when it is perceived simply by the mind without words or symbols[27] (emphasis added).

8. When Moses ordained God's revelations as laws and ordinances, this was part of his "carnal" concern with the material goals of a system of law and order, and when Moses spoke of God as ruler, king, merciful, just, it was because he conceived of God in terms of

[23]Ibid., pp. 18–19.
[24]Ibid., Chap. IV, p. 64.
[25]Ibid.
[26]Ibid.
[27]Ibid.

human nature;[28] whereas, if Christ proclaimed God's revelations as laws, or described God as "lawgiver, or prince, and styled Him as just, merciful, etc." it was because Christ "accommodated Himself to the comprehension of the people, . . . it was doubtless in concession to human weakness," and "merely in concession to popular understanding, and the imperfection of human knowledge."[29]

9. The ceremonials and ritual observances of Judaism are contemptuously dismissed as having "nothing to do with blessedness and virtue," and as being significant to the Hebrews only for "their temporal bodily happiness and the tranquility of their kingdom."[30] In connection with this polemic, Spinoza invokes the prophet Isaiah's stern condemnation of the emphasis on rituals and of the sins against moral and ethical principles, as if this prophecy of Isaiah's were not part of the Judaism that Spinoza was downgrading;[31] whereas mild and gentle treatment that is hardly a model of consistency is accorded to

> the Christian rites, such as baptism, the Lord's Supper, festivals, public prayers, and any other observances which are, and have always been, common to all Christendom; if they were instituted by Christ or His Apostles (which is open to doubt), they were instituted as external signs of the universal church, and not as having anything to do with blessedness, or possessing any sanctity in themselves. . . . [Though] such ceremonies were not ordained for the sake of upholding a government, they were ordained for the preservation of a society.[32]

10. Spinoza, who, out of his early and thorough training in Judaism certainly knew better, uses the word *Pharisees* as a term of opprobrium, which is the way it is used in the New Testament and in much of Christian literature. It is the *Pharisees* who, "in their ignorance, thought that the observance of the state law and the Mosaic law was the sum total of morality;" the *Pharisees* "continued practicing these rites after the destruction of the kingdom, but more with a view of opposing the Christians than of pleasing God."[33] The *Pharisees* "vehemently contend that the Divine gift (of prophecy) was peculiar to their nation."[34] Christ, Spinoza says approvingly, "convicted the

[28]Ibid.: "[S]uch qualities are simply attributes of human nature, and utterly alien from the nature of the Deity."

[29]Ibid., pp. 64–65.

[30]Ibid., Chap. V, p. 69.

[31]Ibid. The reference here is to Chapter I of Isaiah, which Spinoza surely knew to have become part of the synagogue liturgy as the Prophetic portion read on the Sabbath that precedes the Fast of Av.

[32]*Treatise,* Chap. V, p. 76.

[33]Ibid., pp. 71–72.

[34]Ibid., Chap. III, p. 52.

Pharisees of pride and ignorance."[35] Though Moses Maimonides lived centuries after the age of the *Pharisees*, in attacking him Spinoza refers to him derisively as a *Pharisee*.[36]

11. Moses "does not teach the Jews as a *prophet* not to kill or steal . . . but solely as a lawgiver and judge." The command not to commit adultery

> is given merely with reference to the welfare of the state;[37] for if the moral doctrine had been intended with reference . . . also to the tranquility and blessedness of the individual, Moses would have condemned not merely the outward act, but also the mental acquiescence, *as is done by Christ*, who taught only universal moral precepts, and for this cause promises a spiritual instead of a temporal reward.[38]

12. Moses and the Mosaic doctrine are hostile to philosophy,[39] whereas veiled hints seem to imply that Jesus was a philosopher and that his doctrines are more hospitable to philosophy.[40]

13. In connection with his characterization of Judaism's *particularism*, which Spinoza presents as a doctrine of *separatism and hostility to other peoples*, he asserts that Judaism taught its adherents that "they should separate themselves from the rest of the nations: wherefore it was commanded to them, 'Love thy neighbor and hate thine enemy,'" a verse taken from Matthew 5:43.[41] Spinoza reproduces the verse without pointing out the *falsehood* in it, and in a context in which he associates himself with it. For *Spinoza's own words*, just before the words that he cites from Matthew, are "wherefore it was commanded to them," thus conveying his agreement with Matthew's *false* allegation that the Jews were, in fact, so commanded. Surely Spinoza knew better. Surely he knew full well that there is no such teaching in Jewish Scripture, and surely he knew equally well that, indeed, more typical of Hebrew Scriptural teaching is the commandment: "When you see your enemy's beast of burden fallen under its heavy load, you shall help him to relieve the burden."[42] Surely, also, he was fully familiar with the precept in the Biblical Book of Proverbs

[35]Ibid., Chap. II, p. 41.

[36]Ibid., Chap. XV, p. 190.

[37]Ibid., Chap. V, p. 70.

[38]Ibid.

[39]Ibid., Chap. XI, p. 164: "[O]ther Apostles preaching to the Jews, despisers of philosophy, adapted themselves to the temper of their hearers, and preached a religion free from all philosophical speculation." Chap. II, p. 39: "Moses . . . taught them . . . a rule of right living; inculcating it not like a philosopher, as the result of freedom . . ."

[40]See above, notes 17 and 20.

[41]*Treatise*, Chap. XIX, p. 250.

[42]Exodus 30:4 and 5.

(24:17) that was later restated as a Rabbinic admonition in the *Ethics of the Fathers:* "Do not rejoice at the stumbling of your enemy . . ."[43]

14. While there are numerous contradictions in *The Treatise,* a number of which various commentators have tried to explain, there is one major, glaring, inexplicable one that is directly related to Spinoza's application of a "double standard" of evaluation as between Judaism and Christianity. The late Professor Leo Strauss, in his essay, "How to Read Spinoza's Theologico-Political Treatise,"[44] tries to explain some of these apparent contradictions by attributing to the philosopher the intent to conceal some of his ideas. However, the dimensions of the contradiction pointed to below are too large for the Strauss-type of explanation to fit.

Spinoza's political philosophy, as formulated in Part IV of the *Ethics,*[45] and repeatedly in *The Treatise* (especially Chapters XIX–XX), requires of the citizen almost unquestioning *obedience* to the State. In Scholium 2 to Proposition 37 in the Fourth Part of the *Ethics,* Spinoza says (basing his view here on III, 30 and IV, 7) that a person can be prevented from doing injury to another person only "by fear of a greater injury," and that in a civil state "law . . . and the prescriptions of a common rule of life" need to be supported "not by reason . . . but by penalties." "In a civil state . . . *Sin* is nothing but disobedience . . ." and "obedience is *merit* in a citizen" (italics in original). In his philosophy of religion, also, Spinoza emphasizes the role of religion as teacher, guide, and force for the implementation of rules of moral conduct: "Revelation has obedience for its sole object."[46] It would have been natural and consistent, therefore, for Spinoza to have spoken approvingly of Judaism's emphasis on *law,* on practical commandments, on ethical conduct, and on obedience to moral principles. Instead, he disparages Judaism's doctrines as coercive, enslaving, material, nonspiritual.[47] Moreover, instead of criticizing them, as consistency would have required him to do, he speaks in laudatory terms about the *antinomian* aspects of Christian doctrine, calling them spiritual and liberating. He also speaks approvingly of the high position that Christian teaching assigns in its moral hierarchy to emotions like *pity,* which, in the *Ethics,* he had called "evil and unprofitable" in a man "who lives according to the guidance of reason,"[48] an emotion

[43]*Pirke Avot* IV, 24.

[44]Leo Strauss, *Persecution and the Art of Writing* (Glencoe, Illinois: The Free Press, 1952), pp. 142–201.

[45]Barukh Spinoza, *Ethics,* Part IV, Propositions 36, 37, and the *Scholia.*

[46]*Treatise,* Preface, p. 9.

[47]See above, paragraphs numbered 1–10, and notes 12, 16, and 18.

[48]*Ethics,* IV, 50.

of which he says that "a man who lives according to the dictates of reason endeavors as much as possible to prevent himself from being touched by pity."[49]

It should be abundantly clear that this presentation of a sampling out of what we have called the Syllabus of Spinoza's Errors was not intended either as an apologia for Judaism, or as a polemic against Christianity. Spinoza's critique of aspects of Judaism and his endorsements of aspects of Christianity are, for those who might be interested in them, subjects to be studied and evaluated objectively, on their own. But this is not our focus here. Rather, it is his *uncritical* endorsement of some doctrines that he imputes to Christianity, with no more rational or empirical evidence adduced to support *these* doctrines than is available for the support of the doctrines which he deplores in Judaism to which they are invidiously juxtaposed; it is his utterly amazing use of a double standard of evaluation in which he disparages doctrines in Judaism and lauds the same doctrines in Christianity; and it is the *puzzling contradictions* between principles central to his own philosophy and the principles implicit in his attacks on Judaism, that the above recital is designed to point to, and to point also to the need to explain this strange behavior on the part of a philosopher whose other works, especially the *Ethics*, as well as his reputation, have habituated us to expect from him objectivity, detachment, precision, rationality, logical consistency, judiciousness, and fairness.

III

What *is* the explanation? It is necessary, first, to dispose of two explanations that have been suggested or that suggest themselves, and that seem quite inadequate. The first is that in *The Treatise* Spinoza was really attacking *all* religion when it presumes to exercise control over philosophy, especially Christian religion. But, since Hebrew Scripture is part of Christian Scripture, in attacking the former, Spinoza, in fact, also attacked the established Christianity of his day and its attempts to control philosophical thinking, without making his major goal too obvious. There is, no doubt, a certain amount of truth in this theory, and we shall return to a phase of it forthwith. But it does not seem to account for either the full sweep of the attack against Judaism in *The Treatise* or for the biting, caustic tone in which it is often phrased; nor does it account for the encomiums that are so repeatedly showered on Jesus as compared with Moses, and, directly

[49]Ibid., Corollary.

as well as by implication, on Christian doctrine as compared with Judaism.

The second explanation suggested is that the ideal, universal religion that he sketched in *The Treatise*,[50] which Leo Strauss characterizes as neither Judaism nor Christianity but a kind of de-theologized Christianity,[51] required, in Spinoza's opinion, the abrogation of Jewish or Mosaic law because of its particularism. On the other hand, since Jesus was interpreted by him to be a *teacher* rather than a *legislator*, and to have taught universal moral principles, Christianity is not incompatible with the Spinozist universal religion. Once again, while this may have some relevance, it does not suffice as an adequate explanation of Spinoza's almost virulent anti-Judaism.

The conclusions suggested below reflect assessments by earlier commentators such as Luzzato, Hermann Cohen, and, to some extent, Leo Strauss, and the explanations proposed are essentially characterological and are not complimentary to Spinoza. For, over and above the *intellectual* deficiencies that he exhibited in some of his attacks against Judaism, these attacks and his consistent, undisguised hostility seem to be explicable only as overt manifestations of character weaknesses and defects that belie the traditional portrait of Spinoza's personality, discussion of which may appear shockingly iconoclastic.

1. Spinoza never overcame the blow of his excommunication (and of the excommunication and subsequent suicide of Uriel Acosta, about which he knew from his childhood days), and carried its trauma with him for the rest of his life. His resentment and hostility against what he perceived as the intellectual narrowness and religious intolerance of the Jewish community and of the Judaism that it espoused, manifested themselves in vindictiveness and even a hatred against Judaism that is reflected and articulated in *The Treatise*.

2. Spinoza was consumed by a *fear* of the Christian authorities, of their deep-seated prejudice and hostility against dissenting and heretical ideas, and their power to inflict upon dissenters, including himself, severe reprisals (here he shared the fears of the Jewish community that were, in part, the reason for its excommunicating him). By making Judaism the principal and manifest object of his attack, feeling himself, as he did, absolved from loyalty or responsibility to it by virtue of its repugnant exclusionary act, he could perhaps hope to deflect from himself the hostility of the Christian authorities with their built-in anti-Jewish attitudes.

[50]*Treatise*, Chap. XIV, pp. 186–187.

[51]Leo Strauss, *Spinoza's Critique of Religion*, tr. by E. M. Sinclair (New York: Schocken Books, 1965), Preface, p. 20.

3. His fears also led him to try to *curry favor* with his Christian readers, to a kind of political *sycophancy* in which he tried to please them and the Christian authorities by reiterating many of their traditional denigrations and distortions of Judaism. As Leo Strauss puts it (reflecting here also Hermann Cohen's view):

> Spinoza, attempting to achieve the liberation of philosophy in a book addressed to Christians, cannot but appeal to the Christian prejudices which include anti-Jewish prejudices; he fights Christian prejudice by appealing to Christian prejudices; appealing to the Christian prejudice against Judaism, he exhorts the Christians to free essentially spiritual Christianity from all carnal Jewish relics . . . Generally speaking, he makes the Old Testament, against his better knowledge, the scapegoat for everything he finds objectionable in actual Christianity.[52]

4. His fear and his political sycophancy are also reflected in the statement that appears both at the end of the Preface to *The Treatise* and at the conclusion of its closing chapter:

> I feel bound to declare here . . . that I have written nothing, which I do not most willingly submit to the examination and judgment of my country's rulers, and that I am ready to retract anything which they shall decide to be repugnant to the laws or prejudicial to the public good. I know that I am a man, and, as a man, liable to error, but against error I have taken scrupulous care, and striven to keep in entire accordance with the laws of my country, with loyalty, and with morality.[53]

This declaration seems hardly consonant with the received image of Spinoza as the courageous, saintly, and solitary fighter for freedom of ideas, or with the "wholly free and disillusioned spirit," as George Santayana characterized him in his justly celebrated essay, "Ultimate Religion." Santayana's tribute attains a memorable level of eloquence when he says that, in addition to "our great debt to Spinoza for his philosophy of nature,"

> there is, I think, something for which we owe him an even greater debt; I mean, the magnificent example he offers us of philosophic liberty, the courage, firmness, and sincerity with which he reconciled his heart to the truth.[54]

It will strike some readers as almost sacrilegious to suggest that Santayana's essentially accurate characterization of Spinoza in his

[52]Ibid.

[53]*Treatise*, Preface, p. 11.

[54]George Santayana, *Obiter Scripta: Lectures, Essays and Reviews* (New York: Charles Scribner's Sons, 1936), pp. 280–297.

philosophical doctrines on metaphysics and epistemology, in the theory of mind, and in ethical theory, does not reflect with complete accuracy Spinoza's character structure and personal qualities, or his pronouncements on other subjects. Even in the face of the received, traditional image of Spinoza's personality, with which Santayana's eloquent description appears to agree, it may not be altogether an act of desecration to consider the possibility of weaknesses and defects coexisting with unmistakably luminous and inspiriting philosophical genius.

For almost 200 years Spinoza's reputation has been the captive of the Romantic imagination in Europe. Deservedly idealized on the basis of the exalting and inspiring purity of the doctrines of his *Ethics* that were discovered by the Romantics about a century after his death, Spinoza became a hero and a saint for the leaders of the Romantic movement in Germany—Lessing, Jacobi, Novalis—with Goethe as its principal figure. The adulation spread across the English Channel, reaching Coleridge, Wordsworth, and others in the Romantic period of Britain's thought and literature, moved across the Atlantic, and bequeathed to us the idealized portrait of Spinoza as saintly, courageous in his solitariness, flawless in his integrity and honesty, and leading an exemplary personal life that reflected the exalted *amor dei intellectualis* of the *Ethics. The Treatise* has been read, when it *was* read, through the prism of the *Ethics*, which filters out the reprehensible elements in *The Treatise* that were sketched above, as philosophically trivial and uninteresting. Significantly, these same anti-Jewish elements were not altogether filtered out for the Christian readers of *The Treatise.* His contemporaries, and Christian readers in the 18th and 19th centuries, found confirmation, in Spinoza's disparagement of Judaism, of many of the stereotypical anti-Jewish attitudes that they had received from the tradition and culture in which they grew up. Moreover, it was a confirmation that came from, of all people, a person who presumably should know, namely, Spinoza, whom they never failed to identify as a Jew.

To those non-Jews who espoused a post-Emancipation liberalism that included the advocacy of equal civil and political rights for Jews in Europe, *The Treatise* provided a most attractive and congenial rationale for their latent discomfort about *the to them unexpected phenomenon of continuing and persistent post-Emancipation Jewish group existence,* and a justification for their semi-conscious wish that this phenomenon would just disappear and cease to be a source of irritation to them. For many Western Jews, on the other hand, afflicted by a sense of "uncertainty of belonging" (Kurt Lewin's phrase)[55] in post-Eman-

[55]Kurt Lewin, *Resolving Social Conflicts: Selected Papers on Group Dynamics* (New York: Harper & Brothers, 1948), pp. 177–185. "Not the *belonging to many groups* is the cause of the difficulty, but an *uncertainty* of belongingness" (p. 179 [emphasis in the original]).

cipation Europe, and carried along by the wave of assimilation and apostasy that swept over them, the denigration of Judaism in *The Treatise* provided added justification for their Jewish self-hate and for their removing themselves beyond the periphery of the Jewish group. Other Jews, though deeply troubled by the hostility to Judaism in *The Treatise,* nonetheless held on to Spinoza as part of Jewry because the great acclaim accorded to him as a philosopher by the non-Jewish world, and the exemplary nobility of character ascribed to him, gave them a sense of added dignity in their Jewishness and furnished them with a publicly acknowledged self-validation as Jews that they greatly desired.

However, if, in the interest of historical accuracy, we demythologize and deromanticize Spinoza, and see him plain, warts and all, we may be helped in our search for a rational and responsible approach to the question whether he was a *Jewish* philosopher, through the application of the crude criteria suggested earlier. The demythologized Spinoza is a man whose towering, brilliant, and inspiring genius as manifested in the *Ethics,* and whose nobility of vision as expressed also in the opening paragraphs of his *De Intellectus Emendatione,* as well as in many phases of his personal life, are marred by his understandable resentment and vindictiveness against the people and religion that had banned him, and from whom he proceeded to alienate himself completely; marred by understandable fears of the dogmatic and punitive Calvinist authorities of his day; marred by an obsequiousness toward aspects of Christian doctrine that led him, in *The Treatise,* to employ double standards of judgment, to contradict and traduce some of his own central doctrines, and to titillate Christian anti-Jewish prejudices with which he surely was fully familiar; and marred, as Hermann Cohen pointed out,[56] by the damage that his diatribes against Judaism in *The Treatise* wreaked on the perceptions and assessments of Judaism in the thought and some of the writings of Western Europe during the following two centuries, including the assessment of Judaism by even so fair and decent a person and philosopher as Immanuel Kant.[57]

The deromanticization of Spinoza makes it necessary for us also to observe how aspects of his socio-religio-political thought are marred by faulty assessments. Leo Strauss pointed out that Spinoza's adum-

[56]Cf. above, note 3.

[57]See Hermann Cohen, *Die Religion der Vernunft aus den Quellen des Judentums* (Leipzig: Gustav Fok, 1919), p. 391: "Spinoza's polemic became the source of a fundamental misunderstanding of Jewish religion . . . It was from Spinoza that Kant drew his information and his judgment on Judaism" (my translation). Cf. also, Nathan Rotenstreich, *The Recurring Pattern: Studies in Anti-Judaism in Modern Thought* (New York: Horizon Press, 1964), p. 25.

bration of a new, ideal, universal religion made him "a symbol of that emancipation which was to be more than emancipation but secular redemption."[58] For Spinoza's Romanticist disciples, including many Jews in 18th and 19th century Germany, there was the hope, says Strauss, that as a result of his ideas "the non-Jewish world, having been molded to a considerable extent by Spinoza," would "become receptive to Jews who were willing to assimilate to it."[59] This must have been Spinoza's own hope too, certainly *for himself,* and was, no doubt, a consideration of no minor importance in his decision, after the Jewish community's reprehensible act of excommunication, to sever his relationships from the Jewish community entirely, and to live among non-Jews.

Accordingly, we are justified in inquiring whether his life among non-Jews was more congenial and satisfying than it would have been had he managed somehow to remain within the Jewish community. Were the masses of the non-Jews more open and hospitable to his startling and independent and unorthodox ideas than the masses of the *Jews* would have been? Did he find the world of the *non-Jewish* elite, its scholars and intellectuals, more hospitable to his doctrines than the *Jewish* elite and intellectuals were or would have been? The fact is, of course, that, in spite of the measure of intellectual eminence which he achieved among some scholars, and with the exception of the treatment accorded to him by the few who befriended him (some only temporarily) and corresponded with him, his life among non-Jews was largely that of an exile. His views were suspected, attacked, condemned, and reviled. He was forced to refrain from publishing the *Ethics* in his lifetime and, in the interest of his safety, *The Treatise* had to be published anonymously. We are led to a sadly ironic conclusion when we speculate on what treatment, far worse than excommunication, would have been meted out to Spinoza had he published these two works under his own name during his lifetime. He perceived and publicly deplored exclusiveness and bigotry in his own people, disparaged even the creative and constructive elements in non-exclusivist Jewish particularism, and went to the extent of falsely distorting it, as in his shabby use of the verse from Matthew. But he bracketed his vision of a universalist religion and social order with a version of Christianity, underplaying the destructive, menacing particularisms in the Christian world around him to which he refers in the Preface, that world with its virulent bigotries and cruel persecutions, that placed his own safety in jeopardy, and that never failed to identify him as Spinoza, *the Jew.* Spinoza misread

[58]Strauss, *Spinoza's Critique of Religion,* Preface, p. 11.
[59]Ibid.

the realities of religio-socio-political forces, and failed in his assessment of the possibility of extreme universalist liberalism, a utopian idea that, in his thought, became an impediment to developing a doctrine of a pluralism of non-exclusivist particularisms. To borrow the words of Jacob B. Agus, Jewish existence in the Diaspora "no longer possessed any rhyme or reason" for him. Clearly, this was a consequence of his delusively or opportunistically motivated notion that a world purged of "carnal" Jewish particularism would become an Eden of dogma-free and sacrament-free Christian universalism.

5. *Was Spinoza a "Jewish" Philosopher?*

In Spinoza's onslaught on Judaism, his principal vehicle was his book, *A Theologico-Political Treatise* (referred to below as *The Treatise*). The "Syllabus of Spinoza's Errors" against the Jews and Judaism, contained in that book, was laid bare in some detail in the preceding issue of this journal.[1] A heavy burden of guilt was shown to rest on his shoulders, and the personality portrait of Spinoza that emerged in our exposition is a less admirable one than the portrait of him handed down to us by the Romantic Imagination of the late 18th and the 19th centuries. It would thus seem that, if Spinoza and his *Treatise* had bequeathed to us only his calculated calumnies against Judaism and the Jewish people, we would have been amply justified, indeed morally obligated, to dismiss him as nothing more than a traitor and slanderer.

But let us suppose that these calumnies and diatribes were purged from *The Treatise*; manifestly a substantial work of no minor significance would still remain. Suppose now that we sought to answer the question posed in our title, "Was Spinoza a *Jewish* Philosopher?," but this time by applying the three criteria suggested in our previous essay to Spinoza as the author of the *Ethics*, the *Short Treatise*, the *Emendation of the Intellect*, most of his *Letters*, and the purged *Treatise*. What would our answer be?

It needs to be noted in the first place that, of course, not all of the criticisms or polemics against Judaism in the *Treatise*, either among those reviewed in the "Syllabus of Spinoza's Errors," or among those

[1]Cf. Isaac Franck, "Spinoza's Onslaught on Judaism," *Judaism*, 28, 2 (Spring 1979): 180. [See the preceding essay in the present volume. (Note by W.G.)]

Judaism: A Quarterly Journal of Jewish Life and Thought, vol. 28, Summer 1979, pp. 345–352.

left unmentioned, are inherently reprehensible, deplorable, or unjustified. With some of these criticisms many Jewish thinkers, loyal and devoted Jews, will agree (*va'ani hakatan b'tokham,* myself, in all modesty, among them). The criticisms are reprehensible in the context of *The Treatise* because, while they are directed against putative flaws in Judaism, these very same flaws, when manifested in Christianity, are simply not attacked by Spinoza, or are reinterpreted by him in a favorable light without supporting evidence. They thus exemplify the double standard pointed to in our earlier essay.

Moreover, it must also be noted that, if we apply the second of the proposed three criteria, namely,

> the philosopher's intent to contribute to the advancement of Jewish thought, affirmatively or through criticism; . . . his philosophical ideas and doctrines . . . [having been] addressed principally to an audience of committed Jews . . .,

there would certainly be strong and cogent reasons for concluding that Spinoza was not a Jewish philosopher. Whatever may have been his hopes and intentions before the excommunication, certainly afterward he did not address his writings to a Jewish audience. There is no known evidence in any of his work or in his correspondence that he had any desire to contribute to the advancement and improvement of Jewish thought. He displayed no interest in the survival and continuity of Judaism and of the Jewish people, except for this almost parenthetical remark in *The Treatise:*

> I would go so far as to believe that . . . they [i.e., the Jewish nation] may even, if occasion offers . . . raise up their empire afresh, and that God may a second time elect them.[2]

But this is no more than an aside, uttered without any discernible enthusiasm or even concern, and hardly justifies the elevation of Spinoza to the pantheon of pioneers of modern Zionist thought, as some have tried to do.

He became so completely estranged from Judaism that his universalist utopia entailed an assimilationist program leading to the disappearance of Judaism. *As to the Jewish people,* Leo Strauss (again associating himself with Hermann Cohen) said that while

> Spinoza may have hated Judaism, he did not hate the Jewish people, and thought of the liberation of the Jews in the only way in which he could think of it, given his philosophy.[3]

[2]*Treatise,* Chap. III, p. 56.

[3]Leo Strauss, *Spinoza's Critique of Religion,* tr. by E. M. Sinclair (New York: Schocken Books, 1965), Preface, p. 21.

However, even if we were to follow Strauss in his less than zealous or cogent apologia for Spinoza here, the "thought of liberation" that he ascribes to Spinoza could mean only two possible expectations, "given his philosophy": either some vague, speculative, utterly parenthetical "Zionist" type of solution, or the absorption of the Jews into the general population. Either expectation (if Spinoza really gave them any thought) would, in fact, have been an evasion, inasmuch as it would have obviated for Spinoza any motive, and absolved him of any obligation, to contribute to the advancement of a theory or philosophy of Jewish group existence.

But if, his intentions—or, rather lack of intentions—notwithstanding, we concluded, nonetheless, on the basis of other criteria, that Spinoza *was* a Jewish philosopher, then, clearly, by virtue of his failure to fit the second of our criteria, we would have to call him a *Jewish* philosopher *malgré lui,* in spite of himself, rather than by intent or free choice.

What remains, then, is to try to apply the other two suggested criteria: *the first,* did the philosopher's inquiries, ideas, and doctrines arise out of the matrix of Jewish thought and experience? And *third,* did his inquiries and ideas contribute, in fact, to the advancement, enrichment, or clarification of some of the concepts, ideas, and doctrines in subsequent Jewish thought? The application of the first of these criteria can be disposed of rather quickly. One need only read H. A. Wolfson's classic two-volume study, *The Philosophy of Spinoza,*[4] to see that, in the treatment of almost every one of his major ideas in the *Ethics,* the *Short Treatise,* and the *Emendation of the Intellect,* whatever his other philosophical antecedents may have been, Spinoza was also reflecting and responding to ideas in the Hebrew Bible, Rabbinic texts and teachings in the Talmudic period, and the long expanse of philosophical thought in Judaism, from Philo to Leo Hebraeus, from Saadia to Crescas and Albo.

Earlier scholars, e.g., M. Joel in the 1870s[5] and Jacob Klatzkin in the early 1920s,[6] were among the pioneers in exhibiting the deep roots of Spinoza's thought in the mainstream of Judaism. Moreover, *The Treatise,* ignoring the defects dwelt on earlier, is itself concerned with, and is a response (too often a flawed and saddening one) to, problems that had agitated Jewish life and thought very deeply and for many centuries, e.g., the nature of the language of Scripture, the problem of miracles, the meaning of prophecy, religious faith versus supersti-

[4]Harry Austryn Wolfson, *The Philosophy of Spinoza* (Cambridge, Mass.: Harvard University Press, 1934), 2 volumes.

[5]M. Joel, *Zur Genesis der Lehre Spinozas* (Breslau: 1871).

[6]Yaacov Klatzkin, *Barukh Spinoza: Hayav, S'farav, Shitato* (Barukh Spinoza: His Life, Books, System) (Berlin, 1923; reprinted Tel Aviv: Massadah, 1954).

tion, the meaning of the election of Israel, ethical laws and ceremonial laws, the authorship and the authority of the *humash,* the relationship of faith to reason, the relationship of theology to philosophy, the freedom of intellectual inquiry, the freedom of religious worship and observance. If we now add to this abbreviated catalogue even a very brief and random sampling of other technical metaphysical and epistemological issues dealt with by Spinoza in the *Ethics* and in other works, and also indicate how his treatment of them reflects earlier Jewish thought and thinkers, we may find sufficient ground for a tentative conclusion.

1. Spinoza's classification of human knowledge into three (or four) kinds clearly echoes similar attempts at classification in Saadia's *Beliefs and Opinions,*[7] in Maimonides' *Guide*[8] and his early brief treatise on *Logical Terminology,*[9] as well as in the work of later medieval Jewish philosophers.

2. His sketch, in the *Emendation,* of how the human mind developed its instruments of thinking from the simplest to the more complex stages, in which he uses as analogy the problem of how the first hammer was made since it, in turn, required another hammer with which to do so, etc., seems interestingly to reflect the concern of some of the ancient Rabbis about *zvat bizvat assuyah,*[10] the genesis of the first pair of pliers that required other pliers with which to make them.

3. Spinoza's doctrine that God is both Extension *and* Thought was *his* resolution of the controversy in Jewish thought about the Divine Attributes and the question whether there is any materiality in God, with Maimonides teaching the uncompromising doctrine that there is no materiality in God and branding as heretics those who did ascribe materiality to Him, though others disagreed.

4. The question of whether God is transcendent or immanent (or both), and Spinoza's doctrine of immanence, reflected Rabbinic and philosophical debates in Judaism that culminated in some of the Kabbalistic doctrines during the 16th century.

5. Spinoza's proofs of the existence of God reflect, as Wolfson amply shows, not only the discussions in Greek, Christian and Arabic thought, but, most intimately, the discussions by Maimonides, Crescas and other medieval Jewish thinkers.

[7]Saadia Gaon, *The Book of Beliefs and Opinions,* tr. by Samuel Rosenblatt (New Haven, Conn.: Yale University Press, 1948), pp. 16–18.

[8]See Leon Roth, *Spinoza, Descartes and Maimonides* (Oxford: The Clarendon Press, 1924), Chapter IV, "Maimonides and Spinoza," #5 ("The Grades of Natural Knowledge in Maimonides"), pp. 129–134.

[9]Moses Maimonides, *Millot Hahigayon* (Treatise on Logic), critically edited and translated by Israel Efros (New York: American Academy for Jewish Research, 1928) [published as Vol. VIII of the *Proceedings of the American Academy for Jewish Research*], Chapter VIII, p. 47.

[10]*Pirkei Avot* (Ethics of the Fathers), V, 9.

6. Spinoza's argument against the common belief that "God Himself directs all things to some sure end" and that "God has made all things for man that he may worship God"[11] reflects philosophical disputations in earlier Jewish philosophy, and takes a position similar to that of Maimonides and Gersonides. (Maimonides: "The true opinion is . . . not to believe that all things exist for the sake of man."[12] Spinoza actually uses the same words as Maimonides does.)

7. Spinoza's doctrine of Determinism is *his* resolution of the problem of free will, a problem implicit in Scripture, treated in Rabbinic discussions in the Talmudic period, and dealt with by Maimonides and Crescas both as a metaphysical problem, and also in relation to the question of man's moral responsibility.

8. Spinoza's arresting notion of *Amor Dei Intellectualis* is surely an apex, not only of his own philosophy, but, also, of the philosophies of Maimonides and Crescas, and represents a major trend in Jewish philosophical thought with which Spinoza was thoroughly familiar.

9. His identification of God and Nature, his revolt against the psycho-physical dualism of Cartesian and Christian thought, and various other doctrines too numerous to mention, are rooted in his early training in the religious and philosophical thought of Judaism that unmistakably constitute an overwhelmingly great part of the philosophical frame of reference within which Spinoza's genius functioned. So much, then, for criterion number one.

The attempt to apply criterion number three will also have to be brief, sketchy, and only suggestive. Did Spinoza's inquiries and ideas contribute to the advancement, enrichment, or clarification of ideas and doctrines in subsequent Jewish thought? The answer here will depend, in the first instance, on whether you look upon Jewish thought as an open system or a closed one. It seems to me that those who insist, and there are some who do, that it is a *closed* system distort the authentic mainstream of Jewish thought. They ignore many pivotal markers in the development of its religious and philosophical articulation such as, to recall only a few: 1) the passage in Tractate *M'nahot,* which tells of God's drawing aside the curtain of the future in order to enable Moses to see Rabbi Akiba teaching Torah to his students, and Moses feeling weak and embarrassed because he could not understand the doctrine that Akiba was teaching some 1300 years later;[13] 2) the Rabbinic principle enunciated in the Talmud that *"ailu v'ailu divrei elohim hayim"*[14] (*both* conflicting doctrines are the

[11]Spinoza, *Ethics,* I, Appendix.

[12]Maimonides, *Guide of the Perplexed,* III, 13.

[13]Babylonian Talmud, *M'nahot,* 29b.

[14]Jerusalem Talmud, *B'rakhot,* Chapter 1 (Shulsinger Edition, New York, 1948), 3a.

words of the living God); 3) Maimonides' comment that the gates of interpretation are still open;[15] 4) Bahya Ibn Pakuda's assertion that we are under obligation to investigate theological and philosophical problems by rational methods, each according to his powers and capacities, and those who neglect to do so belong to the class of those who fall short of wisdom;[16] or 5) Joseph Albo's view that "every intelligent person is permitted to investigate the fundamental principles of religion and to interpret the Biblical texts in accordance with the truth as it seems to him."[17]

In the light of such repeated commitments, there would seem ample justification for the assertion made recently by Judge Haim Cohen, a Justice in Israel's Supreme Court, that "The great contribution that Spinoza made to the history of Jewish thought is the proposition that the essence of Jewish law is freedom of Jewish thought and conscience."[18]

At the conclusion of his massive work on Spinoza, H. A. Wolfson credits him with four acts of daring:[19] 1) he declared that God has the attributes of extension as well as of thought; 2) he denied design and purpose in God; 3) he insisted on the complete inseparability of soul from body; and 4) he insisted on the elimination of freedom of the will from human actions. From a rigidly static point of view it must be supposed that these doctrines are heterodox, some even heretical. However, as was pointed out above, each of them has been espoused, with greater or lesser zeal, by one or more religious and philosophical thinkers in Jewish intellectual history prior to Spinoza, without their having been denied a place in this history. Spinoza's pushing these ideas to the unfolding of some of their further, or perhaps ultimate, implications opened up new possibilities for the pursuit of additional probing into these perilous areas by subsequent Jewish thinkers.

The late Harav Avraham Yizhak Hacohen Kook will serve as an illustration. While he was certainly critical of Spinoza, believed that the excommunication was justified, and ascribed great danger to Spinoza's excessive rationalism and complete depersonalization of God, Harav Kook nevertheless noted the "admirable force" in Spinoza's thought and said that it was no wonder that this force had made its appearance especially in the thought of *a Jew* and "that the

[15]Maimonides, *Guide of the Perplexed*, II, 25.

[16]Bahya ben Joseph ibn Pakudah, *Duties of the Heart*, tr. by Moses Hyamson (New York: Philipp Feldheim, 1965), Volume I, *Shaar Hayihud* (Part I), Chap. III, pp. 66–67.

[17]Joseph Albo, *Sefer Ha'Ikkarim* (Book of Roots), tr. by Isaac Husik (Philadelphia: Jewish Publication Society, 1946), Volume I, Book I, Chap. 2, p. 55.

[18]*Congress Monthly* (March–April, 1978): 10.

[19]H. A. Wolfson, *The Philosophy of Spinoza*, Vol. II, Chap. XXI, pp. 331–339.

idea of God's unity had struck such deep roots in his soul."[20] Harav Kook taught that "True *Being* is Divinity . . . that *Being* in its entirety is Divinity and there is absolutely nothing except God . . . that everything is included in God," and that this is a monotheistic doctrine "inclined to a pantheistic interpretation, cleansed of its defects."[21] Clearly, this doctrine was in part stimulated by Spinoza's doctrine of *Deus sive Natura,* which, in turn, is likely to have reflected, in part, his familiarity with Kabbalistic doctrine, such as Moses Cordovero's principle that "God is all reality, but not all reality is God."[22] Which came first in the development of his thought is less important than the fact that Spinoza's philosophy, with which Harav Kook was more than perfunctorily familiar, may be seen here as a link between 15th century Kabbalistic teaching and the 20th century thought of Harav Kook.

Spinoza's incisive psychological insights in the *Ethics;* his philosophy of man in the *Ethics* and other works; his rejection of Christian and Cartesian psycho-physical dualism, and insistence on the *unity* of man; his sober and illuminating focus on the psychological and societal problems of controlling man's emotions and passions, through the employment of reason[23] on the one hand, and of religion's teaching and guidance on the other (ignoring his self-contradictions in the *Treatise*) resonate in the contemporary philosophy of man by the late Rabbi Abraham J. Heschel, with its emphasis on the *mizvah,* on being commanded, as antidote to man's self-idolization in our current cult of "need-psychology."[24]

Certainly one of the greatest contributions of Spinoza to Jewish theology is his uncompromising reinforcement of the de-anthropomorphization of God, as taught by Maimonides in the *Guide,* as well as by others. It is interesting that Martin Buber, who certainly disagreed, found it necessary to confront Spinoza, and to declare that "in his theory of the divine attributes . . . (he) seems to have undertaken

[20]Avraham Yizhak Hacohen Kook, *Adar Hayakar V'ikvei Hazon* (The Mantle of Splendor and the Tracks of the Sheep) (Jerusalem, 1967), pp. 153 ff. (my translation).

[21]Avraham Yizhak Hacohen Kook, *Orot Hakodesh* (Lights of Sanctity) (Jerusalem, 1964), Volume II, p. 399 (my translation).

[22]Moses Cordovero (1522–70). Cf. Gershom G. Scholem, *Major Trends in Jewish Mysticism* (New York: Schocken Books, 1954), pp. 252–253, and p. 409, note 19. Cf. also Gershom G. Scholem, *Kabbalah* (New York: Quadrangle/The New York Times Book Co., 1974), pp. 144–152. [The Kabbalah and Pantheism: "The Single most definite statement in Cordovero's treatment of the problem can be classed as panentheistic: 'God is all that exists, but not all that exists is God'" (page 150).]

[23]See Isaac Franck, "Spinoza, Freud, and Hampshire on Psychic Freedom," in *Thought, Consciousness, and Reality: Psychiatry and the Humanities,* Volume 2, ed. Joseph H. Smith, M.D. (New Haven: Yale University Press, 1977), pp. 257–309 (especially 257–272, and 300–306). [See the next essay in the present volume. (Note by W.G.)]

[24]Abraham Joshua Heschel, *Who Is Man?* (Stanford, Cal.: Stanford University Press, 1965). Also: *Man Is Not Alone: A Philosophy of Religion* (Philadelphia: Jewish Publication Society, 1951), pp. 179–190, 207–215, 217–224. Cf. also: *God in Search of Man: A Philosophy of Judaism* (Philadelphia: Jewish Publication Society, 1956), pp. 397 ff.

the greatest anti-anthropomorphic effort ever essayed by the human spirit."[25]

The impact of Spinoza's critical study of the Bible as a *human* document, *from an historical perspective,* is incalculable for the world of scholarship in general, and for Jewish religious thought in particular. That Spinoza was the father of the "Higher Biblical Criticism," and developed its principles in the first instance, is universally acknowledged, though he himself did not always adhere to them scrupulously in *The Treatise* in which he enunciated them. Of course, Spinoza was familiar with some precedents for his empirical method of Biblical study, in traditional Biblical commentators like Rashi and Abraham Ibn Ezra. But formulation of the full-fledged theory of this approach to the study of the Bible had to wait for him. The method displeased those who were rigidly literalist in the interpretation of Scripture as a Divine document, but the enrichment that it brought to the religious and historical study of the Bible, in the following centuries and down to today, is, to repeat, incalculable.

Do such considerations suffice to qualify Spinoza as a Jewish philosopher, on the basis of criterion number three? It seems to me that the heterodox or heretical character of many of his ideas should not result, in his case, any more than in the case of earlier philosophers, in the excision of his work from the spectrum of Jewish thought, though, as we know, such ideas or doctrines have often been the focus of protracted and bitter controversy. Luzzato was as extreme in his attack on Maimonides as on Spinoza. Of course, the reprehensible misdeeds that were committed against Judaism and the Jewish people in parts of *The Treatise* cannot be lightly dismissed, and the fact that the reactions which they have provoked have taken the form of the radical rejection of Spinoza from the body of Jewish philosophy, by some leading Jewish thinkers, is quite understandable. As Jacob Klatzkin, translator of Spinoza into Hebrew, said about Spinoza's *Treatise,* "This book is a trap into which a great man stumbled. It is a deed which is unbecoming to him."[26] However, these misdeeds do not cancel out or invalidate the greatness of his other work, nor do they constitute clear justification for his ejection from the mainstream of Jewish philosophy. But, on the other hand, recognition of the luminous, incandescent greatness of his other work should not prevent us from perceiving him, deromanticized and demythologized, as a flawed man, with weaknesses of character, fears, and temptations, succumbing to defective judgments that were morally repugnant and

[25]Martin Buber, *Eclipse of God: Studies in the Relation Between Religion and Philosophy* (New York: Harper & Brothers, 1952), pp. 23–24.

[26]Yaacov Klatzkin, *Barukh Spinoza,* p. 51 (my translation).

philosophically at variance with some of his own fundamental principles.

To summarize, then. *Against* Spinoza's classification as a *Jewish* philosopher, two considerations have been adduced:

1) His misdeeds against Judaism and the Jewish people in the *Tractatus Theologico-Politicus.*

2) The absence of any interest or intent on his part to contribute to the progression of Jewish thought; therefore, if he *is* a Jewish philosopher, he is that in spite of himself, and not by his own choice.

In favor of classifying Spinoza as a Jewish philosopher, two other considerations have been adduced:

1) A great many of his philosophical ideas arose out of the matrix of Jewish thought and experience.

2) Many of his ideas can be seen to be contributions to the later development and advancement of Jewish thought.

Can there be a definitive, categorical answer? Perhaps we might employ as an analogy the familiar historical case of the third century heretic, Elisha ben Avouyah. Before his renunciation of the tradition, the public avowal of his heresy, and his alleged collaboration with the Romans against his own people,[27] Elisha, a man of profound learning and great intellectual and spiritual stature, had been an esteemed and revered colleague among the Rabbinic sages of his day. It is of surpassing significance, first, that notwithstanding his public renunciation, heresies, and allegedly traitorous acts, a number of Elisha's pre-heretical teachings and precepts have been preserved, were not excised from the ancient Talmudic-Rabbinic texts, and are extant today in that body of literature as it has come down to us. Second, Elisha's friend and former pupil, the great sage, Rabbi Meir, continued in friendship and scholarly discussions with him even after the defection. This ongoing association no doubt caused many a raised eyebrow. However, one of their Rabbinic contemporaries, on a visit to Babylonia, reported that, in Palestine, "they say: 'Rabbi Meir ate the date and threw the pit away.'" In this connection, the Talmud tells us that another Rabbinic contemporary, the notable Raba, explicating a verse in the *Song of Songs,* declared that

> . . . just as in the case of the nut, though it is spoiled with mud and filth, yet are the contents not detestable, so in the case of the scholar, although he may have sinned, yet is his Torah not detested.

And Rabbah b. Shila, still another contemporary, said "Rabbi Meir found a pomegranate; the fruit within it he ate, and the peel he discarded."[28] So let it be with Barukh Spinoza.

[27]Louis Finkelstein, *Akiba: Scholar, Saint and Martyr* (New York: Covici, Friede Publishers, 1936), pp. 77, 254, and footnotes on pp. 325 and 349.

[28]Babylonian Talmud, *Hagigah,* 15 b.

III. Freedom

6. *Spinoza, Freud, and Hampshire on Psychic Freedom*
7. *Einstein and the Idea of Freedom*
8. *Freedom Versus Determinism in Psychotherapy*

6. *Spinoza, Freud, and Hampshire on Psychic Freedom*

That there are interesting and suggestive resemblances and parallels between Spinoza's philosophy of mind and Freud's psychoanalytic psychology has been remarked by a number of writers in the philosophical and psychological literature of the last half-century.[1] That these resemblances and parallels are more than *curiosa* or of merely passing historical interest is reflected in the explorations of some of the substantive significance of these relationships by such writers as David Bidney (1940) and Lewis S. Feuer (1958). But no one has probed the philosophical import of these relationships more incisively or more persistently than Stuart Hampshire, first in his book on Spinoza (1951), then in his volumes entitled *Thought and Action* (1960) and *Freedom of the Individual* (1965), and also, at various times during the past fifteen years, in a succession of penetrating papers, which were eventually gathered together and published in the volume *Freedom of Mind* (1971).

The titles of these volumes are significant. They reflect Hampshire's own ongoing investigations into the philosophy of mind, the nature of human action, the relationships between unconscious processes and man's reason, the meaning and extent of psychic freedom, and thus into the conditions of moral responsibility. A most fascinat-

[1]See, for example, Hamblin-Smith (1925); Alexander (1927); Rathbone (1934); Brill (1940); Bernard (1946). [References are listed in full at the end of the essay. (Note by W.G.)]

Joseph H. Smith (ed.), *Thought, Consciousness, and Reality* (New Haven: Yale University Press, 1977; vol. 2 of the series "Psychiatry and the Humanities," issued by the Forum on Psychiatry and the Humanities, Washington School of Psychiatry), pp. 257–309.

ing ingredient in these investigations is Hampshire's skillful shuttling back and forth between the philosophico-psychological insights of Spinoza and the psychoanalytic discoveries of Freud, as well as his reliance on and unraveling of the philosophical implications of both. Indeed, Hampshire's relentless and brilliant pursuit of the problem of psychic freedom in Spinoza's deterministic universe may well be interpreted to have as its end the conversion of Spinoza, whom H. A. Wolfson called "the last of the medievals" and "the first of the moderns" (p. vii), into a contemporary, late twentieth-century philosopher.

Some of Hampshire's contributions in this still densely overgrown territory of the philosophy of mind, and also some difficulties entailed by his analyses and conclusions, will be explicated in the present essay with the help of a review of relevant portions of Spinoza's doctrine and of Freud's theories, and of their relation to Hampshire's philosophy of human thought and action.

We may utilize as our point of departure the traditional philosophical and psychological question, "Under which conditions is a person a free and responsible agent?" and Hampshire's answer to it as formulated in *Thought and Action*. Distinguishing between *necessary* and *sufficient* conditions, Hampshire says:

> At least two conditions are necessary for saying of a man that he is a relatively free agent and responsible for his actions. First, that he generally know clearly what he is doing. . . . Secondly, there must be a comprehensively wide range of achievement open to him, in which he would succeed if he tried. . . . But are these two conditions jointly sufficient conditions for saying that a man is a free and responsible agent? Or is there some further condition required. . . . This condition is ordinarily taken to be the problem of free will. [pp. 180–81]

Among contemporary American philosophers who have criticized the theory and assumptions of the doctrine of free will, it was John Hospers, in a paper that has been widely reprinted, who systematically and cogently marshaled some of the evidence, based principally on psychoanalytic theory, for a radical skepticism about the availability to men of such conditions as are suggested by Hampshire in the above quotation. Hospers begins by directing our attention to unconscious processes:

> I want to mention . . . a factor that I think is of enormous importance and relevance: namely, unconscious motivation. There are many actions . . . for which human beings in general . . . are inclined to hold the doer responsible, and for which, I would say, he should not be held responsible. The deed may be planned, . . . nonetheless his behavior was brought about by unconscious conflicts developed in infancy, over

> which he has no control and of which . . . he does not even have knowledge. He may even *think* he knows why he acted as he did, he may *think* he has conscious control over his actions, he may even *think* he is fully responsible for them; but he is not. [p. 114; emphasis in the original]

Hospers then presents as additional illustrations several other varieties of unconscious motivations. From these he proceeds to his second point, namely, that each of us is "the product of causes in which his volition took no part." None of us, the "normal" person or the neurotic, is the author of his own character.

Irrespective of whether this character is a consequence of heredity or early environment, we cannot with justification *blame* the person who is unable to overcome the defects in his character any more than we can *praise* ourselves (or others) for the ability to overcome them. Whether one is the kind of person who can exert the effort and overcome these deficiencies—hereditary or environmental—is itself a product of heredity or of early environment. "We did not give ourselves this ability; and if we lack it we cannot be blamed for not having it" (p. 126). Hospers continues:

> All this is well known to psychoanalysts. They can predict, from minimal cues that most of us don't notice, whether a person is going to turn out to be lucky or not. . . . as a physician [the psychoanalyst] can soon detect whether the patient is lucky or unlucky—and he knows that whichever it is, it *isn't the patient's fault.* [p. 126; emphasis in the original]

Thus, if Hospers is right, what Hampshire calls "a comprehensively wide range of achievement . . . in which [a person] would succeed if he tried" can hardly be open to the person. Serious doubts are thus raised about the second of Hampshire's necessary conditions for someone's being psychically free and a responsible agent.

This distillation of Hospers's skeptical scrutiny of the assumptions of psychic freedom—which he insists is not being presented as an argument *for* determinism (p. 127)—helps bring into sharp focus, in compelling contemporary terms, a central problem common to Spinoza, Freud, and Hampshire. Since man's behavior is so overwhelmingly governed or dominated by unconscious and irrational or nonrational processes and motives, since emotions, fantasies, passions, and aberrations, the nature and causes of which are unknown to us, keep us in bondage for so much of our lives, is there anything in man's constitution through the exercise of which a person can liberate himself from this bondage and attain a measure of psychic freedom?[1a] Is there any methodology, or technique, or therapy by means of which a person can achieve control over and dominate his unconsciously and irrationally motivated passions, and become a free agent responsible for his own actions?[1b]

It seems of more than historical interest that these three thinkers, writing at different times—almost three hundred years separating Hampshire from Spinoza—and launching their respective investigations from different historical and conceptual frames of reference, grappled with essentially the same problem. And it is of surpassing philosophical and psychological significance that all three converge upon what is essentially, in its paradigmatic structure, the same conclusion. The paradigm of their common conclusion, if we decide for the moment to ignore the differences and divergences among them, is that, ultimately, the only source and guarantee of the very limited portion of freedom from bondage to the passions that can be attained by man is in the exercise of *reason,* of man's fully conscious cognitive faculties, in the arduous pursuit and discovery of the *causes* of these passions; and in their modification through one's rational, cognitive *reflection* upon them.

This does not imply that, in propounding this paradigm, either Spinoza, or Freud, or Hampshire indulges in or propagates the illusion that its employment always, or even often, leads to successful results. They decidedly do not. Indeed, the differences that appear discernible in their respective assessments of the likelihood of success are among the important divergences that will be expounded for each of the three. However, a remarkable element to be noted in this paradigm of human liberation from obsessive emotions and passions, shared by these three explorers of man as a thinking being, is that the paradigm revolves around the transcendently important fact of man's *reflexive thought,* of what Spinoza so unostentatiously and yet with such stunning fecundity called *idea ideae.*[2]

But here again a caveat is in order. Reason as the antidote to the passions is far from foolproof, because of its own built-in limitations. Too often reason is impotent to deal with the passions because reason itself is subject to corruption by these passions, and often turns out to function in their service through the self-deceptive mechanism of rationalization. The differences in the degree to which Spinoza,

[1a]This passage in Dr. Franck's essay is quoted, and utilized in a discussion of overcoming the obstacles to freedom, in William Gerber, *Serenity* (Lanham, Md.: University Press of America, 1986), p. 90. See also, in the present volume, another essay of Dr. Franck's, in which this language is used in another context, *post,* p. 161. [Note by W. G.]

[1b]This passage is quoted and used on p. 252 of Gerber's book (see the preceding footnote). [Note by W.G.]

[2]*Ethics,* part II, Proposition 21, Scholium.

Freud, and Hampshire, respectively, recognize this limitation make an instructive study, and I shall refer to this later. Nonetheless, their recognition of these limitations notwithstanding, it is reason—cognitive, fully conscious, reflexive thought—that is, in their view, man's only weapon for the conquest of his emotions and for his attainment of fragmentary psychic freedom. It is therefore not inaccurate to speak of Spinoza, Freud, and Hampshire, in this special sense of the term, and in this context, as "rationalists."

Now, it goes without saying that the paradigm suggested is a simplification, distilled out of the rich complexity of Spinoza's, Freud's, and Hampshire's works. It epitomizes the "ideal type construct," the "limiting case," for our understanding of the odyssey of a person from being passion-dominated to being guided by reason, or the painful, often tragic, obstacle-strewn pilgrimage of the individual from the stranglehold of the emotions to a rational understanding of their causes, and to their subsequent modification. Understandably, therefore, the formulation of the paradigm cannot but fail to reflect the person's resistances to the attainment of the aims envisioned in it, the individual's frequent regressions and reversions to the tyranny of the emotions in the course of this process, and even following the successes—often partial and limited successes—in the struggle. Of necessity, the formulation of the paradigm also fails to convey the perpetual state of dynamic tension—between reason and the passions—that characterizes human life, according to the image of man painted by Spinoza, Freud, and Hampshire. In what follows, an attempt will be made to sketch, for each of these men, some of the problems of liberation from our unconsciously motivated compulsions; the methodologies and therapies for the attainment of such liberation and the evidence for their availability; and the explicit or implied assessment by each thinker of the extent of psychic freedom attainable by man.

II

Part 4 of Spinoza's monumental work the *Ethics* has as its title: "Of Human Bondage, or On the Strength of the Emotions." The fifth and concluding part of the book is entitled: "Of the Power of the Intellect, or On Human Freedom." Ignoring Spinoza's important metaphysical theory at this point, even though it constitutes the indispensable matrix for his psychological and ethical doctrines, we can see from these titles that an overarching goal of Spinoza's in the *Ethics* is to outline a therapeutic method through which reason, or the intellect, can overcome the tyranny of the emotions, and through which a person can achieve a certain measure and a certain kind of psychic freedom. Man, Spinoza points out repeatedly, is dominated by his emotions and passions to such an extent that of a person so dominated "we say that he is delirious or mad." Such emotions as "avarice, ambition, lust, etc., are nothing but a kind of madness."[3] Passions "indicate our impotence,"[4] and a person who is dominated by passions "is ipso facto not free."[5] "A man is necessarily always subject to passions,"[6] asserts Spinoza. Man's struggle for psychic freedom is therefore perennial.

Are any of these emotions and passions, for Spinoza, the products of *unconscious* processes and motivations? This is a subject of dispute among commentators. Bidney, in his book *The Psychology and Ethics of Spinoza,* appears undecided (pp. 40, 391–92). First he claims that "the notion of an unconscious mind" or "the notion of an independent [unconscious] mental force determining human behavior" "did not occur to . . . Spinoza." But, on the other hand, Bidney does acknowledge that the mind, according to Spinoza, is sometimes ignorant of some *mental* causes of some of its ideas. Bidney therefore concedes that "this would imply the notion of unconscious ideas"; but at the same time he persists in his view that Spinoza "nowhere makes use of the unconscious as a mental force in conflict with conscious ideas" (p. 392).

But Feuer, in his book *Spinoza and the Rise of Liberalism,* not only credits Spinoza with the "discovery of the distinction between conscious and unconscious forces in man's psychological life" (p. 210), but also argues that the conception of the unconscious "was worked out by Spinoza in order to distinguish between the free man and the slave" (p. 299, n. 55). He further suggests that "Leibnitz took over from Spinoza the hypothesis of unconscious mental states" (ibid.).

There would be little point in entering more extensively here into this textual problem except to note that, like Feuer, Hampshire's reading of Spinoza clearly ascribes to him the affirmation of unconscious processes and motivations.[7] Spinoza's language appears to me to admit of no other interpretation. One illustration is his distinction between "appetite" and "desire":

> there is no difference between appetite and desire, except that desire is generally related to men in so far as they are conscious of their appetites, and it may therefore be defined as appetite of which we are conscious.[8]

[3]*Ethics,* IV, 44, Scholium.
[4]Ibid., Appendix, Paragraph #2.
[5]Parkinson, p. 33, n. 3.
[6] *Ethics,* IV, 4, Corollary.
[7]*Spinoza,* pp. 139–44.
[8]*Ethics,* III, 9, Scholium.

> We said above . . . that desire is appetite with a consciousness of itself.[9]

Manifestly, therefore, if desires are appetites of which we are conscious, this implies that there are appetites of which we are not conscious, and the notion of unconscious motivation as an element in the Spinozist psychology is clearly established.

Spinoza's method for overcoming the domination of unconsciously motivated and irrational emotions and passions, and for liberation from them, is through the person's employment of reason in the search for and acquisition of the cognitive knowledge of the *causes* of his passions, and in the utilization of this knowledge to deprive them of their force and modify them. This is the essence of Spinoza's therapeutic program, as announced in his preface to Book 5 of the *Ethics:*

> I pass at length to the other part of the *Ethics* which concerns the method or way which leads to liberty. . . . I shall treat of the power of reason, showing how much reason itself can control the emotions, and then what is freedom of mind or blessedness. . . . I shall occupy myself here . . . with the power of the mind or of reason, first of all showing the extent and nature of the authority which it has over the emotions in restraining them and governing them. . . . We shall determine by the knowledge of the mind alone the remedies against the emotions. . . .

For man is capable of discovering and knowing the nature of his emotions and passions and their causes: "there is no emotion of which we cannot form some clear and distinct conception."[10] While our knowledge of our emotions and their causes results in only *partial* control over them, a matter to which we shall return shortly, Spinoza displays no doubt about the availability to us of this power: "every one has the power, partly at least, if not absolutely, of understanding clearly and distinctly himself and his emotions, and consequently of bringing it to pass that he suffers less from them."[11]

When, through knowledge of the causes of our passions, the passions themselves become an object of our intellectual scrutiny and reflection, they are susceptible to change. "A passion ceases to be a passion as soon as we form a clear and distinct idea of it."[12] Spinoza's therapeutic principle is thus rooted in man's capacity for *reflexive* knowledge, in Spinoza's doctrine of *idea ideae.* In Spinoza's system, the human being is one single entity, and what we call mind and body are two distinguishable aspects of the same single entity. What

[9] Ibid., Definitions of the Emotions, #1, Explanation.
[10] *Ethics,* V, 4, Corollary.
[11] Ibid., Scholium.
[12] *Ethics,* V, 3.

we call the mind is "the *idea* of the body." As the *idea* of the body, the mind has knowledge of its body. But the mind also has knowledge of itself, it has an idea of itself. "This idea of the mind is united to the mind in the same way as the mind itself is united to the body."[13] The very fact of knowledge entails *reflexive* knowledge, thought about thought, or *the idea of the idea,* and this reflexiveness of thought is, to use Hampshire's phrase, "indefinitely open-ended."[14] To quote Spinoza again:

> the idea of the mind, that is to say, the idea of the idea is . . . just as a person who knows anything, by that very fact knows that he knows it, and at the same time knows that he knows that he knows it, and so on *ad infinitum.*[15]

This, briefly and most inadequately sketched, is Spinoza's version of the paradigm of a person's liberation, or self-liberation, from bondage to unconsciously motivated and irrational passions. But Spinoza was fully aware of the great power of the passions, and of the resistances and difficulties in the path of overcoming them and thus becoming free. He understood the weakness of reason in its search for the causes of the emotions and passions, and its frequent failure, total or partial, to achieve their modification through the mechanism of reflexive knowledge. Forming a "clear and distinct idea" of a passion—that is, reflexive knowledge of it—is a *necessary condition* for it to cease to be a passion, but it is often, in fact, not a *sufficient condition.* He points out that "an emotion cannot be restrained nor removed unless by a contrary and stronger emotion."[16]

Accordingly, we must note that Spinoza's therapeutic strategy includes reason's utilization of the energy and power of the emotions, by employing desirable emotions to overcome spurious and undesirable ones. For the instrumental purposes of therapy, self-knowledge alone is not sufficient. For he again directs our attention to the fact that "no emotion can be restrained by the true knowledge of good and evil in so far as the knowledge is true, but only in so far as it is considered as an emotion."[17] When we succeed in transmuting true reflexive knowledge into an active emotion that is more powerful than the particular passions of which we ourselves are not the cause—which are caused by forces outside us, and to which we happen to be enslaved—only then will we possess power over the irra-

[13]*Ethics,* II, 21.
[14]*Freedom of the Individual,* 2d ed., "Postscript," pp. 119, 127, 129, 140–41.
[15]*Ethics,* II, 21, Scholium.
[16]*Ethics,* IV, 7.
[17]*Ethics,* IV, 14.

tionally held passions—"the power, namely, by which it is possible, in so far as they are passions, if not actually to destroy them, at least to make them constitute the smallest possible part of the mind. . . ."[18] And thus the *partial* psychic freedom we are capable of will be attained.

This exposition of Spinoza's theory of psychic liberation has left untouched the question of its relation to Spinoza's metaphysical determinism. The problem is a knotty one, and there is an understandable temptation simply to acknowledge its existence and refrain from any attempt to discuss it, on the ground that it is beyond the purview of this essay. However, a brief discussion may at least help to place the problem in perspective.

The problem can be stated, following one of Hampshire's formulations, as follows. A person, by his power and exercise of reflexive thought on his own beliefs, emotions, and passions, and through his thereby becoming conscious of their previously unconscious causes, *can* modify them—that is, he *can* do this in one sense of the word "can," namely, in the sense that he possesses the requisite instruments of thought; but does it follow that the person *can* use these instruments of self-liberation in the sense that there is no external system of causes or concatenation of forces that will prevent him from using them, and that thus makes his psychic freedom impossible?[19] Most Spinoza scholars before Hampshire ascribed to Spinoza the view that the latter *can* is not available to man, since what he does or does not do is governed by a deterministic system of universal causation. According to these interpreters, the psychic freedom Spinoza talks about is only that which is contained in the knowledge a person can achieve of the universal necessity of the causes that completely and ineluctably determine his own emotions and actions, as well as all other events.

Wolfson may provide us with an illustration. In his classic study of Spinoza's philosophy, Wolfson, on the one hand, tells us that, for Spinoza, "reason, and the knowledge which springs from reason, is a means whereby man can . . . overcome the assaults of his own emotions" (vol. 2, p. 330). He speaks of reason as "an instrument of self-mastery." On the other hand, Wolfson takes Spinoza to be saying that:

[18] *Ethics,* V, 20, Scholium.

[19] Hampshire's statement of the thesis of determinism that is implicit in the above question is of value here: "The thesis of determinism is that every case of success and every case of failure in self-liberation is to be explained by some antecedent natural causes, and that, given these antecedent conditions, the outcome could not have been different from what it actually was." "Spinoza's Theory of Human Freedom," in *Spinoza: Essays in Interpretation,* p. 41.

> reason is the blind tool of nature, and is not an instrument wielded by man as a free agent. . . . To act according to reason . . . does not imply freedom of the will. . . . When Spinoza urges man to act according to reason . . . he does not mean thereby an exhortation to man to exercise his free will; with him it is only an exhortation to man to acquire the proper kind of knowledge upon which reason is nurtured, so that it may grow in strength and assert itself in its full power when called into action. At the challenge of the emotions reason springs into action in the same manner as our eyelids close at the sudden approach of danger to our eyes. [p. 232]

Reason, therefore, according to Wolfson's Spinoza, seems to act no less automatically than do the emotions or passions whose causes we do not know because they lie outside us and we can in no way control them. For Spinoza, whose metaphysical theory is that of a *monistic* universe, with the terms "God" or "nature" *(Deus sive natura)* signifying the totality of the universe, reason itself, as Wolfson properly points out, is a part of nature, "and it follows from the necessity of the attribute of thought" (Wolfson, p. 232). Whether or not reason will "spring into action" at the challenge of a person's emotions is not determined by the person. And all reason can do is lead us to a knowledge or understanding of the emotion and its causes, and of its inevitability as part of the universal causality of God or nature. Or, to use an illustration of essentially the same view from an essay by a contemporary American philosopher, for Spinoza

> the human affects or emotions *are* natural phenomena, continuous with all nature. . . . man is not a "kingdom within a kingdom," but rather wholly within *one* kingdom, nature. He is not a disturbance or a break in the continuity and unity of nature; and therefore, there is no realm in which man has absolute dominion, or "freedom of will," in violation of the universal determinism of the natural world. [Wartofsky, p. 342; emphasis in the original]

And yet, this honorable tradition of Spinoza interpretation fails to explain some of Spinoza's own language in the concluding pages of part 5 of the *Ethics,* when he writes about psychic freedom. He contrasts the *false* notion of freedom, which in reality is psychic bondage, with true freedom of mind. "Most persons seem to believe that they are free in so far as they may obey their lusts. . . . they would prefer to let everything be controlled by their passions, and to obey fortune *rather than themselves.*"[20] In contrast to those who passively let their passions or fortune control them *"rather than themselves,"* Spinoza ties

[20]*Ethics,* V, 41, Scholium; emphasis added.

together his fundamental enterprise in this part of the *Ethics* in the following summary:

> I have finished all I wished to explain concerning *the power of the mind over the emotions,* or the freedom of the mind.[21]

It is not knowledge alone, of the emotions and their causes, that Spinoza speaks of as he concludes the *Ethics,* but rather "the power of the mind over the emotions"—that is, a person's power to some extent *to obey himself,* and it is this that is equated with *"freedom of the mind."*

Hampshire seems to me essentially correct when he says that for Spinoza a person's knowledge of the causes of his emotions and actions is not in itself freedom, and that "knowledge of the causes of suffering" does not by itself bring liberation from suffering. For, "liberation consists in the substitution of a free activity and of self-assertion . . . for a passive reaction."[22] And, to return now to the beginning of this exposition of Spinoza's theory of psychic freedom, the "activity and self-assertion," as well as the modifications of the passions and irrational compulsions, are possible by virtue of the reflexive thought, the *idea ideae,* man's capacity to inspect and evaluate his own thoughts, beliefs, and emotions.

Does this mean a departure from, a break in, Spinoza's claimed rigorous metaphysical determinism, and a significant inconsistency in Spinoza's philosophy? I believe it does, and that its source is in Spinoza's failure to think through the full implications of the attribute of *Thought,* one of the two attributes, the other being the attribute of *Extension,* which together are the two constitutive aspects of the universe, or of nature, that are known to man. According to Spinoza, the infinite number of other attributes of the totality of nature are not known to man. There are two implications of the attribute of thought as conceived by Spinoza that make this attribute different from the attribute of extension and, theoretically, also different from any of the other hypothetical attributes. These two differences between the attribute of thought and the other attributes exhibit an inconsistency in the structure of Spinoza's system of metaphysical determinism.

The first of the two differences was noted by Spinoza's contemporary, von Tschirnhaus, in his correspondence with Spinoza,[23] and was never dealt with by Spinoza either in the extant correspondence or in the *Ethics.* Von Tschirnhaus points out that since there are an

[21]Ibid., 42, Scholium; emphasis added.

[22]Hampshire, "Spinoza and the Idea of Freedom," p. 308.

[23]Letters 63 and 70, *The Correspondence of Spinoza,* pp. 304–06, 336–39.

infinite number of attributes, each of those attributes and its modifications must have, associated with them, the attribute of thought, and thus "the attribute of Thought is made to extend itself more widely than the rest of the attributes."[24] Or as Frederick Pollock said in his work on Spinoza, "in other words, Thought, instead of being co-equal with the infinity of other Attributes, is infinitely infinite, and has a pre-eminence which is nowhere explicitly accorded to it" (p. 161).[25] Now, while this difference does appear to be inconsistent with Spinoza's deterministic system as a whole, I agree with the judgment of E. M. Curley, in his book *Spinoza's Metaphysics,* that "the special status which our interpretation accords to the attribute of thought is not a difficulty. On the contrary, it is a requirement of any adequate interpretation that it account in some way for the undeniable fact that thought does have a special position among the attributes" (p. 150).

The second respect in which the attribute of thought differs from the other attributes is contained in the fact that, unlike extension (or, theoretically, any other attribute), thought can be *reflexive:* there can be thought about thought, the *idea ideae,* and it is by virtue of this special characteristic of thought that a person, reflecting on his own thoughts, emotions, and so forth, has the capacity to modify them. *Extension* is not reflexive. There is no extension about extension; there is nothing about the body that is analogous to *idea ideae.* This difference constitutes another break in the metaphysical determinism Spinoza propounded, with the result that freedom is not, in fact, foreclosed in his system, and psychic liberation, though only partial and fragmentary, becomes a genuine possibility.

III

The anticipations of Freudian doctrine in the Spinozist theory of mind—of man's bondage to the passions and of the road to the mind's partial liberation from them—are not difficult to perceive. It was Freud, the master cartographer of the human personality, who demonstrated empirically and clinically the presence of unconscious processes and powerful irrational, aggressive, destructive impulses and inner compulsions among the psychological constituents of man. His demonstration of their existence and pervasive power over us is, of course, one of Freud's most important and lasting contributions to our knowledge of human nature.

[24]Ibid., Letter 70.

[25]Cf. also Ruth Lydia Saw, *The Vindication of Metaphysics,* p. 79.

However, Freud also stressed the importance and forcefulness of reason and rationality in man's make-up. He depicted the individual as always in an ongoing, dynamic state of tension between unconscious, irrational impulses and the dictates of reason and rationality to control those impulses. A person's knowledge of the existence of his unconscious impulses and motivations, and his understanding of their nature, ultimately are the most important equipment for *realistically* coping with them and controlling them. Some of the unconscious and repressed elements, according to Freud, cannot be eliminated: it is part of Freudian theory that they are ineradicable.[26] But what Freud is talking about is their *control,* regulation, and partial *subjugation* through man's reason and rational processes. This, Freud believed, was now possible because a promising beginning had been made in our knowledge and understanding of man's own irrationality.

It is worth noting parenthetically that the possible, though most often only partial, victories of reason over our unconscious and irrational impulses are of fundamental significance for Freud not only in his role of descriptive psychologist and explorer of the nature of man. They are also, for Freud the moralist, as they are for Spinoza, a moral desideratum, perhaps man's highest ethical goal, the attainment of which would be impossible without a person's knowledge of, and reflexive thinking about, his unconscious motivations.

The goals of psychoanalytic therapy involve man's reason, rationality, and reflexive thought in a role of crucial and essential importance. In short, its twin goals are: first, to lead the patient, through the uncovering psychoanalytic process, to a rational, cognitive knowledge and understanding of the real, previously repressed, causes and motivations of his neuroses, irrational feelings, emotions, attitudes, and behavior; second, through his use of his own reason, through his reflection upon these previously unconscious and now uncovered causes, to make possible his overcoming and controlling them and achieving complete or partial liberation from their tyranny. Thus, the goals of therapy and the goals of ethics coincide in Freudian doctrine

[26]*New Introductory Lectures* (1933), pp. 104, 105. Freud states here that the repressed, irrational elements in the id are "virtually immortal." He also refers to "the indisputable fact that the repressed remains unaltered by the passage of time." This has often been interpreted to mean that, subsequent to the infantile or early childhood experience that may be judged to have been the origin of a particular repression, the repressed elements remain forever *unaffected* by later experiences. I have argued elsewhere *(Human Nature in Humanistic Psychology)* that this is a misinterpretation of Freud's doctrine. The most cogent evidence against it, I believe, is implicit in the therapeutic process and experience of psychoanalysis, which, to the extent that it is at all successful, is an experience that *affects* or even modifies the particular repressed elements.

as they do in Spinoza's, and may, without distortion, be said to be essentially *rationalist* in character. Of course, neither for Spinoza nor for Freud, so far as psychic freedom is concerned, is the goal mere knowledge or intellectual insight alone. For Spinoza, the goal is the successful exercise of "the power of the mind over the emotions." In Freudian terms, the goal is the self-understanding that is accompanied by emotional insight achieved by the process of "working-through."

If what has been sketched here is essentially accurate, then clearly this part of Freudian theory, and the very logic of psychoanalytic therapy, reflects our previously formulated paradigm of the individual's attainment of psychic freedom. Clearly also, the affinities between the Spinozist and Freudian theories of psychic liberation are compellingly significant, and of more than casual historical interest.

The brevity and generality of this capsulated version of aspects of Freudian doctrine now make it necessary to fill in a few details, and to provide at least some references to textual sources out of the voluminous and complex corpus of Freud's writings.

However, a certain difficulty has to be cleared away in any discussion of Freud's fruitful analysis of the human personality. It is that his writing is infected by a persistent flaw—namely, his frequent and disconcerting hypostatization of the basic concepts he employs. With distracting frequency he uses such locutions as: "*The* id *knows* no values,"[27] "*The* ego *has taken over* the task,"[28] "from a dynamic point of view *it* [the ego] *is weak,*"[29] "*The* super-ego *seems to have made* a one-sided selection,"[30] "*the* id . . . *is* totally non-moral, . . . *the* ego . . . *strives* to be moral, and . . . *the* super-ego . . . *can be* hyper-moral and thus *becomes* . . . ruthless,"[31] "*the* unconscious *is a special realm with its own desires.*"[32] Such hypostatizations make it seem that for Freud these concepts are *things, concrete entities,* and this opens him up to misunderstanding and misplaced interpretations of his meaning. Because of his metaphorical use of language in reference to these concepts, some critics have taken Freud to be saying that within each of us there are "subsidiary personalities" (B. F. Skinner, pp. 78, 79)—*homunculi,* independent little men within us—who act, as it were, apart from the total person.

This is a misreading of Freud. My own view is that his basic concepts are what in the literature of the philosophy of science are fre-

[27]1933, p. 105.
[28]1933, p. 106.
[29]1933, p. 107.
[30]1933, p. 89.
[31]*The Ego and the Id* (1923), p. 79.
[32]*A General Introduction to Psycho-Analysis* (1920), pp. 101–02.

quently called "theoretical constructs," and that fundamentally Freud intended them as such, in spite of the many, many instances in which his linguistic usage gives the appearance of his having hypostatized or reified the concepts. Secondly, my reading of Freud is that, for him, these concepts essentially refer to and are shorthand symbols for *psychic processes, dynamic* psychic processes, which much if not most of the time are in dialectical-reciprocal tension with each other within the individual person. These processes are distinguishable from each other only in conceptual discourse but are actually inextricably intertwined and overlapping, often pulling the individual in opposite, apparently contradictory directions, but often also paradoxically reinforcing each other in the total, mysterious, dialectical structure of the person.[33]

If, then, we keep in the forefront of our attention the dynamic, process-character of such Freudian terms as "id," "ego," "super-ego," and others that we shall have occasion to refer to, then manifestly it is in the interrelationships and interactions between id-processes and ego-processes that the Freudian version of the individual's struggle for and attainment of psychic liberation may first be discerned. Freud has often been taken to be a psychic determinist, in part for the reasons implied in the essay by Hospers referred to earlier, but even more because he insisted that all human acts—even the most trivial, seemingly capricious, and apparently inexplicable ones, such as slips of the tongue, lapses of memory, and dreams—have reasons or causes, and are in fact explicable in terms of unconscious processes that give rise to them.[34] However, according to Freud, some margin of freedom from the tyranny of these deterministic inner compulsions, even though very limited indeed, is attainable through the controls that the person's ego-processes succeed in exercising over his id-processes.

The id, for Freud, "contains the passions";[35] "it may be said of the id that it is totally non-moral."[36] "The id stands for the untamed

[33]This reading of Freud is expounded at greater length, and much more thoroughly, in my work on human nature. Suffice it to say at this point that, notwithstanding Freud's multiple and regrettable hypostatizations, or his seemingly static, *spatial* depiction of id, ego, and super-ego in his famous diagram (1933, p. 111; 1923, p. 29), Freud does sometimes use the phrase "unconscious *processes,*" or "unconscious mental *processes*" (1933, p. 99 and passim; *An Outline of Psycho-Analysis* [1940], pp. 37, 51, and passim), and in at least one passage he speaks of the super-ego as a "*function* in the Ego" (1933, pp. 86–87).

[34]Compare such works of Freud's as *The Psychopathology of Everyday Life* (1901), *Wit and Its Relation to the Unconscious* (1905), *The Interpretation of Dreams* (1900–01), and *A General Introduction to Psycho-Analysis* (1920). See also Arlow, "Psycho-Analysis as Scientific Method," pp. 201–11, especially pp. 204 ff.

[35]1923, p. 30.

[36]1923, p. 79.

passions," "it is the obscure inaccessible part of our personality," "a chaos, a cauldron of seething excitement," "it has no organization . . . only an impulsion to obtain satisfaction for the instinctual needs," "the id knows no values, no good and evil, no morality."[37]

The ego represents reason, and it is the function of the ego-processes to cope with and control the id and free the person from bondage to it. "The ego represents what we call reason and sanity,"[38] "the ego stands for reason and circumspection,"[39] "The ego develops from perceiving instincts to controlling them, from obeying instincts to curbing them."[40]

In this struggle of reason to control the "untamed passions," the contest is not an even one, according to Freud. "From a dynamic point of view [the ego] is weak,"[41] Borrowing a simile from Plato, Freud describes this struggle as follows:

> One might compare the relation of the ego to the id with that between a rider and his horse. The horse provides the locomotive energy, and the rider has the prerogative of determining the goal and of guiding the movements of his powerful mount toward it. But all too often . . . we find a picture of the less ideal situation in which the rider is obliged to guide his horse in the direction in which it itself wants to go.[42]

But instructive as is Freud's realistic assessment of the weakness of reason in the struggle to curb the passions, no less instructive is his juxtaposition of this weakness and reason's ultimate and irreducible efficacy and strength:

> We may insist as much as we like that the human intellect is weak in comparison with human instincts, and be right in doing so. But nevertheless there is something peculiar about this weakness. The voice of the intellect is a soft one, but it does not rest until it has gained a hearing. Ultimately, after endlessly repeated rebuffs, it succeeds. This is one of the few points in which one may be optimistic about the future of mankind, but in itself it signifies not a little.[43]

This realistic and moderate optimism in a man who often was driven to overstating his highly pessimistic discoveries about human nature (because his contemporaries were so scandalized by them and

[37]1933, pp. 107, 103, 104, 105.
[38]1923, p. 30.
[39]1923, p. 107.
[40]1923, p. 82.
[41]1933, p. 107.
[42]1933, p. 108.
[43]*The Future of an Illusion* (1927), p. 93.

so insistently denied their existence) is deeply anchored in Freud's faith in the liberating possibilities of the psychoanalytic therapy, limited though they are. "Psychoanalysis," he tells us, "is an instrument to enable the ego to push its conquest of the id further still."[44]

At one point, Freud's faith in the possibilities of psychoanalytic therapy as facilitator of reason's liberating triumph over unconscious compulsions is articulated in words that have the resonance of a manifesto: "the therapeutic efforts of psychoanalysis [have as] their object . . . to strengthen the ego . . . to widen its field of vision, and so to extend its organization that it can take over new portions of the id. Where id was there shall ego be."[45]

On what, then, is this faith based? What is it that psychoanalytic therapy does which, when it *is* successful, makes possible the psychic liberation from the "marshland of unreason" (Allport, p. 99), the repressed and unconsciously remembered episodes out of one's remote past, the painful and disabling fantasies that dominate the lives of all of us? A major part of Freud's answer is that, through the uncovering techniques of psychoanalysis, the person is led to an increase in his self-knowledge, to recollection of the repressed and forgotten event or events that are the focus of his fears or aversions, to rational understanding of the unconscious causes of his compulsions and of their irrational character and illegitimate origin, and to the conscious determination to eject them. The unconscious impulses, and the repressed elements to which they are related, Freud tells us, "can only be recognized as belonging to the past, deprived of their significance, and robbed of their charge of energy, after they have been made conscious by the work of analysis, and no small part of the therapeutic effect of analytic treatment rests upon this fact."[46]

A few brief illustrations of Freud's own language on the role of reason and the intellect in the end product of successful analytic therapy can be found in these quotations from *An Outline of Psycho-Analysis:*

> [The therapeutic process] thus puts us in a position . . . to extend, by the information we give him [the person being analyzed], his *ego's knowledge of his unconscious.* [p. 65; emphasis added]

> The method by which we strengthen the patient's weakened ego has as its starting point an increase in *the ego's self-knowledge.* [p. 70; emphasis added]

[44]1923, p. 82.
[45]1933, pp. 111–12.
[46]1933, p. 104.

> As a rule we [the analyst] put off telling him of a construction or explanation until he himself has so nearly arrived at it that only a single step remains to be taken. [p. 71]

> it often happens that our patient will immediately confirm our construction and himself recollect the internal or external event which he has forgotten. . . . As regards this particular matter, *our* knowledge will then have become *his* knowledge as well. [p. 72; emphasis Freud's]

> The overcoming of resistances [to the therapeutic uncovering process] . . . is worthwhile, since it brings about a favorable modification of the ego. . . . And we have at the same time worked in the direction of undoing the modification which had been brought about under the influence of the unconscious; for whenever we have been able to detect its derivatives in the ego, we have drawn attention to their illegitimate origin and have urged the ego to eject them. [p. 74]

> we induce the patient's thus enfeebled ego to take part in *the purely intellectual work of interpretation,* which aims at provisionally filling the gaps in his mental resources. . . . we restore order in his ego, by detecting the material and impulses which have forced their way in from the unconscious, and *expose them to criticism by tracing them back to their origin.* [pp. 76–77; emphasis added]

There is hardly any need for additional documentation, though it is available in abundance, to enable us to see in bold relief the pivotal role that Freud assigns to reason, to the intellect, to conscious self-knowledge, to reflexive knowledge by the individual himself (not by the therapist) of the previously repressed and unremembered events that have been functioning as the spurious causes of his problematical behavior. The modification of that behavior is made possible through reflexive thought about those causes. The operation of the "rationalist" paradigm of psychic liberation is thus evident in Freud's theory, as it is in Spinoza's. It is insightfully summarized in Philip Rieff's observation, in a chapter entitled "Politics and the Individual," that "There remains for Freud perhaps the highest rationality: knowledge of the irrational" (p. 264). Rieff, who elsewhere speaks of Freud's "aseptic rationalism" (p. 370), also draws our attention to the function of the patient's *talking* in the course of psychoanalytic therapy as part of Freud's rationalism, because talking is a medium of communicating *conscious* thoughts:

> Talk is therapeutic in itself. By talking about the instincts, Freud says, we do not cause the instinctual demand to disappear . . . but we do accomplish a "'taming' of the instinct."[47] Through talking about sexual-

[47]Rieff gives as his reference here Freud's "Analysis Terminable and Interminable" (1937), p. 326.

> ity, we can control it, so the healthy man can choose to express his sexual appetite and yet not be irrationally driven by it. Self-mastery being a function of self-consciousness, by making sexual desires conscious, says Freud, we gain mastery over them to a degree no system of repression can possibly equal.[48] Talk—language—is the essential medium of consciousness, and therefore the essential means of liberation. [p. 368]

However, Freud's single-mindedness in the explication and defense of psychoanalysis as a theory of, as well as a therapeutic methodology for, the individual's attainment of freedom from bondage to the id-processes goes hand in hand with a sober and realistic understanding of the paradigmatic character of the essential theory, its adumbration of what we referred to earlier as the "limiting case," or the "ideal type construct," of this species of liberation. Repeatedly Freud warns us that "it is true that we do not always succeed in winning,"[49] that "the therapeutic efficiency of psychoanalysis is limited by a whole series of important factors,"[50] that the patient's "resistances against our work . . . persist through the whole treatment."[51]

Moreover, there is another reason why the Freudian theory of psychic liberation is inextricably tied to the recognition that the freedom attained is most often only partial, limited, and even temporary. This theory must be understood within the matrix of Freud's larger theory of human nature. Man, as mentioned earlier, is portrayed by Freud as an inordinately complex dynamic being. Each person is host to a restless multiplicity of psychic processes in a perennial state of multidirectional tensions. Some of these processes may be understood as constantly in opposition to each other, as is most clearly illustrated in the dialectical tensions between ego-processes and id-processes, between reason and irrational inner compulsions. It is noteworthy that Freud's language about this particular relationship, in, for example, *An Outline of Psycho-Analysis,* consistently and repeatedly employs metaphorical words of conflict, such as *struggle, battle, winning, losing.* But, as I indicated, even these two psychic processes are not always to be dichotomized as mutually exclusive, because they themselves are imbedded in an intricate network of interrelated mental processes and forces, sometimes in dialectical opposition but shifting at times from opposition to mutual reinforcement.

Ernest Jones claimed that "Freud was an obstinate dualist" (vol. 3, pp. 266 ff.) in his view of the instincts, and of other psychic forces as

[48]Rieff's reference here is to "Psycho-Analysis" (1923), p. 252.
[49]1940, p. 78.
[50]1933, p. 210.
[51]1940, p. 73.

well. Though there is much evidence to support Jones's view, I believe it to be a simplification. It seems to me that the evidence points to an essential *pluralism* in Freud's portrayal of the human personality. Jones's contention is based on the undisputed evidence he adduces that Freud's analyses so often eventuate in sets of paired or twin explanatory concepts, such as:

Primary system	versus	Secondary system
Pleasure principle	versus	Reality principle
Death instinct or Thanatos	versus	Life instinct or Eros
Irrational	versus	Rational
Unconscious	versus	Conscious
Id-processes	versus	Ego-processes

Jones concludes from such examples that, according to Freud, the dynamic tensions within the person's psychic life are always bipolar. But this seems to me too mechanical and simplistic an interpretation of Freud's intention, in spite of Freud's frequently dualistic conceptual terminology, and in spite of his own references to the notion of dualism.[52]

Freud's accounts of the dynamic nature of our psychic life contain both implied and direct admonitions against strict dichotomizations of mental processes, as well as references to their multiple interminglings. For example, "subtle and intricate intellectual operations . . . and the solution of a difficult mathematical problem . . . can be carried out preconsciously and without coming into consciousness . . . [or even] during sleep."[53]

In addition to pointing out this intermingling of intellectual operations of a technical type, generally assumed to be manifestations of consciousness par excellence, with states of unconsciousness, Freud mentions another kind of intermingling, this time in connection with a person's moral or social conduct: "There are people in whom the faculties of self-criticism and conscience . . . are unconscious, and unconsciously produce effects of greatest importance." Thus, both the ego and the super-ego are sometimes included in some people's

[52]For a similar point of view with reference to Freud's alleged *dualism*, see Roy Schafer, "An Overview of Heinz Hartmann's Contributions to Psychoanalysis," especially pp. 426–29. I am grateful to Dr. Joseph H. Smith for bringing Schafer's paper to my attention.

[53]1923, p. 12. Henri Poincaré, the French mathematician and philosopher of science, reports several such episodes of solutions arrived at without conscious calculation, and during sleep, in connection with complicated mathematical problems with which he had been wrestling (*The Foundations of Science*, pp. 387–94).

unconscious processes. This leads Freud to the perhaps surprising conclusion that "we shall have to say that not only what is lowest but also what is highest in the ego can be unconscious."[54]

Other examples of intermingling include the phenomena of *ambivalence*—that is, the "clinical observation . . . that love is with unexpected regularity accompanied by hate" and "also that in many circumstances hate changes into love and love into hate";[55] the frequent inseparability of sadism from masochism;[56] and the working of Eros and the Death-Instinct both together and against each other "to produce the phenomena of life."[57] These and countless other illustrations can be cited in support of the assertion that the Freudian theory of man does not *dichotomize* or *fragmentize* the individual. It emphasizes the pivotal presence of continuous, unquiet, dynamic tensions of multiple mental forces and processes in opposition and interaction within the human personality, without introducing into it sharply demarcated, absolute compartments.

What is true about the interplay of these various psychic processes and propensities is also true about the interplay between our reason and our irrational inner compulsions, between the ego-processes and the id-processes. Even after successful psychic liberation, complete or partial, from passions, obsessions, fears, and neuroses through the application of reason and the employment of newly acquired self-knowledge, the person remains a commingling of the two. In the Freudian theory, reason hardly ever stands alone, either when its processes achieve some measure of victory over the id-processes, or when it ends up defeated.

Like Spinoza, Freud recognizes that emotions or passions can be overcome only with the aid of stronger emotions, and that the intellect, or rational calculation, can overcome the power of the destructive passions when it is wedded to constructive emotion. In a significant section of his *Civilization and Its Discontents* (1930), Freud emphasizes the point that "necessity alone, the advantages of common work"—that is, rational determinations of what is desirable—would not in themselves hold people together. But he asserts that there is hope for society's overcoming the destructive effects of the pleasure principle, the tendency to sexual aggression, the instinctual cravings of the id, the general instinct of aggression and self-destructiveness, and other unconscious compulsions present in the psychic structures of its individual citizens. This hope arises as a result only of the existence in the individual of the forces of Eros, which aim to "bind to

[54]1923, pp. 32–33.
[55]1923, p. 59.
[56]1933, p. 143.
[57]*An Autobiographical Study* (1925), p. 103.

one another libidinally" individuals, families, races, nations—that is, to bind them into a great unity of humanity.[58] In the struggle for psychic liberation, no less than in the struggle for sociopolitical freedom, the possible successes of reason depend heavily on its having attached to it a constructive emotional dimension.

Finally, the attainment of psychic liberation from irrational compulsion is often completely subverted, or substantially impaired, through the insidious collaboration of reason itself, in the form of what we call "rationalization." Among the defenses, evasions, and self-justifications in which individual humans indulge, when there are guilt feelings or ambivalences about the justifiability of some of their actions, is the self-deceiving stratagem of rationalization. To the best of my recollection, Freud himself used this term only once, in the *New Introductory Lectures*, and he used it there in a different sense from the meaning assigned to it today and from the sense in which it is being used here.

However, though the term "rationalization" as now understood was not used by Freud, the psychological mechanism was described by him many times. In essence, it is the process of finding some justifiable explanation or alibi to others, and especially to oneself, for doing something that is inconsistent with what is socially approved, or in good taste, or expected normal behavior. For example, a person who gives an unusual amount of money, time, and leadership to a boys' club, presenting the appearance of generosity and community-mindedness, may in fact be covering up a repressed and unconscious tendency toward a homosexual interest in young boys.

In this rationalized behavior, the intellect collaborates with an unconscious, irrational, sexual compulsion and desire, permitting the unconscious emotion to dominate the person's life and providing apparently rational explanations for his actions. Thus, as Hospers characterizes the phenomenon,

> One's intelligence and reasoning power do not enable one to escape from unconsciously motivated behavior; it only gives one greater facility in rationalizing that behavior; one's intelligence is simply used in the interest of the neurosis—it is pressed into service to justify with reasons what one does independently of the reasons. [p. 117]

Evasions and self-deceptions occur with amazing frequency in everyday life, in interpersonal relations, in facing unpleasant imperatives in the course of one's work, and in resisting the therapeutic process when it approaches too closely the uncovering of the real causes of

[58]1930, p. 102.

neurotic behavior. I will later comment on rationalization in connection with Hampshire, but it is sufficient to make the point here that Freud's recognition of the mechanism of rationalization is another explanation of his conviction that the psychic freedom attainable by an individual is only partial, temporary, and a fragile achievement, easily fractured and destroyed.

IV

It remained for Stuart Hampshire to uncover and to exhibit instructively and cogently some further implications for psychic freedom that are contained in Spinoza's doctrine of *idea ideae,* of reflexive thought, and that are also contained in Freud's account of the relationships and interactions between the rational ego-processes and unconscious id-processes in the intricate structure of the human personality, and of the methods and goals of psychoanalytic therapy. Hampshire's own theory of psychic liberation from passions and unconscious compulsions is deeply rooted in the theories of Spinoza and Freud. Like theirs, and perhaps even more avowedly and explicitly, his theory reflects, in its essential outlines, the "rationalist" paradigm of psychic liberation suggested at the beginning of the present discussion.

Hampshire is concerned with the broader issues of human freedom and moral responsibility, and a major part of his published work is devoted to the elaboration, in a variety of ways and with striking ingenuity, of the major thesis that the source of human freedom is knowledge, and that the exercise by man of knowledge, including self-knowledge, makes a thoroughgoing determinism untenable. Some indication of this is contained in Hampshire's adumbration of the purpose of his book, *Thought and Action:*

> To show the connection between knowledge of various degrees and freedom of various degrees is the principal purpose of this book. "Why should that which I do with full knowledge of what I am doing alone constitute that which I do with full freedom?"—this question will only be answered by the whole argument. [p. 133]

In the interest of a more thorough understanding of this thesis, as it applies to the issues that are our major concern here, it will be useful first to explicate one of Hampshire's arguments concerning human freedom—namely, that freedom of the mind cannot be denied even on the hypothesis of a metaphysical materialism, when we undertake to explain intentions, beliefs, attitudes, desires, and so forth.

Hampshire developed this argument, in two somewhat different ways, in his ingenious and provocative papers, "Freedom of Mind" and "A Kind of Materialism," presented originally as lectures in 1965 and 1969, respectively, and included in the volume *Freedom of Mind*. As Hampshire says in the earlier paper, according to one interpretation of the materialist hypothesis, when the explanation of emotions is involved, it is assumed that for every state of mind, or for every emotion, there exists a distinct physical state of the organism that is invariably correlated with it. Thus, with the emotion of anger, for example, there is an invariably correlated physiological state that can be produced or removed by certain physical stimuli, with immediate corresponding effects on the emotion.

According to this hypothesis, we would find in all cases "that subjects cease to be angry with *x*, and to be angry with *x* because of *y*, if the appropriate physical change is made; they only consider *y* as a reason for being angry when they are in the appropriate physical state; and when they are in the appropriate physical state, they always find some reason for being angry with someone."[59] If this materialist hypothesis were verified, then the state which we had been calling anger would be explained as the perception of a certain physical state. Thus, when I am angry I am in fact perceiving a modification of my body, "in the same sense that we feel a bruise . . . or a heavy object on our back."[60]

Now, suppose I, who am angry at Jones, come to know about this mechanism—that is, about the physiological cause of the emotion called anger. Such knowledge would enable me to make inferences from my state of mind to a cause external to my state of mind. I would, accordingly, as a result of my quest for an explanation of my emotion of anger, now have knowledge of the physiological states involved, but I would also then have a different psychic state correlated with my new knowledge of the *explanation* for my emotion of anger. What began as my anger with Jones for something he had done would now have become an awareness of a changed physiological state, "in relation to which Jones's action was merely an inessential occasion." Because I would no longer believe that Jones's behavior was a necessary ingredient to my anger, it would follow that I would no longer be angry with Jones for what he had done. In this sense, my acquisition of knowledge of the (materialist) explanation has changed my emotion, or my state of mind, and the experience or phenomenon which we had first set out to explain in accordance with standard scientific procedures would vanish and remain unex-

[59]*Freedom of Mind*, p. 16.
[60]Ibid., p. 17.

plained, leaving an ambiguous and seemingly inexplicable break in the putatively universal, deterministic system of explanation. Moreover, "once convinced of the truth of the scientist's explanation," I would have to "determine [my] attitude to Jones's action all over again."[61]

For this reason, says Hampshire, there is "an unclarity, or even an ambiguity," in any claim that psychic states, or intentional states, are in principle explicable like any other natural phenomena by reference to covering laws in a deterministic system of explanation. This is especially true of intentional states, because the subject's knowledge of the explanation of his emotion by reference to a covering law within a deterministic system will by itself change the psychic state that is ostensibly being explained. Thus, "the intentional description, which incorporates the subject's thought of a cause [of the intention], will have to be changed, as the subject's beliefs change."[62]

The discovered physiological causes of the emotion—say the subject's anger—"are the causes of that independently identifiable state which the subject previously classified as anger, thereby explaining the state in a way which he now knows to have been erroneous. The causes of *that* state which he has previously classified as anger will no longer be the causes of anger."[63]

This consequence of a person's acquisition of knowledge about the explanation of his own emotions, beliefs, attitudes, desires—that is, his acquisition of *reflexive knowledge*—is peculiarly true of the explanation for intentional states generally. A person's knowledge or beliefs about the explanation of his own intentional state, or a change in the person's beliefs about the explanation, "modifies the descriptions applicable to the phenomenon explained, and also modifies the explanation itself."[64] Hampshire's instructive illustration here makes the point even clearer:

> If a man comes to believe that his state of confidence in the excellence of his performance is wholly explained by a confidence-engendering pill which he has taken, he will no longer be so confident of the excellence of his performance. . . . the change in the subject's belief about its cause will constitute a change in his state of mind.[65]

Essentially these same generic complexities are entailed, as noted above, in all suggestions of hypotheses that propose causal, deter-

[61]Ibid., p. 19.
[62]Ibid., p. 20.
[63]Ibid.
[64]Ibid., pp. 15–16.
[65]Ibid., p. 15.

ministic explanations for intentional states and processes. The difficulties, and the inescapable break they expose in the deterministic hypothesis, always become manifest when the individual reflects on proposed explanations of his own psychic processes, in this way exercising his capacity for *reflexive knowledge.* One's reflexive knowledge of an assumed causal mechanism in one's own psychic, and especially intentional, processes constitutes a change in the effect of the mechanism. And "this is the complexity," says Hampshire, "which makes a place, as Spinoza suggested, for freedom of mind."[66]

The ingenuity of this argument in support of the principle that reflexive knowledge is the source and necessary condition of freedom of mind is matched in other arguments for this principle elsewhere in Hampshire's books and papers, but they cannot be developed here. The principle, of course, is predicated in the first instance on Spinoza's fertile contribution to philosophical psychology; this contribution, as reformulated in Hampshire's most recent paper, "The Explanation of Thought," says that "thoughts, whether beliefs or desires, may always be made the objects of second-order thoughts, beliefs about beliefs, desires about desires; and what a person believes about the nature and causes of his thoughts, including his beliefs, to some extent modifies the thoughts" (p. 8). In this essay he also reiterates his insistence on the fundamental differences between psychological explanations and explanations of physical phenomena:

> psychological explanation has at least one peculiarity that distinguishes it from explanation of physical states and events: that man's knowledge of, and his beliefs about, the factors determining his own states always modifies these states. . . . [p. 3]

> The causal connections are not established, as are causal connections between physical events, by referring to laws correlating independent events, but by laws referring to internal connections between thoughts, connections that make the thoughts seem intelligible. [p. 11]

> [reflexiveness] is *one* distinguishing feature of psychological explanation, which may be a good basis for saying that deterministic conceptions cannot finally be applied without restrictions to mental events: the subject's knowledge of the cause always, in his own case, to some degree modifies the effect. [p. 3]

However, in addition to elaborating new features of the traditional *freedom versus determinism* controversy through his emphasis on the reflexiveness of mental states as opposed to physical states, Hamp-

[66]Ibid.

shire also brings his incisive analytic tools to work on the specific problem of liberation from the tyranny of unconscious motivations and compulsions. It is on this problem that Hampshire's unfolding of the Spinozist concept of *idea ideae* brings additional and revealing illumination, as well as on the concomitant problem of moral responsibility. This is helped by Hampshire's introduction of a new term, "stepping back," which in one part of its meaning is expressive of the Spinozist idea of "reflexive thought." When a person thinks about his thoughts, when he reflects on or deliberates about any strong impulse or desire that he experiences, tries to evaluate it and determine by means of his "second-order" thoughts what the causes are of the desire under his scrutiny and what his ensuing actions ought to be, it is as if his reason has *stepped back* from the experienced desire and has carried out its evaluation from a second-order position. Hampshire makes frequent use of the term,[67] and I shall have occasion to use it in the ensuing pages and to explain it more fully.

Hampshire draws on Freud for the evidence that much of the life of each of us is under the domination of unconscious policies and purposes. "We commonly do not know what we are trying to do." There are many instances in which a person "may be said to be pursuing a policy, and executing a plan, without in any sense knowing that that is what he is doing."[68] The person is powerless to control or change these policies, and his actions are often inconsistent with his sincerely professed intentions. The effects of these unconscious processes and compulsions are not limited to manifestly abnormal or neurotic behavior. According to Hampshire, their effects are observable across a wide spectrum of seemingly "normal" behavior:

> Freudian psychology may have provided good experimental reasons for believing that sane men are in many situations incapable of recognizing or of controlling influences upon their conduct that may often be evident to others. . . . [69]

That there is here a problem of freedom of the mind versus psychic bondage is clearly disclosed by the fact that the meaning and direction of the subject's anomalous or seemingly normal behavior and policies, though they are not understood by the subject himself, often are clearly understood by others, particularly his psychoanalyst. If I needed to be told what I was doing, Hampshire insightfully observes, and if someone knew and understood what I was doing better than I did, it would follow that I was not a free and fully responsible agent.

[67]For example, *Thought and Action*, pp. 189–90 and passim; *Freedom of the Individual*, p. 89 and passim.

[68]*Thought and Action*, p. 132.

[69]Ibid., p. 191.

> Only with knowledge comes the opportunity of choice and therefore full responsibility. If I did not know what I was trying to do, no possibilities of deliberate change were open to me.[70]

It is therefore natural for Hampshire to assert categorically that "the most powerful argument against the reality of freedom is the old argument that has been given some new basis in . . . interpretations of the work of Freud and his followers."[71]

What then is the therapy? Essentially, for Stuart Hampshire, it is the same "rationalist" therapy that we found in Spinoza and Freud. It is, to repeat, the individual's exercise of reason and knowledge, especially reflexive self-knowledge, in discovering the causes of his unconsciously propelled passions, and in achieving their ejection or modification. The essential paradigm of psychic liberation is the same for all three. If there are any significant differences that distinguish Hampshire's doctrine from Spinoza's and Freud's, they are *first,* that Hampshire develops some rather subtle and penetrating analyses of implications of *reflexive knowledge* through an examination of the notion of *self-prediction* and of what it tells us about freedom of mind generally. The *second* difference consists in Hampshire's comparatively greater confidence about the *efficacy* of reason and reflexive knowledge in actually breaking through and eliminating or modifying a person's unconsciously motivated compulsions. This also seems to me to entail, as a consequence, Hampshire's comparatively greater confidence with respect to the moral responsibility and accountability to which a person may be held. In short, it would appear to me that Hampshire's doctrine may be said to be more "rationalist" than those of Spinoza and Freud.

Regrettably, a discussion of Hampshire's argument to show that the impossibility of *self-prediction*[72] constitutes another break in the possibility of determinism cannot be included here.

In what follows, the outlines of Hampshire's theory of psychic liberation will be presented, including a brief account of one of its moral implications. Some critical assessments of the "rationalism" of Hampshire's theory will bring the discussion to a conclusion.

Both conceptually and clinically, the *necessary* condition of psychic freedom, for Hampshire, is knowledge. One of Hampshire's difficulties is that he sometimes writes as if he believed that knowledge is also the *sufficient* condition of freedom, but to this I shall return in my

[70]Ibid., p. 132.

[71]Ibid., p. 178.

[72]*Thought and Action*, pp. 169–76, 187–91; *Freedom of the Individual*, pp. 73–91; Pears, pp. 80–104.

concluding paragraphs. However, the therapeutic knowledge, the knowledge that eventuates in psychic freedom, is for him, as it is for Spinoza and Freud, *self-knowledge:*

> A man becomes more and more a free and responsible agent the more he at all times knows what he is doing. . . .[73]

> The more reliable and extensive my inductive knowledge is, including self-knowledge, the less likely I am to attempt a course of action which, unknown to me [and therefore inaccessible to my free control], I cannot carry through. The more I learn of the conditions on which my passions and abilities depend, the narrower the gap between that which I set myself to do, and that which I actually achieve, will become.[74]

For Hampshire, this kind of reflexive knowledge is also a necessary condition for the improvement and freedom of thought generally, not only for freedom from the tyranny of emotions and passions:

> As self-consciousness is a necessary prelude to greater freedom of the will, so is it also a prelude to a greater freedom of thought.[75]

> The improvement of thought always requires reflection, the formation of ideas of ideas, and a critical self-consciousness; there is no other method.[76]

As to the methodology for getting hold of the reflexive knowledge required to become psychically liberated, Freudian psychoanalytic therapy is in full accord with Hampshire's theory of psychic freedom. From the standpoint of this theory, "Freudian psychology is no more than an extension of reflection in order to bring to consciousness repressed wishes and beliefs."[77] Here is a fuller statement of Hampshire's systematic placement of psychoanalytic theory and therapy within the framework of his own theory of psychic freedom:

> The new positive science of human conduct, psychoanalysis . . . is founded upon a peculiar form of memory and a peculiar form of self-consciousness of the subject. It might even have been predicted that it must take this form, if it is to be knowledge that explains to the subject why he has the purposes he has. As an applied science, psychoanalysis identifies the increasing freedom of the agent to control his

[73]*Thought and Action,* p. 177.
[74]*Freedom of the Individual,* p. 90.
[75]*Thought and Action,* p. 312.
[76]"The Explanation of Thought," p. 16.
[77]Ibid.

> own conduct and states of mind with an extended self-consciousness, with a capacity to recognize in memory motives and purposes that he had not recognized before. Psychoanalysis therefore provides a reflexive knowledge of the workings of the mind that fits into the philosophical definition of freedom in terms of self-knowledge.[78]

The bringing to consciousness, to self-awareness, and to the critical scrutiny of reason through second-order thoughts, of the previously unrecognized causes of one's emotions and behavior—the loosening from the grip of repression of long-forgotten memories of long-forgotten events, and their identification as the source of attitudes or compulsions—makes possible a liberation from them, and a new freedom for the subject to direct his thoughts and behavior rationally. This process, says Hampshire, inasmuch as its goal is self-conscious, deliberate action, entails as a necessary ingredient our stepping back in our thinking in order to scrutinize, via second-order thoughts, not only the causes of our previously compelled behavior but also "the possible ends that we may attempt to achieve,"[79] "the new possibilities."[80] In a sense it would probably be correct to say that, from a critical point of view, Hampshire's "stepping back" idea is similar to or at least overlaps with what the psychoanalyst would call the patient's "objectification" at a certain point in the analytic process. But it is broader than that. Hampshire's stepping back is unavoidable if the psychoanalytic uncovering process does not stop at only identifying and understanding the causes of the problematic behavior but endeavors to bring about changes from the earlier situation. As Hampshire explains:

> About the "stepping back" and secondary decisions; any inductive knowledge that a man acquires of the determinants of his behavior, which are other than his own decisions, changes the situation as he confronts it; he sees that certain possibilities which he had believed to be open, are closed. But he now has to decide what he is to try to do in the new situation. He is not absolved from further decision, just because he now realizes that the primary decision would have been inoperative. This is the "stepping back," which opens new possibilities of things that he might now do. . . . [81]

Whether Hampshire's "rationalist" implication that the uncovering process of psychoanalytic therapy, and its liberation of the subject from his compulsions, must in fact "inevitably" result in either a

[78]*Thought and Action,* p. 255.
[79]Ibid., p. 189.
[80]*Freedom of the Individual,* p. 89.
[81]In Pears, p. 98.

"change" in the subject's behavior or in an inescapably *deliberate* decision on his part to leave the situation as is, constitutes an interesting problem. Is it truly "necessary" or "inevitable" that the subject will make a new decision? In what sense is the subject "not absolved from further decision" because he now realizes "that the primary decision would have been inoperative"? Is it not possible that the subject will neither take any new action nor rationally and deliberately decide to commit himself to the old situation, but rather will simply and will-lessly and passively continue as before? This possibility is neither contradictory to Freudian theory nor unfamiliar to clinical psychoanalytic experience, though it of course seems repugnant to Hampshire's deeply ingrained "rationalism."

Hampshire's doctrine here is most tempting and provides a suggestive antidote to one phase of Hospers's antilibertarian argument. It was Hospers's contention that since none of us is the author of his own character, the person guilty of immoral or criminal behavior can justifiably claim that he cannot be held responsible for his criminal acts because, he might argue, "I am that kind of person as a result of heredity or environment, and I could not help doing what I did; it was impossible for me—I was not free—not to do it." Hampshire's argument against this kind of position is a provocative one. If I have acquired reflexive knowledge about the kind of person I am,

> I cannot have this last kind of knowledge without a policy, a strategy, being required of me as my response to the situation now recognized. . . . I can always be asked when I first recognized these features of my situation. From this moment onwards, I am responsible for changing or not changing my policies in one direction rather than another. . . . It is unalterably impossible that we should either explain or excuse our present or future voluntary and deliberate action by referring to the influences bearing upon us, unless we are explaining or excusing in advance an unexpected failure to achieve that which we shall genuinely try to achieve.[82]

> [Therefore] my character is still something for which I am responsible. . . . If I had thought that my history, and the external causes influencing me, were . . . bad in their effects, I at least could have tried to find the means to prevent or minimize their effect. . . . I am faced with the choice of acquiescing or of trying to find the means of diverting or minimizing their effects.[83]

This is Hampshire's "stepping back," and his confidence that the reflexive knowledge that is part of it will unavoidably result in a free

[82]*Thought and Action*, pp. 188–89.
[83]Ibid., p. 187.

choice. But it does not always happen, and Hampshire's phenomenological description of the stepping back process, with its features of required moral responsibility, fails to demonstrate that the subject, having become aware of these features, was not still bound by some compulsion to repeat the crime, did indeed have the freedom to change, and was disingenuous in his self-prediction that he would inevitably repeat the crime.

Perhaps, in this dispute between Hospers and Hampshire, one might be driven to support an unpopular separation—namely, between being held morally responsible and being subject to punishment. Perhaps, if *ex hypothesi* the subject did phenomenologically experience the stepping back and the moral features of the situation but nevertheless did not change, we would hold him *morally* blameworthy for not changing; but on the basis of the Hospers-Clarence Darrow hypothesis that the subject, in spite of his rational, reflexive awareness of the moral features of the situation, was nonetheless under psychic compulsion and not free to refrain, he should not be subjected to severe punishment.

The purpose of this discussion of Hampshire versus Hospers was to help focus on what I earlier called Hampshire's greater confidence (compared to Spinoza and Freud) in the "rationalist" paradigm of psychic liberation. Not that Hampshire is oblivious to the failures of reason to prevail: he is not, as is evident in numerous passages in his writings. But an extract from his most recent paper illustrates his relative sanguinity. Hampshire points out that a person, when asked about his belief or desire or any other kind of thought, "may be self-deceived, or he may make a mistake," but in the self-same passage he goes on to claim categorically that "he is at least privileged in respect to conscious thought. He will modify his beliefs and desires, and they will change, as he reflects on their causal connections. He will even on occasion be ashamed of the causal dependences when he reflects on them, and he will consequently disavow and change what he has discovered to be his previous thinking."[84]

One carries away an impression from this and other passages that too often, for Hampshire, self-conscious thought and reflection on the causes of desires and passions automatically result in the subject's triumph over and liberation from these desires and passions. Such a doctrine would suggest that he holds the exercise of reason and reflexive thought to be the *sufficient* condition for psychic freedom, and would be provocative of many doubts, as we shall see below.

This brings us back to the thesis that knowledge is the *necessary* condition of freedom. We can take it to be part of Hampshire's thesis,

[84]"The Explanation of Thought," p. 9.

as it is of Spinoza's and Freud's, that every person's achievement of psychic freedom from unconsciously caused compulsions is a case of the person's having exercised his reason, his reflexive knowledge, and the resulting self-modifying power of his thought—that without this kind of knowledge and thinking the liberation could not have taken place. But is the converse of this statement also and always true? Is every case of a person's self-knowledge, of reflexive thinking, of his having become conscious of predictions of his behavior, also *necessarily* a case of his becoming liberated from the tyranny of a passion, or of modification of his behavior? Are there not many cases of the subject's ignoring the acquired reflexive knowledge, even defying it, or resisting and evading any modification of his behavior by various strategies of self-deception and rationalization? Are knowledge and intention identical? Are all intentions conscious? What of *unconscious* purposes? Hampshire says:

> I cannot escape the burden of intention, and therefore of responsibility, which is bestowed upon me by knowledge of what I am doing, that is, by recognition of the situation confronting me and of the difference that my action is making. As soon as I realize what I am doing, I am no longer doing it unintentionally.[85]

Strictly speaking, all Hampshire is entitled to say here is that as soon as I realize what I am doing, "I am no longer doing it *unknowingly.*" I may be doing it knowingly, but at the same time be governed by some *unconscious purpose,* the existence of which Freud demonstrated most persuasively and Hampshire would of course not deny.

Another observation forces itself upon the student of Hampshire's work, especially when it is seen through the Spinozist and Freudian perspectives—namely, that he attributes to *reason,* which is so significant in his doctrines, a central and strange exclusivity in relation to psychic liberation. There is in his texts insufficient evidence of his recognizing, as Spinoza did, that an emotion can be overcome only by a contrary and stronger emotion, and that therefore reason is in need of the collaboration of emotion. Except for a brief reference to a person's first-order desire for alcohol being eliminated "because other desires were being frustrated by alcoholism,"[86] no other outstanding illustration comes to mind of any attention being given to this important psychologico-philosophical point for any theory of psychic liberation. Absent also is any noteworthy attention to the intricate interminglings, in man's complex and dynamic structure, of reason and unreason, ego and id, Eros and Thanatos, love and hate, sadism

[85]*Thought and Action,* p. 175.

[86]*Freedom of the Individual,* p. 134.

and masochism. For the most part Hampshire does not comment on the ambivalences and tensions that characterize human existence and are so compellingly relevant to the understanding of both the strong resistances to and the hoped-for triumphs of psychic liberation.

It is perhaps this overemphasis on the role of reason, not as a moral desideratum but as a force in man's psychological structure, that may account for Hampshire's unsatisfactory treatment of the phenomenon of *Akrasia*,[87] a term that is discussed at some length by Aristotle[88] and is variously translated as "Incontinence," "Imperfect Self-control," "Moral Weakness," or "Weakness of Will." Aristotle's problem was to try to explain how it was possible for a person to display the puzzling moral weakness implicit in his asserting that he knows that to do X would be a mistake or evil, and his proceeding at the same time to *do* the very act called X. Aristotle pointed out that Socrates had denied the existence of the problem on the ground that such a person did not really have the "knowledge" that doing X was evil; he was obviously ignorant or mistaken about this.

Aristotle's attempt to resolve this paradox need not detain us here. But Hampshire's explanation simply does not have the ring of reality:

> a man cannot be sincere in accepting the conclusion that some course of action is entirely mistaken, if he at the same time deliberately commits himself to this course of action. . . . a man cannot without absurdity *say* of himself that he is convinced . . . [that the action would be a mistake but that] he will do exactly this . . . mistaken thing.[89]

Human beings often display precisely this kind of moral weakness. We may recall, for example, the familiar case of Saint Paul, who in his Epistle to the Romans (7 : 19) made just such a public confession, "I do not do the good I want, but the evil I do not want to do is what I do," without either insincerity or absurdity *necessarily* characterizing his declaration. Hampshire's judgment here seems obviously predicated on the assumption of total or overwhelmingly great *rationality* in man, and consequently of the impossibility of self-contradiction—or of the coexistence of two mutually opposed intentional states—infecting the human psyche; but men are obviously self-contradictory with disconcerting frequency.

And finally, a brief comment must be made about the relationship between reason and rationalization. Hampshire does take cognizance of the phenomenon of rationalization as one of the impediments that lie in the way of a person's efforts to know what he is doing, to act

[87]Ibid., pp. 71 ff.
[88]*The Nicomachean Ethics,* book 7, especially chap. 3.
[89]*Freedom of the Individual,* p. 71; Hampshire's emphasis.

freely, with full self-consciousness and rational, reflexive self-knowledge. However, here too his overemphasized rationalism gets in his way. He suggests that if one reflexively becomes convinced that in his "rationalized" situation his "regret, shame, discouragement, disapproval, hope, confidence, admiration [are] utterly inappropriate to their subjects, *the state of mind must disappear,*" and further, that "when the subject recognizes that the object does not have the properties that are required . . . [he] cannot still regret *that which he now knows not to be regrettable.*"[90] But this does not always happen. The state of mind in which the "rationalization" prevails often does not disappear, and we often do precisely continue to regret that which we know "not to be regrettable."

For it is a well-known feature of rationalization that the intellect collaborates with the process, and that reason in fact often helps find spurious self-justifications for continuing the self-deception. Reason itself may turn out to be fickle and may permit itself to be used in the service of the unconsciously motivated purpose. In the process of rationalization, reason may in fact conspire to circumvent itself, furthering conclusions or actions that are really advancing the unconscious passion or compulsion or delusion. The subject thus maintains the illusion that cognition and reason have triumphed immaculately, whereas in actuality they have not. Since Hampshire's texts do not always remark on these dangers inherent in the rigid reliance on reason as the ultimate arbiter of truth, goodness, and right, residual questions about this frequently exclusivist "rationalism" are unavoidably raised.

However, even after these deviations from the rationalistic paradigm have been noted, and man's resistances to its guidance are seen in their naked force, and even after the extreme narrowness and fragility of the margin of psychic freedom that can be achieved have been recognized, the ultimate fact still remains that such psychic freedom is always a product of, or a function of, the exercise of reason, of reflexive thought. Ultimately, it is only by the employment of reason that we can detect, identify, penetrate, expose, or explode rationalizations, so that the self-deceptions may be made transparent, the falsity held up to one's own and perhaps to public scrutiny, and the mask of rationalization torn off.

In the final analysis, therefore, it is only reason, imperfect and open to misuse though it is, that remains the ultimate guide and tribunal to which man must repair in order to distinguish between freedom and servitude, good and evil, right and wrong, truth and falsehood. Hampshire's seemingly overstated emphasis apart, it is only true

[90]Ibid., pp. 94 ff.; emphasis added.

knowledge, reflexive thought—especially when we succeed in imparting to it an emotional dimension—that is able to overcome or at least to restrain our damaging or pathogenic emotions or compulsions. Psychic freedom, to the limited extent that it is attainable—whether we pursue the quest for it via Spinoza's insights, or via Freud's clinical discoveries, or via Hampshire's penetrating inquiries—is shown to be attainable only when the necessary condition is present, namely, *the exercise of reason.* In this sense, a theory of psychic freedom must rest on the bedrock of the fundamental and indispensable rationalism shared by these three seminal thinkers.

References

Alexander, B. "Spinoza und die Psychoanalyse." *Chronicon Spinozanum* 5 (1927):196–203.

Allport, G. W. *Becoming: Basic Considerations for a Psychology of Personality.* New Haven, Conn.: Yale University Press, 1955.

Aristotle. *The Nicomachean Ethics.*

Arlow, J. A. "Psychoanalysis as Scientific Method." In *Psychoanalysis, Scientific Method and Philosophy,* edited by S. Hook. New York: Grove Press, 1960.

Bernard, W. "Freud and Spinoza." *Psychiatry* 9 (1946):99–108.

Bidney, D. *The Psychology and Ethics of Spinoza.* New Haven, Conn.: Yale University Press, 1940.

Brill, A. A. "Reminiscences of Freud." *Psychoanalytic Quarterly* 9 (1940):177–83.

Curley, E. M. *Spinoza's Metaphysics: An Essay in Interpretation.* Cambridge, Mass.: Harvard University Press, 1969.

Feuer, L. S. *Spinoza and the Rise of Liberalism.* Boston: Beacon Press, 1958.

Franck, I. *Human Nature in Humanistic Psychology.* Unpublished.

Freud, S. *The Interpretation of Dreams (1900–01); The Psychopathology of Everyday Life (1901); Wit and Its Relation to the Unconscious (1905).* In *The Basic Writings of Sigmund Freud,* translated and edited by A. A. Brill. New York: Modern Library, Random House, 1938.

——— . *Beyond the Pleasure Principle* (1920). Translated by C. J. M. Hubback. London: Hogarth Press and Institute of Psycho-Analysis, 1948.

——— . *A General Introduction to Psycho-Analysis (1920).* Translated by J. Riviere. Garden City, N.Y.: Garden City Publishing Co., 1938.

——— . "Psycho-Analysis (1923)." In *Standard Edition of the Complete Psychological Works,* vol. 18. London: Hogarth, 1955.

——— . *The Ego and the Id (1923).* Translated by J. Riviere. London: Hogarth Press and Institute of Psycho-Analysis, 1947.

______ . *An Autobiographical Study (1925).* Translated by J. Strachey. London: Hogarth Press and Institute of Psycho-Analysis, 1948.

______ . *The Future of an Illusion (1927).* Horace Liveright and Institute of Psycho-Analysis, 1928.

______ . *Civilization and Its Discontents (1930).* Translated by J. Riviere. New York: Jonathan Cape & Harrison Smith, 1930.

______ . *New Introductory Lectures on Psycho-Analysis (1933).* Translated by W. H. J. Sprott. New York: Norton, 1933.

______ . *Collected Papers.* New York: Basic Books, 1959. Vol. 5, "Analysis Terminable and Interminable," edited by J. Strachey, 1937.

______ . *An Outline of Psycho-Analysis (1940).* Translated by J. Strachey. New York: Norton, 1963.

Hamblin-Smith, W. "Spinoza's Anticipation of Recent Psychological Developments." *British Journal of Medical Psychology* 5 (1925):257–78.

Hampshire, S. *Spinoza.* Baltimore: Penguin Books, 1951.

______ . *Thought and Action.* New York: Viking Press, 1960.

______ . *Freedom of the Individual.* 2d ed., with postscript. New York: Harper & Row, 1965.

______ . *Freedom of Mind.* Princeton, N.J.: Princeton University Press, 1971.

______ . "Spinoza and the Idea of Freedom." In *Spinoza: A Collection of Critical Essays,* edited by M. Grene. Garden City, N.Y.: Anchor Books, Doubleday, 1973.

______ . "Spinoza's Theory of Human Freedom." In *Spinoza: Essays in Interpretation,* edited by E. Freeman and M. Mandelbaum. LaSalle, Ill.: Open Court Publishing Co., 1975.

______ . "The Explanation of Thought." In *Psychiatry and the Humanities,* vol. 2 ("Thought, Consciousness, and Reality"), edited by J. H. Smith. New Haven, Conn.: Yale University Press, 1977.

Hospers, J. "What Means This Freedom?" In *Determinism and Freedom in the Age of Modern Science,* edited by S. Hook. New York: New York University Press, 1958.

Jones, E. *The Life and Work of Sigmund Freud.* 3 vols. New York: Basic Books, 1953.

Nelson, B., ed. *Freud and the 20th Century.* New York: Meridian Books, 1957.

Parkinson, G. H. R. "Spinoza on the Power and Freedom of Man." In *Spinoza: Essays in Interpretation,* edited by E. Freeman and M. Mandelbaum. LaSalle, Ill.: Open Court Publishing Co., 1975.

Pears, D. F., ed. Dialogue, "Freedom and Knowledge," by I. Murdoch, S. Hampshire, P. L. Gardiner, and D. F. Pears. In *Freedom and the Will.* New York: St. Martin's Press, 1963.

Poincaré, H. *The Foundations of Science.* Translated by G. B. Halsted. Lancaster, Pa.: Science Press, 1946.

Pollock, F. *Spinoza: His Life and Philosophy* (1899). 2d ed. New York: American Scholar Publications, 1966.

Rathbun, C. "On Certain Similarities Between Spinoza and Psychoanalysis." *Psychoanalytic Review* 21 (1934):1–14.

Rieff, P. *Freud: The Mind of the Moralist.* Garden City, N.Y.: Anchor Books, Doubleday, 1961.

Saw, R. L. *The Vindication of Metaphysics: A Study in the Philosophy of Spinoza.* London: Macmillan, 1951.

Schafer, R. "An Overview of Heinz Hartmann's Contributions to Psychoanalysis." *International Journal of Psycho-Analysis* 51 (1970):425–46.

Skinner, B. F. "Critique of Psychoanalytic Concepts and Theories." *Minnesota Studies in the Philosophy of Science,* vol. 1 ("The Foundations of Science and the Concepts of Psychology and Psychoanalysis"), edited by H. Feigl and M. Scriven. Minneapolis: University of Minnesota Press, 1956.

Spinoza, B. *Ethics.*

______. *The Correspondence of Spinoza.* Translated and edited by A. Wolf. London: George Allen & Unwin, 1928.

Wartofsky, M. "Action and Passion: Spinoza's Construction of a Scientific Psychology." In *Spinoza: A Collection of Critical Essays,* edited by M. Grene. Garden City, N.Y.: Anchor Books, Doubleday, 1973.

Wolfson, H. A. *The Philosophy of Spinoza: Unfolding the Latent Processes of His Reasoning.* Cambridge, Mass.: Harvard University Press, 1948.

7. *Einstein and the Idea of Freedom*

Albert Einstein's life and work reflected, in microcosm, the perennial and ever-reenacted struggle for freedom of the human spirit on the stage of recorded human history. In Einstein's case this dramatic struggle revolved around two pivotal and existentially inescapable aspects of the man: Einstein the scientist, and Einstein the Jew. The two are inseparable. They are inextricably intertwined, not only by virtue of being aspects of the same person, but also, and perhaps even more, because they were welded together by features of the cultural milieu into which he was thrust for the greater part of his career; by the cross-winds of doctrine and dogma that buffeted him throughout the midspan of his life; and by the unspeakably tragic events, unleashed by the advent of Nazism, that overtook and engulfed the Jews of Europe in the twelve fateful years of Hitler's Third Reich.

In the course of this year's Centennial observances, Einstein's amazing achievements in physical science are being celebrated throughout the world. But it was only a very short time ago that these same achievements were denounced and vilified as putative exemplars of false, fraudulent "*Jewish* science," which allegedly had, as its conspiratorial goal, the pollution and destruction of the purity of "*Aryan* science." These attacks on Einstein, in which German "scien-

Raphael Jospe and Samuel Z. Fishman (eds.), *Go and Study; Essays and Studies in Honor of Alfred Jospe* (Washington, D.C.: B'nai B'rith Hillel Foundations, 1980), pp. 267–285. Originally presented, in briefer form, at the Smithsonian Institution, Washington, D.C., on March 29, 1979, as the concluding lecture in a series arranged in observance of the Einstein Centennial. A text slightly different from the one printed here was published in *Midstream; A Monthly Jewish Review*, vol. 26, January 1980, pp. 13–20.

tists" were among the major actors, epitomized the Nazi assault on the freedom of scientific inquiry, on the freedom of the intellect, and on the very concept of objective truth, an assault that led inexorably to the ghastly culmination of the gas chambers and crematoria.

His vicissitudes notwithstanding, or perhaps because of them, Einstein had a wonderful sense of humor: an understated, self-effacing, self-deprecating kind of humor. He was a supreme ironist, perceiving with shrewd, Olympian insight many of the follies of the human scene. It will be useful, as a beginning, to single out two of Einstein's witticisms which, when unpacked, and some of their connotations uncovered, may be seen to encapsulate profound reflections on the issues of freedom implicit in the two aspects of his life referred to above. The first of these witticisms is brief. When he was once asked how it was that he came to develop his theories of relativity, his simple reply was: "I dared question an axiom." I have not been able to authenticate this quote. It may be apocryphal. But it is pregnant with implications for our theme.

The other witticism was published in the London *Times* on November 28, 1919. That newspaper had requested from Einstein a description of the results of his theory of relativity, for the benefit of the London public. It was only three weeks after the historic report had been presented at the meeting of the Royal Society about the experimental confirmation of Einstein's theory that light rays are bent in the sun's gravitational field. Let us recall the historical setting. London had just observed the first anniversary of the armistice that had ended World War I, in which Germany had been the enemy. In honoring Einstein, English newspapers tried to ignore every connection between Germany and the scientist they were honoring. Einstein himself deplored this because he hated chauvinistic, narrow-minded nationalism, and he proceeded to twit the *Times* in these words:

> The description of me and my circumstances in the *Times* shows an amusing flare of imagination on the part of the writer. By an application of the theory of relativity to the taste of the reader, today in Germany I am called a German man of science and in England I am represented as a Swiss Jew. If I come to be regarded as a *bête noire* the description will be reversed, and I shall become a Swiss Jew for the German and a German for the English.

Professor Philipp Frank, the distinguished physicist and colleague of Einstein, writing in 1947, supplied this mordant comment on the quote: "At that time Einstein did not anticipate how soon this joke would become true."[1]

[1]Frank, Philipp, *Einstein: His Life and Times*, New York: Alfred A. Knopf, 1949, p. 144.

Out of these two Einsteinian witticisms we may distill some observations about five aspects of the Idea of Freedom: 1) Freedom of Inquiry; 2) Freedom for Error; 3) Freedom of the Intellect; 4) Socio-political Freedom; 5) Freedom of Religion.

I. Freedom of Inquiry

Einstein was a scientist. Above all, science is dedicated to the advancement of knowledge. To say this is to be neither unmindful nor disparaging of applied science and its contributions to the technological advancement of mankind, and to the improvement of the physical life of man on this planet. But what distinguishes the quintessential idea of science from technology is the pursuit by science of knowledge as an end in itself, over and beyond the application of knowledge to instrumental purposes. Philosophers, historians, and scientists have often reminded us, particularly in the past three generations, that the advancement of knowledge is possible only if scientific inquiry is permitted to follow its own course, as an evolving, self-correcting, trial-and-error process. The making of errors and the freedom to make errors are as integral a part of this process as are the recognition of error, its correction, and the progression beyond any given state of knowledge or ignorance. The advancement of knowledge never proceeds in a confident, rectilinear progression from truth to truth. Significant inquiry in any branch of human knowledge entails and requires questioning of what has appeared to be beyond question, probing, daring, and imaginative projection into the realm of the unknown, often at the risk of being in error.

Such courage and such imagination can obviously flourish only in an atmosphere of freedom in inquiry, and can be hopeful of success in advancing human knowledge only when the various intellectual and scientific disciplines are free to apply their own tests of validity and truth, without outside interference, political or otherwise. When freedom of inquiry is frustrated by fear that errors may be punished; by coerced, slavish assent to any set of preconceived ideas, axioms, or norms outside the immanent canons of logical validity, truth, and the methodology of the sciences; by political orthodoxies; or by appeals to a sanctified something called "common sense" as the final authority and arbiter of truth, then the advancement of human knowledge is sure to be arrested or stopped.

It was the late Alfred North Whitehead who, in one of his many discourses on education, focused his attention on the power of education to liberate man from his unexamined assumptions. Out of minds so liberated, out of free inquiry, out of the free testing of conflicting ideas, new knowledge is born. And in his influential book of half a century ago, *Science and the Modern World,* Whitehead also reminded his readers that "a clash of doctrines is not a disaster—it is an opportunity."[2] The import of what is being said here is dramatically and cogently exemplified in the career of Albert Einstein, the scientist. Indomitably and fearlessly he explored the boundaries of man's knowledge of the physical world, often to the discordant accompaniment of the derision of scoffers, and later under the whiplash of abuse, vilification, and what surely would have become physical persecution had he returned to Germany in 1933. (But to this phase we shall return later.) His relentless probing brought physical science to a confrontation with new frontiers in the exploration of the mysteries of the universe we inhabit. His whimsical answer, "I dared question an axiom," goes to the very root of the matter. For one of the essential features of the growth of knowledge is that the axiom of today so often becomes the error of tomorrow, or, if not an error, at best only *partial* knowledge that was in need of correction and revision. In so much of the history of science and philosophy, the paradigmatic defense of the intellectual or scientific status quo of the day has taken the form of an appeal to the inviolability of "common sense." But as Einstein once observed:

> Common sense is actually nothing more than a deposit of prejudices laid down in the mind prior to the age of eighteen. Every new idea one encounters in later years must combat this accretion of so-called self-evident concepts.

Einstein's refusal to be intimidated by the accretion of so-called self-evident ideas, his questioning of axioms, his intellectual daring and adventurousness, may have served as stimulus for the remarkable essay by Thorstein Veblen, American economist and sociologist, entitled "The Intellectual Preeminence of Jews in Modern Europe," published in 1919. It was Veblen's penetrating insight that when the intellectually gifted Jew became "a naturalized, though hyphenate, citizen in the gentile republic of learning," he also became the questioner, the sceptic, the daring prober, and explorer. Having left the "cultural heritage of the Jewish people," and having become "immersed in the gentile culture," the Jew found himself "in the vanguard of modern inquiry" precisely because intellectually he remained an alien, living on the frontiers of European culture. His marginality gave him "the requisite immunity from the inhibitions of intellectual quietism," and "he became a disturber of the intellectual

[2]Whitehead, Alfred North, *Science and the Modern World* (Lowell Lectures, 1925), New York: Macmillan, 1929, p. 266.

peace . . . a wanderer in the intellectual no-man's-land." The young Jew who entered the intellectual life of Europe was "a sceptic by force of circumstances." The first requisite for constructive work in modern science, said Veblen, ". . . is a sceptical frame of mind," and the young Jew was therefore "in line to become guide and leader . . . in that intellectual development out of which comes the increase and diffusion of knowledge among men." It was this psycho-social analysis that Veblen suggested as explanation of the fact that "the Jewish people have contributed much more than an even share of the intellectual life of modern Europe."[3]

Although Veblen made no reference to him by name, the possibility that Einstein was among those Veblen had in mind in this perceptive essay is not to be discounted. Surely there is an instructive similarity between Veblen's characterization of the young Jew who entered turn-of-the-century European science and Einstein's description of himself in a letter to Max Born: "As a man without roots anywhere . . . I have wandered continually hither and yon—a stranger everywhere." And surely Einstein knew that probing into the recesses of the unknown was bound, as he repeatedly pointed out, "to bring ninety-nine fruitless gropings for one successful grasp." Typically, in connection with a certain feature of one of his theories, Einstein remarked: "That was my biggest blunder. Death alone can save us from blunders."[4] We also know from his own writings, and from the public record, that unlike his experience with the *Special* Theory of Relativity in 1905, he made a number of false starts before successfully developing his *General* Theory of Relativity. We also know that he spent the final third of his life in doggedly, tenaciously—but fruitlessly, as it turned out—pursuing his will-of-the-wisp *Unified Field Theory*. Some future scientist may pick up this trail and succeed where Einstein failed, and, in succeeding, this future scientist may establish that Einstein's vision had reached out toward the correct goal. Contrariwise, it may be shown in the future that his idea of a *Unified Field Theory* was, to use Sir Karl R. Popper's terminology, only another "conjecture" that was unproductive.

But seekers after truth in future generations will be able to draw courage and sustenance from his unswerving tenacity, his selfless

[3]Veblen, Thorstein, "The Intellectual Preeminence of Jews in Modern Europe," *The Political Science Quarterly*, March 1919. Reprinted in Veblen, *Essays in Our Changing Order*, New York: Viking Press, 1934; also in *The Portable Veblen*, ed. by Max Lerner, New York: Viking Press, 1958, pp. 467–79.

[4]Quoted by George R. Harrison, "Albert Einstein: Appraisal of an Intellect," *Atlantic Monthly*, Boston, 1955, p. 25. Cf. *Time* magazine, New York, February 19, 1979, pp. 78–79: "Einstein had opted for a stable universe . . . with . . . what he called the Cosmological Constant. A decade later . . . Einstein reversed himself. . . . The Cosmological Constant, he allowed, was the worst mistake of his scientific career."

search for knowledge, his refusal to be diverted from exercising his own intellectual freedom. In spite of fame and world-wide adulation during his life in the United States, he succeeded in avoiding the snares of dogmatism or of the kind of auto-intoxication or self-worship that might have caused a lesser person to try to interfere with, or attempt to restrict, or encroach upon, or be intolerant or contemptuous of, the views or of the freedom of others who dissented from his quest.

II. Freedom for Error

But Einstein's gropings, so many of which were so stunningly successful, and the gropings of most scientific inquirers would be discouraged or killed off if the prober lived in an atmosphere of social, ideological, intellectual, or scientific conformity, in which probing and questioning were frowned upon, and unproductive probings or speculations were punishable as heresy, error, or deviation. In his intellectual autobiography which he contributed to the volume called *Albert Einstein: Philosopher-Scientist* (in the series of volumes entitled "The Library of Living Philosophers"), Einstein wrote movingly about what he called "the holy curiosity of inquiry." He said of it the following: "This delicate little plant, aside from stimulation, stands mainly in the need of freedom; without this it goes to wreck and ruin without fail."[5] And again, in a brief essay entitled "On Freedom," Einstein pointed categorically to freedom of inquiry and freedom for error as necessary conditions for the advancement of knowledge.

> . . . the progress of science presupposes the possibility of unrestricted communication of all results and judgments—freedom of expression and instruction in all realms of intellectual endeavor. By freedom I understand social conditions of such a kind that the expression of opinions and assertions about general and particular matters of knowledge will not involve dangers or serious disadvantages for him who expresses them. This freedom of communication is indispensable for the development and extension of scientific knowledge. . . . In order that every man may present his views without penalty there must be a spirit of tolerance in the entire population. Such an ideal of external liberty can never be fully attained but must be sought unremittingly if scientific thought, and philosophical and creative thinking in general, are to be advanced as far as possible.[6]

[5]Einstein, Albert, "Autobiographical Notes," in *Albert Einstein: Philosopher-Scientist*, edited by Paul Arthur Schilpp (The Library of Living Philosophers, Volume VII), Evanston, Illinois: The Library of Living Philosophers, Inc., 1949, p. 17.

[6]Einstein, Albert, *Out of My Later Years*, New York: Philosophical Library, 1950, pp. 12–13.

There is an important philosophical point implicit in the notion of "Freedom for Error" that is worth noting here because it forms a natural transition to the connection between Einstein and socio-political freedom. The point becomes discernible when we reflect on aspects of the "history of ideas" in Western thought. It has been developed acutely and instructively by the philosopher of science, Sir Karl R. Popper, principally in his superb book *Conjectures and Refutations.*[7]

The way knowledge in general progresses, and especially scientific knowledge, says Popper, is by "unjustified" (that is, not yet justified) and, as it very often turns out, "unjustifiable anticipations, by guesses, by tentative solutions to our problems, by *conjectures.*"[8] These many *conjectures* in the history of science, most of which turn out to be *false,* are, according to Popper, the lifeblood of the progression of science, and, as part of the life of science, these conjectures are "controlled by criticism, that is, by *attempted refutations.*"[9] *Some* of the *conjectures* propounded by scientists (and we must remember that *all* scientific theories are *conjectures*) do survive the *systematic attempts* to refute them.[10] It is instructive to be reminded that every scientific experiment, every effort to test a scientific theory, if it is a *good* experiment, a *good* test, is in fact an attempt to *refute* the theory, that is, to demonstrate that what can be deduced and predicted from the theory is not reflected by the observed facts. I proceed to quote at some length from Popper:

> Criticism of our conjectures is of decisive importance: By bringing out our mistakes it makes us understand the difficulties of the problem we are trying to solve. . . . The very refutation of a theory—that is, of any serious tentative solution of our problem—is always a step forward that takes us nearer to the truth. And this is how we learn from our mistakes. . . . Our own errors provide the dim red lights which help us in groping our way out of the darkness of our cave.[11]

It would seem, therefore, that this fact, namely, that error has a necessary role in the process of the advancement of science, would have been recognized in the world of scientific inquiry, and that such recognition would have resulted in a concomitant recognition of the indispensability of freedom for error. And yet it is a notorious fact of history, more especially of 20th century history, that regimes and

[7]Popper, Karl R., *Conjectures and Refutations: The Growth of Scientific Knowledge,* New York: Basic Books, 1962.

[8]Ibid., p. vii.

[9]Ibid.

[10]Ibid., p. vii; Introduction, pp. 3–30; and Chapter 1, pp. 33–65.

[11]Ibid., pp. vii and 28.

societies have been able successfully, and with fatal effectiveness, to condemn and suppress opposing ideas, not only of a socio-political nature, but also in the realm of the sciences, by proclaiming them to be errors, pernicious and dangerous errors. Such regimes have succeeded in having not only the masses acquiesce in these condemnations, but in getting the class of intellectuals to accept them, and in having many of the intellectuals and scientists even echo them and lead in them. How has this been possible? How was this *Trahison des Clercs,* this *Treason of the Intellectuals* (to borrow the title of a book by the French writer Julien Benda), hatched out of the mainstream of modern Western philosophical and scientific thought to defile and pollute the intellectual environment of 20th century Europe?

Part of the explanation, Karl Popper suggests, is contained in two widely held doctrines about the concept of truth. The first is the doctrine that has come down from Plato, to Aristotle, to Descartes, and in another way to Francis Bacon, which maintained that "truth is manifest," that truth is publicly accessible for man to know effortlessly and "once the naked truth stands revealed before our eyes, we have the power to see it."[12] For René Descartes, this falsely "optimistic epistemology" was based on his theory of *veracitas Dei,* the theory that the *truthfulness of God* makes truth manifest to humans. Francis Bacon, according to Popper, held the doctrine of *veracitas naturae, nature is truthful;* it is an open book, and "a pure mind cannot misread it."[13] This doctrine of manifest truth had remarkably beneficent social and cultural consequences, since it led to the unparalleled intellectual and scientific revolutions of the 17th century, and to the conviction that through knowledge humans might become free. However, this same optimistic but clearly false epistemology also had disastrous consequences. It carried within it the assumption that, since truth is manifest, knowledge, or the possession of truth, did not need any explanation. "But how can we ever fall into error if truth is manifest?"[14] Obviously, the answer lies in a *conspiracy theory of error.* "There are powers conspiring to keep us in ignorance, to poison our minds with falsehood, and to blind our eyes so that they cannot see the manifest truth."[15] This this false epistemology, with its ineluctable corollary of the conspiracy theory of error, can be the basis of all kinds of fanaticism, and may both lead to and be utilized by totalitarian ideologies, seems to me amply clear.

[12]Ibid., p. 5.
[13]Ibid., p. 7.
[14]Ibid.
[15]Ibid.

III. Freedom of the Intellect

There is another widely disseminated doctrine about the concept of truth that Popper draws to our attention. It is "the strange view that the truth of a statement may be decided upon by inquiring into its sources—that is to say, its origin . . . "[16] It canonizes the *genetic* question, in the belief that a knowledge claim may legitimize itself by its pedigree rather than by objective evidence that supports it. Origins and genesis are substituted for validity, according to this doctrine, and for consistency with objective evidence, as criteria of truth. *Some* sources or origins of knowledge-claims are deemed to be ultimate, absolute, and self-validating, for example, those sources that are racially pure or Aryan, or those that are Marxist-Leninist-Stalinist, in origin. But, of course, as Popper insists, "pure, untainted, and certain *sources*" of scientific knowledge do not exist, and "questions of origin or of purity should not be confounded with questions of validity or of truth."[17] ". . . every source, every suggestion is open to critical examination. . . . The proper epistemological question is not one about sources; rather we ask whether the assertion made is true—that is to say, whether it agrees with the facts."[18]

Thus, when we put together these two doctrines concerning the concept of truth, namely, the theory of "manifest truth" with its corollary "conspiracy theory of error," and the view that the truth of a statement is determined by its source, part of the perverse logic behind the 20th century assaults on intellectual freedoms becomes tragically clear. This perverse, convoluted logic is evidenced in two responses to the experimental confirmation of Einstein's theory, one in the Soviet Union and the other in Germany. In 1922 a Soviet philosopher, A. Maximov, who specialized in the physical sciences, wrote in the official Soviet philosophical journal as follows:

> [The] idealistic atmosphere [in Germany] has surrounded and still surrounds relativity theory. . . . The impossibility within the limits of bourgeois society for intellectuals to withdraw from these influences led to the circumstance that the relativity principle served exclusively religious and metaphysical tendencies.[19]

Clearly, the "manifest truth" readily perceived by all intelligent and honest Soviet citizens is Dialectical Materialism, and the *error* of rela-

[16]Ibid., p. 18.
[17]Ibid., p. 25.
[18]Ibid., p. 27.
[19]Quoted by Philipp Frank, op. cit., pp. 145–46.

tivity theory, which must be banished, has as its degenerate source the conspiracy of the bourgeois intelligentsia to foster religion and metaphysics. And at the very same time in Germany some vociferous opinion characterized Einstein's theory as "Bolshevism in Physics."[20] Germany was experiencing the post-World War I trauma of defeat. Those elements which perceived the loss of war as a "stab in the back" were also hostile to Einstein:

> We are not surprised to find that the relativity theory soon began to be regarded as "Jewish" and capable of harming the German people.[21]

Here, in turn, the *manifest truth* is what all good, intelligent, and patriotic Germans would automatically recognize in its pristine Aryan purity, namely, "German Physics" (as we shall see forthwith). And there must obviously be no freedom for the insidious *error* of the relativity theory, which has its origin in the conspiratorial anti-German "Jewish Physics" from which Einstein came.

Some years later, in 1929, Einstein reminisced publicly about his own experiences upon his return to Germany in 1914:

> When I came to Germany 15 years ago, I discovered for the first time that I was a Jew, and I made this discovery through Gentiles more than through Jews. The Jews are a community of people bound together by the bonds of faith and tradition. I saw upright Jews subjected to scorn and contempt, *and my heart bled.*[22]

It is significant that, under the corrosive impact of the anti-Semitism that pervaded German society during that period, even Einstein's unapologetic dignity and pride in his Jewishness may have suffered some erosion. On the one hand, it was as a proud Jew that he publicly spoke his contempt for the assimilationist, grovelling *Zentralverein Deutscher Staatsbürger Jüdischen Glaubens* (Central Association of German Citizens of Jewish Faith), the adherents of which tried to downplay their Jewishness and to curry favor with the German establishment by speaking disparagingly of other Jews (he did later voice his contempt also for the equivalent "American Council for Judaism"). But, on the other hand, different overtones resonate in Einstein's words at the funeral service for Walter Rathenau, the brilliant Jew who had been the Weimar Republic's Minister of Foreign Affairs, and

[20]Ibid., p. 146.
[21]Ibid.
[22]*Fossische Zeitung*, Berlin, 1929. Quoted in "Einstein *Ha'yehudi V'yahaduto*" ("Einstein the Jew and His Jewishness"), by Z'ev V. Oren in *Hadoar* (Hebrew literary weekly), New York, 7 Nissan, 5728, p. 382 (my translation).

who was murdered by nationalist German elements on June 24, 1922. In his funeral speech Einstein said:

> I regret that Rathenau accepted an official post in the German government. In view of ideas and acts with reference to Jews in wide circles of the German people, it is my opinion that the natural reaction of Jews ought to be a dignified withdrawal from the public life of Germany.[23]

It is difficult to assess the extent to which Einstein's advocacy of "dignified withdrawal" was in fact a damning indictment of the German people, or a melancholy voice of a Jew who had been inwardly traumatized and humbled, by the hostility he experienced, into advocating retreat.

This was considerably before the advent of Nazism, but the ultranationalists in Germany were already systematically blaming the Jews for Germany's loss of the war. "There suddenly appeared an organization whose only purpose was to fight Einstein and his theories."[24] A literary magazine highly regarded among nationalists published an article under the title "Bolshevistic Physics" which attacked those, "university teachers among them," who "fell for" Einstein's theories, and said:

> . . . without mincing words, we are dealing here with an infamous scientific scandal. . . . In the last analysis one cannot blame workers for being taken in by Marx, when German professors allow themselves to be misled by Einstein.[25]

The notion of a Nordic-Aryan philosophy and science that is able to observe and interpret faithfully the reality and profundity of nature was given ever-wider circulation, and by contrast, the "fantastic" theories of the non-Nordic Einstein were vilified. When Einstein, under pressure to reply to these attacks, wrote in a Berlin newspaper that it would be senseless to try to answer in a scientific manner arguments that were not meant scientifically and said simply: "If I were a German nationalist, with or without a swastika, instead of being a Jew with liberal opinions . . . "[26] his opponents were infuriated by his having called the thing by its right name. Einstein began to feel uneasy in Berlin. When he was offered a professorship at the University of Leiden in Holland, and was asked whether he wished to leave Berlin, he replied: "Would such a decision be so amazing?

[23]Albert Einstein, *Neue Rundschau*, Berlin, 1922, Volume 2, pp. 815–16. Quoted by Z'ev Oren in *Hadoar*, loc cit., above (my translation).

[24]Frank, Philipp, op. cit., p. 159.

[25]Ibid., p. 160.

[26]Ibid., p. 161.

My situation is like that of a man who is lying in a beautiful bed, where he is being tortured by bedbugs."[27]

The most notorious of those who led the attack against Einstein were two fellow physicists, Johannes Stark and the Nobel laureate Philipp Lenard, who blamed the defeat of Germany on an international conspiracy in which the Jews were alleged to have been the actual wirepullers in the background. Lenard had joined the Hitler group in its early days and was one of the long-time members of the Nazi Party. In the preface to his four-volume work entitled *Deutsche Physik* (German Physics) (1936), Professor Lenard said: "Jewish physics is a deception *(ein Trugbild).*"[28] Later he said that "Jewish physics," represented by

> the pure-blooded Jew Albert Einstein, . . . no longer has a leg to stand on. Nor was it intended to be true. In contrast to the desire for truth by the Aryan scientist, the Jew lacks to a striking degree any comprehension of truth.[29]

In a lecture at Munich, in 1937, Lenard spoke of "the gradual development of a Jewish natural science . . . which . . . tried to deprive Aryan physics of its foundations."[30] In 1938, in the *Journal for General Science,* he attacked "the influence of the Jews on the development of natural science" and stated that "Einstein's theory of relativity offers us the clearest example of a dogmatic Jewish type of theory."[31]

One could multiply illustrations of this kind endlessly, and Professor Philipp Frank offers us many in his book on Einstein, including this *obiter dictum* from the same *Zeitschrift für die gesamte Naturwissenschaft:*

> The Jew would not be himself if the characteristic feature of his attitude, just as everywhere else in science, were not the disintegration and destruction of Aryan construction.[32]

[27]Ibid., pp. 161–62.

[28]Kneller, George Frederick, *The Educational Philosophy of National Socialism,* New Haven: Yale University Press, 1941, p. 251, note 14.

[29]Frank, Philipp, op. cit., p. 252.

[30]Ibid.

[31]Ibid., p. 253. Cf. *Time* magazine, op. cit., above, note 4, p. 78: "Einstein and his 'Jewish physics' became the object of increasingly scurrilous denunciations. Fellow German scientists turned their backs on him—with the exception of a few men like [Max] Planck."

[32]Frank, Philipp, p. 255. As Frank points out, the history of Nazi attitudes to relativity theory is not without its ironic and amusing elements. In the 1920s there were some among Nazi and pro-Nazi political and scientific writers who tried to appropriate relativity to Nazi doctrine by characterizing it as representative of German Idealism and

Aryan science is "manifest truth." Einstein's theories are "error," as is self-evident from their non-Aryan, Jewish, source. Such "error" arose as part of the Jewish conspiracy to destroy the "manifest truth" of pure Aryan science, and must be banished. Here the fate of intellectual freedom for error in the progression of science, and of the socio-political freedom of a religio-cultural minority, thus became joined by virtue of the unified barbaric attack against both.

IV. Socio-Political Freedom

When the freedom for error is destroyed, the paradoxical consequence is that a particular kind of error becomes enthroned and *the freedom for truth* is destroyed, as was the case in Nazi Germany and as has been shown in the U.S.S.R. For the suppression of freedom for error is always enforced, as should be clear by now, ostensibly in the interest of protecting the freedom for a claimed higher truth, a manifest truth. Thus, typically, Hitler and his Nazi Party continued to preach Freedom. However, since their foremost principle was the primacy of politics over all fields of human life and thought, Freedom, *true Freedom,* was to be safeguarded for the State alone, with its Aryan philosophy and institutions. The American philosopher, George Santayana, detected this ingredient in German thought even before Hitler. In a 1915 article, later reprinted (1922) in his volume *Soliloquies in England,* Santayana observed:

> Freedom in the mouth of German philosophy has a very special meaning. It does not refer to any possibility of choice nor any private initiative. German freedom is like the freedom of the angels in heaven who see the face of God and cannot sin. It lies in such a deep understanding of what is actually established that you would not have it otherwise. . . . You are merged by sympathy with your work, your country, and the universe. . . . Your compulsory service then becomes perfect freedom. So that, paradoxical as it may seem, it is only when you conform that you are free, while if you rebel and secede you become a slave.[33]

thus as a useful weapon of National Socialism against materialist philosophy. Later, relativity theory was condemned, on the one hand, as indicative of the alleged preference by Jews for *theoretical deliberations* in contrast with the striving by Aryan Germans for concrete action. On the other hand, Nazi spokesmen most frequently branded Einstein's theories as materialistic and therefore linked with Marxism. (Cf. Frank, pp. 250–51 and 253.)

[33]Santayana, George, *Soliloquies in England,* New York: Charles Scribner's Sons, 1922, pp. 169–70. (Quoted by Frank, op. cit., p. 227.)

The dependence of this doctrine on Hegel's metaphysics and philosophy of history will be obvious to anyone familiar with Hegelian doctrine.[34] The practical application of this doctrine of Freedom to German universities under Nazism was explicated unabashedly by E. Kriek, leader in German pedagogy of the Nazi period:

> It is not science that must be restricted, but rather the scientific investigators and teachers; only scientifically talented men who have pledged their entire personality to the nation, to the racial conception of the world, and to the German mission, will teach and carry on research in German universities.[35]

The same paradoxical consequence has been and continues to be manifested in the Soviet Union. In the years 1937–1964, a Soviet biologist, Trofim D. Lysenko, propounded and, with Stalin's reign of terror supporting him, enforced his phony brand of "Marxist" genetics, with the result that

> The story of Soviet genetics [during this period] is perhaps the most bizarre chapter in the history of modern science . . . it was completely incomprehensible that [the U.S.S.R.] could have entrusted its fundamental agricultural resources to exploitation by an obvious quack.[36]

Lysenko's Marxist-Stalinist genetics thus became the "manifest truth." As a consequence, truth and falsity in Soviet genetics ceased to be determined by critical examination of Lysenko's theory, by experiment, or by confirmation or refutation, but rather by Politburo edicts. Was there any freedom left for competent Soviet geneticists to be *right* under Lysenko's suppression of freedom of inquiry for those who, in his view, were guilty of *error?* The answer is writ large in the tortured annals of Soviet genetics in the Lysenko era, and the conclusion is frighteningly clear. *If there is no freedom for error, the consequence is that there is no freedom for truth.* Under the condition of the banishment of freedom for error, the truth or falsity of scientific theories is determined not through the immanent scientific process of search, experimentation, and refutation or confirmation. Truth and error are

[34]Hegel, George Wilhelm Friedrich, *Reason in History: A General Introduction to the Philosophy of History,* translated by Robert S. Hartman, New York: Liberal Arts Press, 1953, pp. 50–53: "Law, morality, the State, and they alone, are the positive reality and satisfaction of freedom. The caprice of the individual is not freedom. . . . Only the will that obeys the law is free, for it obeys the law and, being in itself, is free."

[35]Frank, Philipp, op. cit., p. 228.

[36]Lerner, I. Michael, in the Foreword to *The Rise and Fall of T. D. Lysenko,* by Zhores A. Medvedev (translated by I. Michael Lerner), New York: Columbia University Press, 1969, p. v.

determined by the ruling political powers and their brand of "manifest truth." The *only* freedom that then remains is the freedom for that error which has become canonized and enthroned by those in power, and freedom for truth is destroyed.

Lest anyone think that the scandalous Lysenko episode is a thing of the past, as was suggested by Zhores A. Medvedev at the conclusion of his book, *The Rise and Fall of T. D. Lysenko,*[37] a sobering report by the Moscow correspondent of *The Washington Post,* dated December 14, 1977, stated that "One year after his death, Lysenko's theories are invoked here by Soviet scientists. . . . This is a stunning development."[38] But more to the point in relation to the tender treatment of Einstein's Relativity Theory by the Nazis and their "scientific lackeys" is another *Washington Post* report out of Moscow, this one dated March 10, 1979, which, in part, reads as follows:

> Fresh and virulent attacks on Jewish mathematicians in the Soviet Union pose a serious threat to the exchange agreements in science and technology. . . . In the last year, Jewish mathematicians have been forbidden to publish articles and travel abroad to attend international meetings. Jewish students have been barred from universities. . . . We even hear reports . . . that histories of Soviet mathematics are being rewritten to exclude the accomplishments of Jews. . . . One of the two mathematicians allegedly suppressing Jews is identified as L. S. Pontryagin, who . . . directs the editorial Board that decides whose articles get published and edits the journal *Matematicheski Sbornik.*
>
> Pontryagin and a few rabid colleagues of his apparently feel that Jews don't represent Soviet mathematics. . . . These people somehow impute a possible disloyalty of Jews who want to emigrate and see a conflict between this desire and the development of a "true native Soviet mathematics."[39]

Shades of "pure Aryan physics"!

V. Freedom of Religion

We may now conclude this discourse with some reflections on Einstein and religious and cultural freedom, and on Einstein the Jew. That socio-political freedom is a necessary condition for the existence of freedom of the intellect and of scientific inquiry, is axiomatic, and Einstein's many utterances on this subject are so well known that we

[37]Ibid., p. 253.

[38]*The Washington Post,* December 14, 1977, p. A25.

[39]O'Toole, Thomas, *The Washington Post,* March 10, 1979, p. A11.

may limit ourselves to the one quoted earlier in this essay. His refusal to return to Germany following Hitler's accession to power and his publicly demonstrative renunciation of his German citizenship were among his ways of translating his beliefs into actions. His embrace of American citizenship was part of his commitment to political freedom and an exemplification of the ancient apothegm, "*ubi libertas, ibi patria*" ("where there is liberty, there is my homeland"). However, it is of surpassing importance to emphasize that, for Einstein, the imperative need for the Freedom of Inquiry had a religious significance as well. For he saw in that freedom the indispensable safeguard for the experience of religious awe and exaltation that give stimulus to the scientific quest. Einstein often voiced his *amazement* at the rational aspects of the physical universe, and this *rational* amazement, co-mingled with emotional admiration, constituted for him one of the most powerful ingredients in authentic religion. Here too it is worth repeating his own words:

> The most beautiful and most profound emotion we can experience is the sensation of the mystical. It is the sower of all true science. He to whom this emotion is a stranger, who can no longer wonder and stand rapt in awe, is as good as dead. To know that what is impenetrable to us really exists, manifesting itself as the highest wisdom and the most radiant beauty which our dull faculties can comprehend only in their primitive forms—this knowledge, this feeling, is at the center of true religiousness.[40]

Einstein often said that he was not religious in the sense of adherence to observances and rituals. His was what he called "cosmic religion." However, for his entire life following his full rediscovery of himself as a Jew, under the impact of the virulent anti-Semitism he observed and felt in Berlin after his return in 1914, Einstein displayed a deep loyalty to, and was continually involved in, activity on behalf of Jewish communities in need, and later in vigorous support of the Zionist program to establish a reborn Jewish state in the Holy Land for the restoration of freedom, dignity, and justice to the Jewish peo-

[40]Quoted by Philipp Frank, op. cit., p. 284, and by Barnett, Lincoln, *The Universe and Dr. Einstein*, New York: Mentor Books, The New American Library, 1952, p. 117. Barnett also quotes the following:

> My religion consists of a humble admiration of the illimitable superior spirit who reveals himself in the slight details we are able to perceive with our frail and feeble minds. That deeply emotional conviction of the presence of a superior reasoning power, which is revealed in the incomprehensible universe, forms my idea of God.

One hears here echoes of Psalm 104.

ple.[41] I use the word "rediscovery" advisedly, because earlier in his life, in his early teens, Einstein had gone through a period of devout observance of the ritual practices of traditional Judaism. Moreover, during the two years of his professorship at the German university in Prague he was a member (though only nominally) of Prague's Jewish community, and maintained warm friendships with some of its leading intellectuals, such as Max Brod, Franz Kafka, and Hugo Bergman.

Though it was German anti-Semitism that shocked him into the rediscovery of his Jewishness, his involvements were motivated and reinforced by his discovery and conviction that Judaism had

> . . . united the Jews for thousands of years . . . [by the bond] of the democratic ideal of social justice, coupled with the ideal of mutual aid and tolerance among all men. Even the most ancient religious scriptures of the Jews are steeped in these social ideals. . . .The introduction of a weekly day of rest . . . [and] the unique accomplishments of the Jews in the field of philanthropy spring from the same source.[42]

In addition, he said, what tied him to Judaism is the high place it assigned in its hierarchy of values to the pursuit of learning and development of the mind, within a framework of intellectual freedom and liberty of conscience:

> [A] second characteristic trait of Jewish tradition is the high regard in which it holds every form of intellectual aspiration and spiritual effort. . . . [The extent of Jewish contributions in these fields is due to] the esteem in which intellectual accomplishment is held among the Jews . . . At the same time a strong critical spirit prevents blind obedience to any mortal authority.[43]

[41]"My relationship to the Jewish people," Einstein stated, "has become my strongest human bond, ever since I became fully aware of our precarious situation among the nations of the world." (Quoted in *Science News*, Washington, D.C., March 31, 1979, Vol. 115, No. 13, p. 213.) To Kurt Blumenfeld, the distinguished German Jewish leader in the two decades following World War I, Einstein explained his commitment to Zionism as follows:

> I am opposed to nationalism, but I am in favor of Zionism. Today I realized why. The man who has two arms and insists on proclaiming that he has a right arm is a chauvinist. But a man who lacks a right arm must do everything possible to find a substitute for it. As a human being I am therefore opposed to nationalism, but as a Jew I will support from this day the Jewish national aims of the Zionists. (Kurt Blumenfeld, "Albert Einstein," *Jewish Frontier*, New York, May 1955, p. 8.)

[42]Einstein, Albert, *Out of My Later Years*, op. cit., p. 249. In an address entitled "Our Debt to Zionism," given in 1938, Einstein stated:

> To be a Jew, after all, means first of all, to acknowledge and follow in practice those fundamentals in humaneness laid down in the Bible—fundamentals without which no sound and happy community of men can exist. (Ibid., p. 262.)

[43]Ibid., pp. 249–50.

It is remarkable with what profound insight Einstein, the physicist, who was not a scholar of Jewish thought and religion, understood the spirit and the ethos of Judaism, and how feelingly he was committed to them. It is in these very features of Judaism that Einstein perceived the explanation of 20th century anti-Semitism. It is only fitting to conclude by quoting his memorable words:

> . . . today . . . it is just *because* we are the people of the Book that we are persecuted. The aim is to annihilate not only ourselves, but to destroy, together with us, that spirit expressed in the Bible . . . which made possible the rise of civilization in Central and Northern Europe . . . [44]
>
> Hence the hatred of the Jews by those who have reason to shun popular enlightenment. More than anything else in the world, they fear the influence of men of intellectual independence. I see in this the essential cause for the savage hatred of Jews raging in present-day Germany. . . . The Nazi group sees the Jews as a nonassimilable element that cannot be driven into uncritical acceptance of dogma, and that therefore . . . threaten their authority because of its insistence on popular enlightenment of the masses.
>
> Proof that this conception goes to the heart of the matter is convincingly furnished by the solemn ceremony of the burning of the books staged by the Nazi regime . . .
>
> [this trend] seeks to base society exclusively upon authority, blind obedience, and coercion. . . . The adherents of this . . . trend are the enemies of the free groups and of education for independent thought. They are, moreover, the carriers of political anti-Semitism.[45]

[44]Ibid., p. 254.
[45]Ibid., p. 252–53.

8. *Freedom Versus Determinism in Psychotherapy*

I should like to review with you today some aspects of an old philosophical problem, the so-called problem of *freedom versus determinism,* but focusing today on this problem as it arises in the theory and practice of psychotherapy. In doing this I shall deal most often with *psychoanalysis,* as a kind of paradigm of psychotherapy, in the hope and belief that what is said here is indeed relevant to psychotherapy generically.

Permit me to begin by stating my conclusion. In propounding it, I do not presume to suggest that this conclusion is original, novel, revolutionary, or earth-shaking. I only suggest that it is true. My conclusion is that, so far as psychotherapy is concerned, the psychotherapeutic enterprise assumes, entails, is predicated upon, and knowingly proceeds on the basis of, two principles simultaneously: 1) psychic determinism and 2) psychic freedom.

1) The principle of *psychic determinism* referred to here is not a doctrine of cosmic, physical mechanistic determinism according to which every event is completely determined, and which claims that, given a knower with *exhaustive* knowledge of every aspect of the *state of the universe* at any given instant in time, the possessor of such exhaustive knowledge would be able to deduce and describe *exhaustively* the state of the universe at any other instant in time, whether 10,000 years earlier or 10,000 years later. Such an idea of determinism was described by Bertrand Russell as follows:

> . . . There are such invariable relations between different events at the same or different times that, given the state of the whole universe

Lecture given in the spring of 1981 before the Department of Psychiatry, School of Medicine, Georgetown University, and on December 1 of the same year at the weekly Scholars' Luncheon of the University's Kennedy Institute of Ethics.

> throughout any finite time, however short, every previous and subsequent event can theoretically be determined as a function of the given events during that time.[1]

I personally do not believe in this kind of determinism, and I do not think that anyone *really* believes in it. The most cogent evidence for this contention is the fact that *no one* ever behaves like that kind of determinist, and those who claim to be that kind of determinist are in fact no exceptions to this generalization. The fact is that *no determinist* ever behaves like a *determinist.*

Underlying all authentic psychotherapy is that principle of *psychic determinism* which says that all human *actions* are inherently and in principle *explicable;* that all human *actions* have *causes,* i.e., *psychic causes,* such as *wishes, desires, purposes, motives, intentions, goals.* Some of these *psychic causes* are *conscious;* many of these *psychic causes* are *unconscious;* many more are unconscious than was suspected before the seminal discoveries made by Sigmund Freud. The *psychic causes* are typically *teleological* in character, and there is no contradiction here between *teleology* and *psychic determinism;* indeed they are entirely compatible. It is part of the enterprise of psychotherapy to help the patient to *discover* the *conscious* psychic causes of his actions and problems, and to help him *uncover,* to the extent to which it is possible, the *unconscious* psychic causes of his actions. The built-in assumption is that there are no uncaused human actions; that even the most trivial human actions have explanations in terms of *psychic causes* that must be sought and, if possible, found.

2) The second principle that underlies psychotherapy, and that functions simultaneously, and in a relation of symbiosis with the first, is the principle of *psychic freedom.* This notion of *psychic freedom,* and the doctrine of *free will,* do not necessarily imply a world of *pure chance,* of *ultimate caprice,* a world in which there flow about, in great abundance, a multiplicity of uncaused events, uncaused causes, uncaused human actions. In such a world, *human actions,* i.e., purposive, intentional, goal-directed actions, could not be sustained, and would be inconceivable.

The psychic freedom that is assumed and affirmed in the psychotherapeutic enterprise is typically the freedom *that a person may be capable of achieving* in his struggle against the *enslavement,* the *bondage* to *unconscious psychic causes* in which a person perennially finds himself. It is not easy to overcome the tyranny of the multiplicity of such unconscious motives, drives, obsessions, compulsions that dominate so

[1]Russell, Bertrand. "On the Notion of Cause, with Applications to the Free-Will Problem." In *Our Knowledge of the External World.* New York: W.W. Norton & Co., 1929, p. 240.

much of our lives. Indeed, it is most *difficult* to achieve such liberation, and too often we are defeated in this struggle. Such victories as we do achieve, such liberation as we do attain, occur when the process of psychotherapy helps the patient—through its uncovering techniques—to achieve the discovery of and *conscious* awareness of the *causes*, the *psychic causes* out of our own past history, that explain our present actions and anxieties—and to the exercise of our *reflexive*, rational thought upon those causes. Stuart Hampshire calls this the patient's "*stepping back*,"[2] and looking at himself and at the previously *unconscious* causes of his present problem, and through his newly achieved knowledge of those causes, hopefully being enabled to triumph over them and be liberated from their tyranny. Such hoped-for achievement of freedom is a *necessary* assumption of, a principle that underlies, all psychotherapy, a principle without which psychotherapy could neither be nor be conceived.

It is both useful and interesting to look at these two seemingly contradictory principles in juxtaposition to the positions advocated by several recent psychologists and psychotherapists. A.A. Brill, a devout disciple of Freud's, asserted that "The rank and file of psychiatrists believe in '*absolute determinism*.'" This Brill held to be antithetical to "the belief of 'most persons' that 'they can do what they want and regardless of motives.'"[3] G. Berg declared that ". . . psychology . . . recognizes that a person's acts, like the acts of any organism or organ, are predetermined by heredity, development, and environment."[4]

In his book, *Crime and the Mind*, Walter Bromberg suggested that "Many psychiatrists feel that no man can really choose a course of conduct, because 'free choice' is determined by each individual's cultural and psychological background, his unconscious impulses, identifications, predetermined wishes and drives. . . . The traditional view of absolute free will cannot be supported clinically."[5]

In more aggressive manifesto-like tones, Charles Berg, a leading English Freudian, in his book *Deep Analysis*, admonishes his colleagues that "To achieve success the analyst must above all be *an analyst*, that is to say he must know positively that all human emotional reactions, all human judgments, and even reason itself, are but the tools of the unconscious; that such seemingly acute convictions which an intelligent person like this possesses are but the inevitable effects of causes which lie buried in the unconscious levels of his psyche."[6] Ernest

[2]See, for example, *Thought and Action*. New York: Viking Press, 1960, pp. 189–90; and *Freedom of the Individual*, 2nd edition. New York: Harper & Row, 1965, p. 80.

[3]Brill, A.A. *Psychoanalytic Psychiatry*. New York: Lehman, 1948, p. 87.

[4]Berg, G. *War in the Mind*. London: Macaulay, 1944, p. 36.

[5]Bromberg, Walter. *Crime and the Mind*. New York: Macmillan, 1965, p. 50.

[6]Berg, Charles. *Deep Analysis*. London: Allen & Unwin, 1946, p. 190.

Jones, psychoanalyst and Freud's biographer, also insists on determinism as the doctrine of psychoanalysis.[7]

However, interestingly enough, B.F. Skinner, the well-known behaviorist, in his book *Beyond Freedom and Dignity*, rebukes certain unnamed Freudians for "*assuring* their patients that they are free to choose among different courses of action and are in the long run the architects of their own destinies."[8]

At this point it becomes important to inquire, what does Freud himself say on this subject? Was Freud a determinist? There are numerous statements scattered throughout the corpus of Freud's work which, read uncritically, would seem to indicate that indeed Freud was a determinist. I choose only two as examples. In the *Psychopathology of Everyday Life* (1901), he said:

> Many persons argue against the assumption of an absolute psychic determinism by referring to an intense feeling of conviction that there is free will. This feeling of conviction exists, but is not incompatible with the belief in determinism.[9]

In the *General Introduction to Psychoanalysis* (1915–1917), Freud declared that ". . . there is within you a deeply rooted belief in psychic freedom and choice . . . this belief is quite unscientific, and . . . it must give ground before the claims of a determinism which governs even mental life."[10] However, the affirmative answer that seems to be indicated by these and other quotations, and that has been given countless times in the literature, requires careful clarification. Indeed, Freud was a determinist, if by determinism we mean that he believed psychological phenomena to be explicable in terms of causes. But Freud is talking about *psychological causation.* He propounded the theory that psychological events do have *causes;* that even psychological events such as dreams, lapses of memory, slips of the tongue, misplacing things, etc., are not to be dismissed as capricious, contingent, unpredictable, inexplicable and *uncaused* events. He believed that these events are decidedly not *uncaused* events. Such events *can be causally* explained through *psychological* causes and explanations. One of Freud's most important contributions was precisely the doctrine that these psychological events and episodes *can* be explained, that

[7]Jones, Ernest. "Free Will and Determinism." In *Essays in Psychoanalysis*, Volume II. New York: International Universities Press, 1964, Chapter VII, pp. 178–89.

[8]Skinner, B.F. *Beyond Freedom and Dignity*. New York: Knopf, 1971, pp. 20–21.

[9]Freud, Sigmund. *Psychopathology of Everyday Life*. Translated by A.A. Brill. In *The Basic Writings of Sigmund Freud*. New York: Modern Library Giants, 1938, p. 161.

[10]______ . *A General Introduction to Psychoanalysis*. New York: Garden City Publishing Company, 1938, p. 95.

they are not *uncaused* mysteries or bizarre occurrences, and that for the satisfactory explanation of such events one does not have to resort to *physical* or *psychological* or *material* causes. If this is what is meant by determinism, then Freud indeed was a *determinist.*

But, of course, this is *psychic determinism.* Unlike the traditional notion of a mechanistic, physical, universal determinism which seems to be incompatible with freedom, psychic determinism is not incompatible with it. And, as related to psychotherapy, and to the question whether a person can change himself with the help of therapy, Freud certainly espoused a doctrine of *freedom,* and to this I will return. It remains a source of perplexity that, given the aims of psychotherapy, so large a number of psychotherapists, and especially psychoanalysts, believe that psychoanalytic theory entails a belief in determinism and in the impossibility of a free choice. Perhaps their views on this matter are the product of their failure to make the distinction between these two senses of determinism.

It is perhaps worth noting that in recent years several philosophers have questioned the assumption of incompatibility between freedom and determinism; among them are A.J. Ayer, P.H. Nowell Smith, and R.E. Hobart. It is not true, they maintain, that no determined acts are free, or that if an act is free then it is not determined.[11] Indeed, it is Hobart's thesis, in a challenging essay entitled "Free Will as Involving Determinism and Inconceivable Without It,"[12] that if an act is free then it is determined. Ayer said that "from the fact that my action is causally determined . . . it does not necessarily follow that I am not free."[13] P.H. Nowell Smith's view is that

> I could not be free to choose what I do *unless* determinism is correct. . . . Freedom, so far from being incompatible with causality, implies it.[14]

The substance of their argument, as elaborated subtly and cogently by Hobart, is that in a so-called "free universe" without causation, *free human action* based on the agent's free decision would be impossible. In a non-causal universe in which all events, including human actions, would be undetermined, capricious, chancy, and unpredictable, those events which we call "human actions" could not properly be called by that name. Such events could not be intentional, purposive, goal-di-

[11]Berofsky, Bernard, editor. *Free Will and Determinism.* New York: Harper & Row, 1966, p. 53.

[12]Hobart, R.E. "Free Will as Involving Determinism and Inconceivable Without It." In *Mind,* XLIII, No. 169 (January, 1934), pp. 1–27.

[13]Ayer, Alfred J. "Freedom and Necessity." In *Philosophical Essays.* London: Macmillan & Co., 1954, pp. 271–84.

[14]Newell Smith, P.H. "Free Will and Moral Responsibility." In *Mind,* LVII, 1948, p. 46.

rected *actions,* because they would be events that *happened to the agent* rather than something the agent did *as agent.* To the extent to which actions are undetermined events in a universe of contra-causal freedom, to that extent they are a loss to human freedom.

> When a person does something, and means to do it, it is the action that *he wants to do,* caused and *determined by his desire,* and because there is causation, his free act can have consequences.

The free action of a person is not some capricious, chance, unpredictable intrusion into his self. It is rather the action of *this self,* this person, this character, in the expectation that the person's wishes and the act's intent will be fulfilled if they conform to the cause-effect relationships that characterize our universe. In a causeless universe of capricious, unpredictable events, free, *intentional human action* would be a meaningless idea, and the accomplishment of the goals of free actions would be impossible.

However, the attack on the doctrine of free will within the context of psychotherapy may be launched from another direction, from within the bastion of psychoanalytic theory itself. Among contemporary American philosophers who have criticized the theory and assumptions of the doctrine of free will, it was John Hospers, in a paper that has been widely reprinted, who systematically and cogently marshaled some of the evidence, based principally on psychoanalytic theory, for a radical skepticism about the availability to human beings of the necessary and sufficient conditions for free will. Hospers begins by directing our attention to unconscious processes:

> I want to mention . . . a factor that I think is of enormous importance and relevance: namely, unconscious motivation. There are many actions . . . for which human beings in general . . . are inclined to hold the doer responsible, and for which, I would say, he should not be held responsible. The deed may be planned, . . . nonetheless his behavior was brought about by unconscious conflicts developed in infancy, over which he has no control and of which . . . he does not even have knowledge. He may *think* he knows why he acted as he did, he may *think* he has conscious control over his actions, he may even *think* he is fully responsible for them; but he is not. (Emphasis in the original)[15]

Hospers then presents as additional illustrations several other varieties of unconscious motivations. From these he proceeds to his second

[15]Hospers, John. "What Means This Freedom." In *Determinism and Freedom in the Age of Modern Science,* edited by Sidney Hook. New York: New York University Press, 1958, p. 114.

point, namely, that each of us is "the product of causes in which his volition took no part." None of us, the "normal" person or the neurotic, is the author of his own character.

Irrespective of whether this character is a consequence of heredity or early environment, we cannot with justification *blame* the person who is unable to overcome the defects in his character any more than we can *praise* ourselves (or others) for the ability to overcome them. Whether one is the kind of person who can exert the effort and overcome these deficiencies—hereditary or environmental—is itself a product of heredity or of early environment. "We did not give ourselves this ability; and if we lack it we cannot be blamed for not having it."[16] Hospers continues:

> All this is well known to psychoanalysts. They can predict, from minimal cues that most of us don't notice, whether a person is going to turn out to be lucky or not. . . . as a physician (the psychoanalyst) can soon detect whether the patient is lucky or unlucky—and he knows that whichever it is, it *isn't the patient's fault.* (Emphasis in the original)[17]

This distillation of Hospers' skeptical scrutiny of the assumptions of psychic freedom helps bring into sharp focus the problem before us in the psychotherapeutic context. Since man's behavior is so overwhelmingly governed or dominated by unconscious and irrational or nonrational processes and motives, since emotions, fantasies, passions, and aberrations, the nature and causes of which are unknown to us, keep us in bondage for so much of our lives, is there anything in man's constitution through the exercise of which a person can liberate himself from this bondage and attain a measure of psychic freedom? Is there any methodology, or technique, or therapy by means of which a person can achieve control over and dominate his unconsciously and irrationally motivated passions, and become *a free agent* responsible for his own actions?[17a]

For a possible answer to *this* question we may turn to two seminal thinkers, closely linked in spite of a 250-year gap between them, namely, Sigmund Freud and Barukh Spinoza. It is of more than antiquarian interest that Freud and Spinoza, writing at different times, and launching their respective investigations from different historical and conceptual frames of reference, grappled with essentially the same problem. And it is of surpassing philosophical and psychological sig-

[16]Ibid., p. 126.

[17]Ibid.

[17a]Regarding the two sentences here which begin "Since man's behavior" and "Is there any methodology," compare Dr. Franck's essay entitled "Spinoza, Freud, and Hampshire on Psychic Freedom," earlier in this volume, p. 101. [Note by W. G.]

nificance that both converged upon what is essentially, in its paradigmatic structure, the same conclusion. The paradigm of their common conclusion, if we decide for the moment to ignore the differences and divergences between them, is that, ultimately, the only source and guarantee of the very limited portion of freedom from bondage to the passions that can be attained by man is in the exercise of *reason*, of man's fully conscious cognitive faculties, in the arduous pursuit and discovery of the *causes* of these passions; and in their modifications through one's rational, cognitive *reflection* upon them.

This does not imply that, in propounding this paradigm, either Spinoza or Freud indulges in or propagates the illusion that its employment always, or even often, leads to successful results. They decidedly do not. Indeed, the differences that appear discernible in their respective assessments of the likelihood of success are most important (but not to be dealt with here).[17b] However, a remarkable element to be noted in this paradigm of *human liberation* from obsessive emotions and passions, shared by these explorers of man as a thinking being, is that the paradigm revolves around the transcendently important fact of man's *reflexive thought*, of what Spinoza called *idea ideae.*[18]

But here again a caveat is in order. Reason as the antidote to the passions is far from foolproof, because of its own built-in limitations. Too often reason is impotent to deal with the passions because reason itself is subject to corruption by these passions, and often turns out to function in their service through the self-deceptive mechanism of rationalization. The differences in the degree to which Spinoza and Freud, respectively, recognize this limitation make an instructive study. Nonetheless, their recognition of these limitations notwithstanding, it is reason-cognitive, fully conscious, reflexive thought that is, in their view, man's only weapon for the conquest of his emotions and for his attainment of fragmentary psychic freedom.

Now, it goes without saying that the paradigm suggested is a simplification distilled out of the rich complexity of Spinoza's and Freud's works. It epitomizes the "ideal type construct," the "limiting case," for our understanding of the odyssey of a person from being passion-dominated to being guided freely by his/her own reason; or the painful, often tragic, obstacle-strewn pilgrimage of the individual from the stranglehold of the emotions to a rational understanding of their causes, and to the freedom to achieve their subsequent modification. Understandably, therefore, the formulation of the paradigm cannot but fail to reflect the person's resistances to the attainment of the aims

[17b]Dr. Franck dealt with these differences in the essay cited in footnote 17a. Regarding the passage here which begins "However, a remarkable element," compare that essay, this volume, p. 102. [Note by W. G.]

[18]Spinoza, Barukh. *Ethics*. Part II, Prop. 21, Scholium.

envisioned in it, the individual's frequent regressions and reversions to the tyranny of the emotions in the course of this process, and even following the successes—often partial and limited successes—in the struggle. Of necessity, the formulation of the paradigm also fails to convey the perpetual state of dynamic tension—between reason and the passions—that characterizes human life, according to the image of man painted by Spinoza and Freud.

It is worth noting parenthetically that the possible, though most often only partial, victories of reason over our unconscious and irrational impulses are of fundamental significance for Freud not only in his role of descriptive psychologist and explorer of the nature of man. They are also, for Freud the moralist, a moral desideratum, perhaps man's highest ethical goal, the attainment of which would be *impossible without a person's knowledge of, and reflexive thinking about, his unconscious motivations.*

The goals of psychoanalytic therapy involve man's reason, rationality, and reflexive thought in a role of crucial and essential importance. In short, its twin goals are: first, to lead the patient, through the uncovering psychoanalytic process, to a rational, cognitive knowledge and understanding of the real, previously repressed, causes and motivations of his neuroses, irrational feelings, emotions, attitudes, and behavior; second, through his use of his own reason, through his reflection upon these previously unconscious and now uncovered causes, to make possible his overcoming and controlling them and achieving complete or partial liberation from their tyranny. Thus, the goals of therapy and the goals of ethics coincide in Freudian doctrine.

Of course, for Freud, so far as psychic freedom is concerned, the goal is not mere knowledge or intellectual insight alone. For Spinoza, the goal was the successful exercise of "the power of the mind over the emotions." In Freudian terms, the goal is the self-understanding that is accompanied by emotional insight achieved by the process of "working through."[19]

If what has been sketched here is essentially accurate, then clearly this part of Freudian theory, and the very logic of psychoanalytic therapy, reflects our previously formulated paradigm of the individual's attainment of psychic freedom.

[19]Freud, Sigmund. *New Introductory Lectures on Psycho-Analysis.* New York: W.W. Norton & Co., 1933, pp. 104–05.

IV. Other Topics

9. *Psychology as a Science: Resolving the Idiographic-Nomothetic Controversy*

I[1]

"What is the subject matter of this science?" is a proper methodological question to ask about any empirical science. The late Gordon W. Allport asked this question about the science of psychology in a special way, and thereby raised the old philosophical problem whether scientific knowledge is knowledge of particulars or of universals. It was Allport's oft-repeated complaint that psychology has given its attention only to universals, has neglected to study the individual, and has therefore been guilty of a serious failure in the fulfillment of its scientific task. Allport's complaint and prescription are reflected in the following two brief quotations:

[1]The author is grateful to Susan B. Haack (University of Warwick) and Allan B. Wolter (Catholic University of America) for their critical reading of this paper, and for their helpful suggestions, a number of which have been incorporated in this revised version; to Kent Bach (San Francisco State) who served as commentator on this paper at the Ann Arbor meeting; and to Laurence B. McCullough (Kennedy Institute of Ethics) for making available to me his dissertation, *The Early Philosophy of Leibniz on Individuation* (unpublished), which was helpful in the clarification of some ideas. The author is especially grateful to Paul F. Secord for his criticisms of the original manuscript and his editorial suggestions.

Journal for the Theory of Social Behavior, vol. 12, March 1982, pp. 1–19. Presented, in briefer form, at the Sixth Annual Meeting of the Society for Philosophy and Psychology, University of Michigan, Ann Arbor, March 15, 1980. An adapted version appears in Jaan Valsiner (ed.), *The Individual Subject and Scientific Psychology* (New York: Plenum Press, 1986), pp. 17–36.

> . . . as long as psychology deals only with universals and not with particulars, it won't deal with much—least of all human personality.[2]

> . . . psychology will become more specific, i.e., better able to make predictions, when it has learned to evaluate single trends in all their intrinsic complexity, when it has learned how to tell what will happen to this child's I.Q. if we change his environment in a certain way.[3]

Accordingly, Allport distinguished between two methods in the study of man, for which he borrowed a pair of terms from Windelband.[4] He called the study of broad, general, universal laws, and the methods employed in this kind of study, *nomothetic,* from the Greek word νόμος—*nomos,* meaning *law,*[5] and the study of individuals and the methods employed by this kind of study, *idiographic,* from the Greek word ἴδιος—*idios,* meaning *one's own, private.*[6] Allport saw contemporary psychology caught in "the dilemma" between "science and uniqueness," and stated the "quandary which confronts us" as follows:

> The individual, whatever else he may be, is an internally consistent and unique organization of bodily and mental processes. But since he is unique, science finds him an embarrassment. Science, it is said, deals only with broad, preferably universal, laws. Thus science is a *nomothetic* discipline. Individuality cannot be studied by science, but only by history, art, or biography whose methods are not nomothetic (seeking universal laws), but *idiographic.* Even the medieval scholastics perceived the issue, and declared *scientia non est individuorum.*[7]

In further amplification of his version of the idiographic horn of the dilemma posed by him, Allport quoted from Kluckhohn and Murray[8] the observation that

[2]Gordon W. Allport, *Personality and Social Encounter* (Boston: Beacon Press, 1960), p. 146.

[3]Gordon W. Allport, "The Psychologist's Frame of Reference," *Psychological Bulletin* XXXVII (1940), p. 17.

[4]Gordon W. Allport, *The Use of Personal Documents in Psychological Science* (New York: Social Science Research Council, 1942), p. 53. Also *Pattern and Growth in Personality* (New York: Holt, Rinehart & Winston, 1961), p. 9, n. 9. Cf. Windelband, W., *An Introduction to Philosophy,* translated by J. McCabe (London: Unwin, 1921).

[5]Henry George Liddell and Robert Scott, *Greek-English Lexicon* (New York: Harper and Bros., 1875), p. 982: "Νόμος, . . . strictly *any thing assigned, distributed, apportioned,* that which one has in use or possession: hence,—I. *a usage, custom,* and *all that becomes law thereby, a law, ordinance,* Lat. *institutum.* . . . At Athens νόμα was the name given esp. to Solon's laws . . . "

[6]*Ibid.*, p. 665: "Ἴδιος . . . *own, one's own, private* . . . "

[7]Allport, *Pattern and Growth in Personality,* op. cit., pp. 8–9.

[8]Clyde Kluckhohn, Henry A. Murray, and David M. Schneider, eds., *Personality in Nature, Society, and Culture* (New York: Knopf, 1959), p. 53.

Every man is in certain respects
a. like all other men,
b. like some other men,
c. like no other man.[9]

It is with the respects in which every man is "like no other man" that this horn of Allport's dilemma is concerned. "Individuality," he insisted, "is a prime characteristic of human nature."[10] Moreover, Allport reminded us,

> The application of knowledge is always to the single case. . . . With all its weaknesses the case study remains the preferred tool of all clinicians, psychiatrists, personnel officers, and consulting psychologists. They find that the single case cannot be reduced to a colligation of scores. Here, then, we encounter a pragmatic reason why idiographic procedures must be admitted to psychological science: practitioners demand them.[11]

Allport would thus appear to have been asking for what might be called a science of individuals, of single cases, of unique beings, of insightful understandings of each individual personality. He pointed out that the social case worker takes an idiographic approach in his work with his client, and that no nomothetist can be helped by the general laws of psychology to know what his wife would like for a gift. "He can make this prediction correctly only by knowing his wife's particular pattern of interest and affection."[12]

In propounding this view Allport revived an old controversy, and evoked the expected spectrum of reactions. The "humanistic psychologists," the "individual psychologists," the "existential psychologists," and others like them, have welcomed Allport's call for an idiographic psychology with jubilation and uncritical acclaim. On the other hand, disdain and derision have come from the camps of positivism and of those with a physical science orientation. Still others, dismissing both the dogmatic "idiographicism" typified by Allport, and the doctrinaire "nomotheticism" of the "scientifically minded," have maintained that psychology as a science is and must be *both* idiographic and nomothetic, and that the putative dichotomy between the two methods is spurious.

This latter view is exemplified on the one hand by the noted psychologist Kurt Lewin, who said:

[9]Quoted by Allport in *Pattern and Growth in Personality*, p. 13.
[10]*Ibid.*, p. 21.
[11]Allport, *The Use of Personal Documents in Psychological Science*, op. cit., p. 58.
[12]*Ibid.*, p. 59.

> Even if all the laws of psychology were known, one could make a prediction about the behavior of a man only if in addition to the laws, the special nature of the particular situation were known. . . . [A task] of equal importance . . . involves the task of representing concrete situations in such a way that the actual event can be derived from [the laws] according to the principles which are given in the general laws.[13]

A more recent psychologist, Merle B. Turner, associating himself with Lewin's view in contrast to Allport's, observes:

> On closer inspection . . . it has appeared that the issues [between nomothetic and idiographic methods in psychology, as propounded by Allport] are not at all clearly drawn. Both idiographic and nomothetic methods of description and understanding are essential. One is to supplement the other.[14]

Manifestly, then, clarity about the relationships between idiographic and nomothetic methods in the science of psychology is not available in abundance. In the pages that follow I shall endeavor to contribute to the clarification of the issue by analyzing some of the contending views referred to above, and by exhibiting the inextricable interdependence between psychological inquiry when it is pursued in a theoretical-conceptual framework, and psychological inquiry when pursued within an operational matrix by psychologists as practitioners. Hopefully, additional light will thus be shed on what I may venture to call the idiographic-nomothetic symbiosis in psychology as a science.

II

In espousing his position Allport seems to have gone back, at least so far as knowledge of *man* is concerned, to a prevalent interpretation of Duns Scotus' doctrine of *haecceitas—thisness*. Duns Scotus (1265–1308) argued that, since the human intellect discovers that individual things are distinct, it follows that in each thing there must be some inherent, fundamental characteristic that differentiates it from all others. Individual things are distinguished from each other in *essence* as well as in existence. Thus, according to Richard McKeon on Scotus' ontology and theory of knowledge,

[13]Kurt Lewin, *Principles of Topological Psychology* (New York: McGraw-Hill, 1936), p. 11.
[14]Merle B. Turner, *Philosophy and the Science of Behavior* (New York: Appleton-Century-Crofts, 1967), p. 290.

> the principle of individuation is in the form, not merely in the matter; the essence of each individual contains the principle of contraction and limitation which restrains the universality of the species: the ultimate reality of the thing which is, contracts the specific form. This is the doctrine of *haecceity*, according to which the characteristics of individuation are not to be found in the quantity or in any other attribute of body . . . but in a formal distinction derived from the thing. . . . Duns Scotus . . . considered that which is as particular, and as known in each case by the haecceity peculiar to the particular thing.[15]

What Scotus himself tells us about the nature of *haecceitas*, in one of his texts, is as follows:

> . . . if you ask "what is this individual thing from which difference is taken? Is it not matter, or form, or the composite?" I reply that every quidditive entity, whether partial or total of any kind, is of itself indifferent, as quidditive entity, to this entity and that one, so that the quidditive entity it is [is] naturally prior to this entity as this. . . . And just as the composite insofar as it is a nature does not include the being by which it is "this," so neither does matter insofar as it is nature, nor form. Therefore, this being is not matter, nor form, nor the composite, insofar as any of these is a nature; but it is the ultimate reality of the being which is matter, or which is form, or the composite. . . .[16]

However, another commentator, Anne Fremantle, after quoting from D.J.B. Hawkins' *A Sketch of Medieval Philosophy*, appends her own view, which is typical of a widespread misapprehension of Scotus' doctrine of *haecceitas:*

> 'Hence, beyond all that in reality corresponds to universals . . . [Scotus] claims that things exhibit a principle of individuality, a *thisness*, which is not reducible to any other factor. The singular adds an entity over and above the entity of the universal. . . . ' We cannot understand anything until we have understood its *thisness*, and the difference between *thisness* and *thatness*. . . . In fact, for Duns Scotus, the individual is the only existing thing, and it is not the being of *being* but the being of the individual which is investigated by philosophy.[17]

Thus, to Scotus' claim that each individual thing has a *haecceitas* that could never be resolved into a class concept has been superadded a

[15]Richard McKeon, ed. and trans., *Selections from Medieval Philosophers*, Vol. II (New York: Scribners, 1930), pp. 305–306.

[16]Johannes Duns Scotus, *The Oxford Commentary on the Four Books of the Sentences*, Book II, Dist. III, p. 599, in Arthur Hyman and James J. Walsh, eds., *Philosophy in the Middle Ages* (Indianapolis, Ind., 1973), pp. 560–604.

[17]Anne Fremantle, *The Age of Belief: The Medieval Philosophers* (New York: Mentor Books, 1955), pp. 183–84.

second doctrine and (incorrectly, I shall argue later) ascribed to Scotus by some commentators, Anne Fremantle among them. This doctrine claims that we can have no understanding of anything until "we have understood its *thisness*," and that only *the individual* is to be studied in our pursuit of knowledge.

III

If this latter doctrine is what Allport meant, namely that since every individual has a *thisness* which cannot be resolved into a class concept, the study of man ought to concentrate on the study of these unique and irreducible individualities—and, as I shall try to show, it is not at all clear that *this* is what he meant—then he would have support from various quarters in current and recent thought. His strongest support may be found in the existentialist school. Allport pointed out that "at bottom the existentialist approach to man is urgently idiographic."[18] He sometimes sounded like an existentialist, as when he uttered such pronouncements as the following:

> . . . *the outstanding characteristic of man is his individuality.* He is a unique creation of the forces of nature.[19]

> Every person deviates in thousands of ways from the hypothetical average man. But his individuality is not the sum of these separate deviations.[20]

> Existence ultimately resides nowhere except in the individual's point of view.[21]

But some existentialists go much further than Allport. They deny the very possibility of science and of systematic thought in general. They appear to say that the only significant kind of human knowledge is the knower's intuitive, insightful apprehension of the individual thing, or the individual person in his pure individuality, in his utter uniqueness. All other knowledge-claims distort and tend to destroy both the knower and the known. Allport himself pointed out that for the existentialists,

[18]Allport, *Pattern and Growth in Personality*, op. cit., p. 557.
[19]*Ibid.*, p. 4.
[20]*Ibid.*, p. 7.
[21]*Ibid.*, p. 557.

> To force existence into a theoretical system is to destroy it. . . . Another's existence cannot be pinned down or communicated by devices; an extrascientific grasp is the best we can hope for.[22]

He made these comments in a footnote, in connection with his reference to a statement by Soren Kirkegaard, which is quoted by Jean Wahl. Kirkegaard stated:

> One might say that I am the moment of individuality, but I refuse to be a paragraph in a system.[23]

But Allport's ascription to the existentialists of the view that "an extrascientific grasp is the best we can hope for" is a misleading understatement which, under critical inspection, reveals that there is in fact a considerable gap between Allport's own views and those of the existentialists, in spite of his emphasis on idiographic knowledge and methods. The existentialist would insist that, for authentic knowledge, a direct, intuitive, "extrascientific grasp" of the other person's concrete uniqueness and individuality is the epistemological ideal and goal we *should* hope for and strive for, and that scientific knowledge of generalizations, abstractions, laws, etc., is only a barrier to such authentic knowledge. On the other hand, Allport's emphasis on idiographic knowledge did not lead him to any rejection of science. At most it resulted in some confusion on his part about the differences between these two kinds of knowledge and the relationships between them, as will become clear in the ensuing discussion. Allport was not without some awareness of the distance between his and the existentialists' views. He pointed out that the existentialist approach to man

> as yet . . . offers no special methods for representing the unique structure of persons. . . . the movement has not yet evolved genuinely novel methods for the representation of individuality.[24]

However, in a footnote to this passage, Allport acknowledged, with a kind of embarrassed self-consciousness, that the existentialists may find his desire for such "methods and representation" quite uncongenial:

[22]*Ibid.*, n. 6.

[23]Jean Wahl, *A Short History of Existentialism*, trans. Forrest Williams and Stanley Maron (New York: Philosophical Library, 1949), p. 4. Quoted in *Pattern and Growth in Personality*, op. cit., p. 557, n. 6 (Allport's footnote gives the wrong page number in the reference to Wahl's book, and the quote from Kirkegaard contains a minor inaccuracy).

[24]Allport, *Pattern and Growth in Personality*, op. cit., p. 557.

> Existentialist writers may dispute this implied criticism. They may say that it is not the purpose of existential analysis to become objective and scientific. To force existence into a system is to destroy it.[25]

For, unlike Allport even when he urged the pursuit of idiographic knowledge, some existentialists seem to be categorical in their rejection of scientific knowledge. This may be seen unequivocally in the epistemology imbedded in Martin Buber's distinction between the *I-Thou* and the *I-It* relationship. Maurice S. Friedman's exposition of Buber's theory of knowledge helps throw into bold relief the existentialist rejection of science, and its claim that the direct, intimate, intuitive I-Thou bond with the concrete particular yields the only real knowledge.[26] In Buber's epistemology, Friedman tells us,

> . . . the philosophical anthropologist . . . must discover the essence of man not as a scientific observer . . .
>
> . . . science investigates man not as a whole but in selective aspects . . . Scientific method is man's most highly perfected development of the I-It, or subject-object, way of knowing. . . . Just for these reasons scientific method is not qualified to discover the essence of man. It can compare men with each other and man with animals . . . This scale . . . can be of aid . . . but not in discovering the uniqueness of man as man.
>
> . . . It is, in fact, only the knowing of the I-Thou relation which makes possible the conception of the wholeness of man.[27]

IV

Allport did not reject the generalized knowledge which comes to us from science and scientific method, though other writers, not only existentialists, who are allied with Allport in the emphasis on idiographic knowledge, are either on the threshold of such rejection, or are deeply enmeshed in it. For example, Adlerian adherents of the school of "Individual Psychology" seem to be implying such a rejection in descriptions like the following:

> Adler's "Individual Psychology would be the idiographic science par excellence."
>
> . . . Adler was not satisfied with probabilities; he wanted a psychological theory which would be adequate for each individual case, the excep-

[25] *Ibid.*, n. 6.

[26] Maurice S. Friedman, *Martin Buber: The Life of Dialogue* (Chicago: University of Chicago Press, 1955), p. 161.

[27] *Ibid.*, pp. 172–73.

> tions as well as the rule. What he aimed at was a truly idiographic psychology . . . [28]

And A.H. Maslow, in his cavalier, swashbuckling manner, announced that

> American psychologists have listened to Allport's call for an idiographic psychology but have not done much about it. Not even the clinical psychologists have. We now have an added push from the phenomenologists and existentialists in this direction, one that will be very hard to resist, indeed, I think, theoretically impossible to resist. If the study of the uniqueness of the individual does not fit into what we know of science, then so much the worse for the conception of science. It, too, will have to endure re-creation.[29]

A clear warning against this extreme idiographic anti-scientism which, paradoxically, some psychologists and other social scientists have wished to insinuate into the social sciences, comes from the pen of Alfred Schutz, a keen student of the methodology of the social sciences:

> It has been maintained that the social sciences are idiographic, characterized by individualizing conceptualization and seeking singular assertory propositions. . . . Some proponents of the [above view] . . . were inclined to identify the methodological situation in one particular social science with the method of the social sciences in general. Because history has to deal with unique and non-recurrent events, it was contended that all social sciences are restricted to singular assertory propositions.[30]

Arguing by analogy, the idiographic anti-scientists contend (and sometimes Allport appears to have contended) that because psychotherapy, social casework, etc., have to deal with the unique and (in many respects) non-recurrent individual person, psychology must work toward singular assertory propositions. That the history of the individual case is of crucial importance for the work of the psychotherapist, case worker, or guidance counsellor, is of course axiomatic. In psychoanalysis in particular, the unique history of the patient is of the

[28]H.L. Ansbacher, "Causality and Indeterminism According to Alfred Adler and Some Current American Personality Theories," *Essays in Individual Psychology*, ed. Kurt A. Adler and Danica Deutsch (New York: Grove Press, 1959), pp. 34, 29.

[29]Abraham H. Maslow, "Existential Psychology: What's In It For Us," *Existential Psychology*, ed. Rollo May (New York: Random House, 1961), p. 56.

[30]Alfred Schutz, "Concept and Theory Formation in the Social Sciences," *Philosophy and the Social Sciences: A Reader*, ed. Maurice Natanson (New York: Random House, 1963), p. 232.

greatest importance. This was shown by Hans Meyerhoff in an interesting paper in which he charted the large areas of overlap between the disciplines of psychoanalysis and history, and in which he made the keen observation that ". . . psychoanalysis 'works' only insofar as we reconstruct the history of the individual case."[31]

Thus, for certain purposes, the direct, idiographic knowledge of the unique, non-recurrent individual person, the person's case history, or the I-Thou insight and *Einfühlung* that take place between close friends, lovers, husband and wife, therapist and patient, are irreplaceable. Moreover, though the existentialists are profoundly wrong in assuming or implying that this kind of idiographic, I-Thou knowledge of individual persons is all the knowledge we need, and that it can somehow constitute a knowledge of *man,* it also seems clear that the generalized, nomothetic knowledge of man through the science of psychology can never reach or exhaust the rich uniqueness and individuality of the person. The existentialists are profoundly right in insisting that a kind of knowledge other than the generalizations of the science of psychology is needed for the "knowledge from within" of the unique individual person. However, by the same token, one has to respond to Allport that this knowledge of the full uniqueness of the individual person "from within" is by itself uncodifiable into *a science of psychology*. This has to be said, because Allport appears to have been confused about aspects of the distinction between idiographic and nomothetic knowledge, and therefore, in the final analysis, his point is unclear.

As was noted above, Allport neither denied nor objected to "the proposition that psychology seeks general laws."[32] His insistence that psychology must deal with individuals was based, as was pointed out earlier, on two considerations, one substantive, the other methodological. The substantive point is his belief in "the real possibility that no two lives are alike in their motivational processes."[33] The methodological point is that even abstract, general, nomothetic science can never escape the individual, since its findings must be applied to the individual object:

> The application of knowledge is always to the single case. We apply the science of engineering only in building particular conduits or bridges. In the human realm we have to particularize our nomothetic knowledge before it is of any value. . . .[34]

[31]Hans Meyerhoff, "On Psychoanalysis as History," *Psychoanalysis and the Psychoanalytic Review,* Vol. 49, No. 2 (Summer, 1962), p. 12.

[32]Allport, *Pattern and Growth in Personality,* op. cit., p. 572.

[33]Allport, *The Use of Personal Documents in Psychological Science,* op. cit., p. 57.

[34]*Ibid.,* p. 58.

> No general principles can ever be applied except to concrete and particular objects. The individual case stands at the gateway and terminus of generalized knowledge.[35]

So far, nothing in these passages suggests any departure from the assumptions and procedures of the sciences generally, including the physical sciences. However, Allport appears to have believed that he was pointing to psychology's need for a departure from the nomothetic procedures of science, when he directed our attention to the fact that

> general laws of human behaviour known to us are altered and sometimes negated by the idiographic knowledge available to us concerning the personality we are studying.[36]

But this is also true of the application of the science of engineering to bridge building. If, upon idiographic examination, a fault is discovered in a beam of structural steel, or some other significant deviation from the required general character of the other beams, the beam is discarded. Or if, as happened a number of years ago, a wind of unusually great force blew down a great suspension bridge, and it was concluded that the bridge's "rigidity" was responsible for the occurrence, the idiographic knowledge about *that* bridge led to the altering of the general laws of bridge building so that future bridges were to be built with less "rigidity" and more "elasticity." Similarly, in automobiles designed in accordance with nomothetic principles defects show up when individual cars are driven by their buyers, and the car design then has to be changed in conformity with revised nomothetic principles of automotive design. New, nomothetically designed airplanes are produced, a crash of an individual plane occurs, and a revised design is substituted in accordance with revised nomothetic principles of aerodynamics. This, therefore, cannot be the point in Allport's insistence that psychology must depart from the nomothetic model of science and deal idiographically with individuals.

The confusion on this point, so often present in Allport's writing, and carried to a thoughtless extreme by some of the existentialists, Adlerians, and Maslow's "humanistic" psychologists, is in part a result of the telescoping of two contentions that need to be separated out. First, is the contention that psychology should be concerned with the individual case, with differences between individuals, etc., which is certainly arguable, and which seems to be what essentially Allport was intent on saying. But the second contention is that *nothing general*

[35] *Ibid.*, p. 150.
[36] *Ibid.*, p. 58.

can be said about individuals and individual differences, a contention that is not plausible, and that in fact was *not* what Allport meant, though others (e.g., Maslow) attributed this to him.

A similar correction has to be made in understanding Duns Scotus' doctrine of *haecceitas.* Scotus did indeed insist, for metaphysical reasons, that each individual thing could be completely described only if we could know its haecceity intellectually. However, the need for haecceity was, in Scotist doctrine, "a logical one." An individual's *haecceitas* is known only to God, and "can be known by man only in a future life."[37] Scotus did not believe that we could even conceptually grasp any individual's unique haecceity, or know it by acquaintance intellectually. We only know *about it* logically, *by description,* as it were. Nor did Scotus think that we could have a *science* of the individual according to his haecceity. Our conceptual knowledge is of the universal. We arrive at an intellectual awareness of individuals by a combination of our sense knowledge and intellectual knowledge. So far as the conditions for scientific knowledge are concerned, Scotus stressed repeatedly that *"scientia est universalium"* ("science is of the universal").

And finally, there is an instructive lesson in the science of astronomy that illustrates the intersection in science of concern with individuals and concern with generalizations and classes. Astronomy is a *physical* science, but it certainly makes claims about *particulars,* the sun, the moon, that planet, or this star, and propounds "singular assertory propositions" about them. But these singular assertory propositions function within a matrix of generalizations about physical objects, their motion, inertia, acceleration, gravitation, speed of light, radiation, mass, energy, chemical interactions and their consequences, etc., etc.

V

The point that Allport seems to have been getting at is something different from the denial that there can be generalizations about individuals, and this *is* a point about psychology. Each individual human being is unique. The individual person is "a system of patterned uniqueness." But it is also a fact, said Allport, that "science likes universals and not particulars."[38] This, for Allport, seemed to present a problem. Let us look at the problem as stated in Allport's own words:

[37]Wolter, Allan B., article on John Duns Scotus, *Encyclopedia of Philosophy,* Paul Edwards, Editor in Chief (New York: Macmillan Publishing Co., 1967), pp. 427–436 (these quotes, pp. 431–32).

[38]Allport, *Pattern and Growth in Personality,* op. cit., p. 9.

> . . . personality itself is a universal phenomenon though it is found only in individual forms. Since it is a universal phenomenon science must study it; but it cannot study it correctly unless it looks into the individuality of patterning! Such is the dilemma.[39]

It is the responsibility of psychology, according to Allport, to investigate "how uniqueness occurs," to study "those processes that bring about uniqueness."[40] Accordingly,

> The reason conventional science is baffled is that it cannot see how the internal organization of the particular can fit into its nomothetic search for general laws.[41]

But Allport strangely failed to see that the investigation of the processes that bring about uniqueness, the quest for the "laws that tell us how uniqueness occurs," is ultimately a *nomothetic* enterprise, the successful pursuit of which will give us *abstract, general knowledge* about how these individual systems of patterned uniqueness come about, rather than knowledge of the idiographic kind (though of course much idiographic investigation has to take place in order to lead to the nomothetic goal of formulating the laws of how uniqueness comes about, but this is true in varying degrees of all empirical investigations). The nomothetic character of this part of Allport's quest was betrayed in his own words, when he said that he had shown "that a general law may be a law that tells us how uniqueness comes about,"[42] or that he had "drawn special attention to those laws and principles that tell how uniqueness comes about."[43]

What remain, therefore, out of Allport's advocacy of the use of idiographic methods in the study of man, are two other contentions:

(a) that "the personal patterns of individuality are unique,"[44] i.e., that each individual person is unique; and
(b) that "the behavior of every individual is lawful in its own right,"[45] that " . . . each personality is a law unto itself. . . . The course of each life is a lawful event, even though it is unlike all others of its class. Lawfulness does not depend upon frequency nor upon

[39]*Ibid.*
[40]*Ibid.*, p. 10.
[41]*Ibid.*
[42]Allport, *Personality: A Psychological Interpretation* (New York: Henry Holt & Co., 1937), p. 558.
[43]Allport, *Pattern and Growth in Personality*, op. cit., p. 572.
[44]*Ibid.*, p. 10.
[45]*Ibid.*

uniformity, but upon necessity. There is a necessary patterning in each life . . ."[46]

VI

Now, before getting on with the main argument of this section, one feels constrained to digress, and inquire what Allport meant by the claim that the behavior of every individual is *lawful* in its own right; that each personality is a *law unto itself;* that the course of each life is *a lawful event;* that this *lawfulness depends upon necessity;* and that there is a *necessary patterning* in each life. There is no trouble with the *obvious* meanings of this claim, which Allport makes clear, namely,

(a) that there is a consistency, a predictability, even a necessity in the behavior patterns of each individual,
(b) that the better you know an individual person, i.e., the more you have studied or experienced the person, the more accurately you will be able to predict that person's behavior.

However, the less obvious and more knotty problem, namely, what are the causal explanations of this consistency and lawfulness, Allport did not probe. He disposed of this problem by brief, almost casual, and dogmatic references to some concepts out of the writings of Aristotle, St. Thomas Aquinas, Spinoza, and Leibniz.

When a body of phenomena is said to display lawful behavior, it is natural to seek explanations for this, to ask what the causes are for this lawful behavior. To the question as to what the causes are for the lawfulness of the behavior of each person, Allport would of course have rejected the behaviorist attempt to give explanations exclusively in terms of physiological causes such as drives and tensions, and of the "law of effect" that refers to reward-and-punishment conditioning. He would also reject the Freudian answer that would explain the lawfulness of each person's behavior in terms of such psychological causation as early childhood experiences, the Oedipal phase, toilet training, etc.

What Allport seems to have suggested is the rather vague theory that there is a kind of *immanent* purposive force within each person that explains the person's lawful, consistent behavior. He invoked Aristotle's doctrines of *orexis* (ὄρεξις) and *entelechy* (ἐντελέχεια), Aquinas' doctrine of *intention*, Spinoza's concept of *conatus*, and Leibniz's notion

[46] Allport, *Personality*, loc. cit.

of the intellect as the source of its own ideas; and his own notion of the person as the source of his own acts. This seems to be a doctrine of immanence with respect to the behavior of the discrete individual which would make of each person a *causa sui*. Such a doctrine is at least dubious, and would require considerable critical scrutiny.

VII

To return now to the main argument, it is difficult to understand why the two contentions mentioned above, namely, that each person is unique, and that his behavior is lawful, require additional idiographic knowledge of individuals. These contentions are themselves generalizations, general laws, and therefore by definition nomothetic in character. Either these two generalizations have been reasonably well established on the basis of empirical evidence, in which case no additional idiographic evidence is needed for their support (except in the sense that the evidence for empirical generalizations of this type is never complete, and the generalization or law or theory always retains the character of a "conjecture"[47]). Or, if the generalizations have not been established well enough, then additional idiographic evidence for their support has to be sought; *but the objective of such a quest would be a nomothetic one, i.e., the establishment of a general law,* and would not differ essentially from the procedures of other scientific investigations. On the other hand, if the therapist, or social case worker, or personnel director needs for his special purposes genuinely idiographic knowledge about *this or that person,* the acquisition of this knowledge would not require extensive idiographic studies of other individuals. Allport himself understood this, as we can see in his assertion that

> We do not need to understand every life in order to discover the lawful regularities in one life. If you have an intimate friend, you may know very well why he behaves as he does . . . because you know the lawful regularities in his life.[48]

Let us, however, further examine Allport's emphasis, and the emphasis of others, on the need for "an idiographic psychology" by making the extreme assumption that, pursuant to this goal, every human being on earth were to be subjected to the suggested idio-

[47]See Karl R. Popper, *Conjectures and Refutations* (New York: Basic Books, 1962), pp. 33–66.

[48]Allport, *Pattern and Growth in Personality,* op. cit., p. 10.

graphic analysis; what kind of knowledge would this hypothetical undertaking yield, and to what uses could it be put? What, as a result of this undertaking, would the science of psychology get that it now does not have? What would the results of this undertaking contribute toward the three contentions stressed by Allport, namely, that the personal patterns of individuality are unique; that the behavior of every individual is lawful in its own right; and that psychology must discover the laws of how uniqueness comes about?

First we must note that since, *ex hypothesi*, every human being on earth would be studied, we would have an instance of what the logic textbooks call "perfect induction," or "complete induction." It would then seem that, if the idiographic studies gave proper attention to properly selected variables, the consolidated results should give us complete and certain knowledge of the laws of how uniqueness comes about. However, as was pointed out above, this would be essentially nomothetic knowledge, knowledge of general, abstract laws of certain aspects of human nature, abstracted from the totality of each of the individual human beings. Moreover, there is no reason to suppose that, for the discovery of the laws of how uniqueness comes about, a study of *all* members of the class of human beings is needed, and that reasonably well-established laws could not be arrived at on the basis of studies of *a sample* of the class. Indeed, if only "perfect induction" could give us these laws, then all future generations of human beings would have to continue being subjected to the idiographic studies advocated by Allport. Thus psychology would finally achieve a *full* knowledge of these laws of how uniqueness comes about only in the ultimate moment of collective self-contemplation immediately before the cataclysm that destroys the entire human race. This seems to me not too unfair a *reductio ad absurdum* of the "call for an idiographic psychology."

As to Allport's contentions that each individual is in some respects unique and that each person is a lawful system, either these have already been established as sound empirical generalizations, or as in the case of other scientific disciplines, psychology must continue its investigations by studying individual human beings (idiographically, if you will) to see whether the two *nomothetic* contentions under discussion are supported by the evidence. Here again, it would hardly require idiographic studies of *all* human beings in order to establish satisfactorily these two generalizations. At most, what it would require is more careful or thoroughgoing study of individuals in order to have a more solid foundation of evidence for the nomothetic generalizations. This does not add up to an "idiographic psychology."

It would seem, however, that the knowledge obtained from such idiographic studies of all human beings *could* have two kinds of uses. First, it would be useful to therapists, social case workers, guidance counsellors, or personnel directors in helping them to a more thorough understanding, and to more accurate predictions of the behavior, of those in the total population who are their patients or clients. In other words, it would be useful to have this idiographic knowledge about those individuals about whom it is important to have individual knowledge for such specific purposes. But this seems hardly more than a tautology, and one is therefore tempted to ask what need there is for universal idiographic studies of individuals other than the patients and clients concerned, and, by the same token, to ask what need there is for an "idiographic psychology." What *is* needed is careful idiographic study of each individual who, for one reason or another, is in need of the attention of the type of practitioner mentioned above, so that the practitioner would know as much as possible about the laws of his patient's or client's inner personality system. If Allport meant that there ought to be more of this done, and that it ought to be done better than it is being done now, then his admonition is probably justified, but, from the point of view of the systematic psychological study of human nature, relatively trivial.

The other use to which idiographic studies of all human beings could be put is in the prediction of the behavior of human beings generally. We can predict the behavior of an intimate friend more accurately than can be done by another person who does not have our idiographic knowledge of our friend; and it is so with each person of whom we possess idiographic knowledge. Accordingly, where the prediction of individual persons' behavior is important, idiographic knowledge of these persons is important. Allport complained that science is greatly disadvantaged in the prediction of the behavior of individuals, "because the best source of that prediction is the past behavior of the individual."[49] His complaint about science continues this theme:

> Where this [scientific] reasoning seriously trips is in the prediction applied to the single case, instead of to a population of cases. A fatal non-sequitur occurs in the reasoning that if 80% of the delinquents from broken homes are recidivists, then *this* delinquent from a broken home has an 80% chance of becoming a recidivist. The truth of the matter seems to be that *this* delinquent has either 100% certainty of becoming a repeater or 100% certainty of going straight. If all the causes in his case were known, we could predict for him perfectly (barring environmental accident). His chances are determined by the pattern of his life and not by the frequencies found in a population at large.[50]

Here Allport was once again saying that if you wish to know about the probable behavior of an individual, you will be better off if you

[49]Allport, *The Use of Personal Documents in Psychological Science,* op. cit., p. 155.
[50]*Ibid.*, pp. 156–57.

have as much knowledge as possible about this individual's personality system, than if you have only statistical generalizations about a class of persons to which he belongs. This is probably right, and it means that if you wish to make predictions about recidivism in the case of 1,000 specific delinquents, your predictions will be better if you have idiographic knowledge of each one of them. But you will then in fact be making 1,000 disparate predictions, and idiographic studies of other individual human beings, whether of all of them or only of a sample of them, are likely to be irrelevant to these 1,000 predictions. Again we end up with the trivial conclusion that it is useful to have idiographic knowledge about those individuals about whom it is important to have individual knowledge for specific reasons or purposes. And again, this does not add up to an idiographic psychology.

VIII

To sum up then. In the study of the nature of man we may acquire knowledge of individuals in their unique and irreducible individuality, and we may acquire general knowledge of aspects of human beings, e.g., traits, or propensities, which are abstracted from the concrete individuals. This is true in all other empirical sciences. However, in the case of human beings, the knowledge of the individual is of especial importance, because the behavior, the future, the fate or destiny of fellow humans in general and of certain individual humans in particular is of importance to us. Idiographic knowledge of the individual person is of crucial importance in the work of therapists, case workers, guidance counsellors, etc., because it is with the individual that these psychologists as practitioners deal. Knowledge of the uniqueness of the unique individual in the sense of *Einfühlung*, of the I-Thou relationship between persons, is of transcendent importance in inter-personal relations, but this is of course the kind of knowledge that one can only *experience* directly and ineffably; and it is hardly possible to talk about it. At best one can try to describe it elliptically, metaphorically. In itself, it is not systematically codifiable.

Manifestly, the study of the nature of man also requires the acquisition of general, abstract knowledge of human behavior; general laws about the psychological constitution of human beings, and about probable human actions under certain conditions. This is the kind of knowledge Allport called nomothetic. Without this kind of knowledge, a science of psychology, and more generally, a science of man, would not be possible. Allport was no doubt right when he said that "*psychological causation is always personal and never actuarial.*"[51] But it is through

[51] *Ibid.*, p. 157.

the study of many instances and many kinds of personal causation, and through codification of them into nomothetic generalizations, that our systematic knowledge of man will increase and deepen. Indeed, just as new idiographic knowledge of individuals may serve as a point of departure for extending and enriching our knowledge of *laws* of human nature, so may nomothetic knowledge of general laws of human behavior make possible deeper and more trustworthy idiographic insights into individuals by facilitating our understanding of the respects in which the individual under study is "like (some or all) other people," and the respects in which he is "like no other men."

Historical knowledge, and the methodology of historical inquiry, have often been said to be strictly idiographic. However, Ernest Nagel rejects such rigid exclusivity. Approaching this issue in connection with his examination of problems on the logic of historical inquiry, Nagel concludes that *natural science* is not purely nomothetic, and that *history* is not a purely idiographic discipline. "It would be a gross error," Nagel tells us, "to conclude that singular statements play no role in the theoretical sciences or that historical inquiry makes no use of universal ones."[52] As to *the natural sciences,* Nagel reminds us that *even they*

> *can assert their general statements as empirically warranted only on the basis of concrete factual evidence, and therefore only by making use of singular statements.* Moreover, many . . . laws of "pure" science have a generality that is at least geographically restricted. . . . Furthermore, some branches of natural science . . . are primarily concerned with spatiotemporal distributions and the development of specific individual systems, and are therefore engaged in establishing statements singular in form.[53] [Emphasis supplied]

On the other hand, so far as history is concerned,

> . . . *the historian's characterizations of individual things assume that there are various kinds of occurrences,* and in consequence that *there are more or less determinate empirical regularities which are associated with each kind and which* differentiate one kind from other kinds.[54] [Emphasis supplied]

Returning to psychology now, the interplay of singular statements and universal statements in the systematic discourse about human

[52]Ernest Nagel, *The Structure of Science: Problems in the Logic of Scientific Explanation* (New York: Harcourt, Brace & World, 1961), p. 548.
[53]*Ibid.*, pp. 548–49.
[54]*Ibid.*, p. 549.

nature and conduct is in fact quite familiar. But what may be worth recalling here, in connection with Allport's call for an idiographic psychology, is the extent to which even therapists depend upon *nomothetic* generalizations to help them better to understand *idiographically* their patients or clients. Anthony Kenny's observation is helpful here, when he says that "Being told that a man acted out of vanity helps us to understand his action . . . because we say to ourselves: 'Yes, of course, men *often* act like that.'"[55] Moreover, the therapist is helped in making predictions about individuals, i.e., *idiographic predictions, by the nomothetic knowledge* he has of regularities and of generalizations concerning the class of similar cases. Jacob A. Arlow's clinical illustration is instructive in this connection, and it is worth quoting from it at length.

> During an initial interview I asked a patient how long he had been married. He answered, "Sixteen months, three weeks." The overly exact quality of this response aroused in me the suspicion that I was dealing with a person whose character structure was colored by obsessional thinking and compulsive traits. To confirm my suspicion I asked further, "How long did you know your wife before you married her?" He answered, "Two years, three months." At this point, inwardly, I make a further set of predictions concerning this individual's mental traits. I guessed that he would be especially concerned with money. . . . A further set of predictions concerned his relationship to cleanliness. I could guess that he would be excessively neat regarding his person and his clothes, tidy in his surroundings, orderly in his manner, and rigorously punctual regarding appointments and the fulfillment of financial obligations. Questioning confirmed each of these predictions in minute detail. But even further predictions can be made on the basis of the minimum hints given by this patient. Such predictions in psychoanalysis . . . have been validated regularly, hundreds of times in psychoanalytic investigations.[56]

The various illustrations in the preceding pages exhibit the paradigmatic interplay and reciprocal illumination between the psychologist's idiographic knowledge of the individual person and his nomothetic knowledge of generalizations about all human beings or about classes of human beings. The illustrations also must lead to the conclusion that the idiographic/nomothetic controversy has been misconceived by the doctrinaire and dogmatic partisans on both sides, as well as by

[55]Anthony Kenny, *Action, Emotion, and Will* (London: Routledge and Kegan Paul, 1963), p. 95.

[56]Jacob A. Arlow, "Psychoanalysis as Scientific Method," *Psychoanalysis, Scientific Method and Philosophy: A Symposium*, ed. Sidney Hook (New York: Grove Press, 1960), pp. 206–207.

those—most often nomotheticists—who cavalierly and impatiently dismiss the whole matter as a "pseudo-issue."[57] It is not a pseudo-issue. The fact that, as was argued above, there is no mutually exclusive dichotomy between these two methods and two kinds of knowledge in psychology, and that they are in fact inextricably intertwined, does not mean that they may not be distinguished from each other in discourse, or that there is no need to understand the nature of the relationships between them. This has been exhibited above, and two additional illustrations should help make the relationships clear.

The nomothetic generalization that all human acts, no matter how trivial, capricious, or inexplicable they may appear to be, acts such as slips of the tongue, memory lapses, or dreams, are in fact explicable in terms of unconscious processes in which they originate, does not *by itself* tell us either that *this patient's lapsus linguae* is of any special significance, nor does it by itself explain what its significance may be in this patient's symptomatology. It is only in the context of and in relation to much other idiographic knowledge about *this patient* that his slip of the tongue may be seen to have a cause or a reason that is explanatory of this and other elements in his behavior. When, in the light of the additional idiographic knowledge of the patient, the slip of the tongue is indeed discovered to be of significance in *this particular case*, this in turn may be seen as another confirmatory instance of the nomothetic generalization, and thus the nomothetic knowledge is enriched.

On the other hand, the intensive idiographic study of each of the 500 juvenile offenders in a particular institution would no doubt help the parole authorities to hazard a prediction of future behavior *in each case* when an offender is up for parole. But such idiographic knowledge and succession of individual decisions will not advance our knowledge of delinquency, confinement, parole, and recidivism, unless it is supplemented by the nomothetic search for trends, invariances, or correlations which may help discover possible relations between certain factors and recidivism. The resulting nomothetic generalization, though only of a certain degree of probability, may lead to the application of this nomothetic knowledge idiographically in the form of revised treatment of this or that offender who has displayed the given characteristic. In short, if psychology as a science pursued nomothetic generalizations exclusively, without interest in the individual case, or if it pursued only the idiographic knowledge of individuals with no interest in nomothetic generalizations, the hoped for achievement of explanation and understanding of human behavior would remain a will-o'-the-wisp.

[57]See, for example, Melvin H. Marx, "Confusion in Attitudes Toward Clinical Theory," *Theories in Contemporary Psychology*, ed. Melvin H. Marx (New York: Macmillan, 1964), p. 313.

10. *Self-Realization as Ethical Norm: A Critique**

The doctrine that self-realization or self-actualization is an ethical norm, that the pursuit of self-actualization is inherently a moral good, that acts of self-actualization are morally right and ought to be performed, is often spoken of as dating back at least to Aristotle, and some attribute it also to Plato. The doctrine had a kind of vogue at the turn of the century. Maurice Mandelbaum, in his rich and comprehensive study, entitled *History, Man and Reason,* states that "the doctrine of self-realizationism . . . tended to dominate Anglo-American philosophical theories of conduct at the turn of the century."[1] This judgment must also include continental and particularly German philosophy, since Mandelbaum includes Fichte and Nietzsche in addition to T. H. Green, F. H. Bradley, Bosanquet, and to some extent John Dewey, in his inventory of protagonists of the doctrine. Among contemporaries I find Stephen C. Pepper, in his 1960 volume entitled *Ethics,*[2] devoting two chapters to an exposition of the "Self-Realization Theory." Somewhat earlier, C. A. Campbell, of the University of Glasgow, in a 1948 lecture, reprinted in his volume entitled *In Defense of Free Will,*[3] mounted a valiant defense of the principle of self-realizationism in ethics—a defense, it seems to me, more distinguished for its

*This paper has benefitted from the comments of the members of the Washington Philosophy Club. I am especially grateful to my colleagues, William A. Banner and Edward Regis, Jr., for their helpful comments and suggestions.

[1]Mandelbaum, Maurice. *History, Man, and Reason.* Baltimore: Johns Hopkins Press, 1971, p. 265.

[2]Pepper, Stephen C. *Ethics.* New York: Appleton-Century-Crofts, 1960.

[3]Campbell, C. A. *In Defence of Free Will.* London: George Allen & Unwin, 1967.

The Philosophical Forum; A Quarterly, vol. 9, Fall 1977, pp. 1–25. Presented, with changes, before the Washington Philosophy Club, as its presidential address, on April 10, 1976.

valor than for its results. More recently, a group of American psychologists, who frequently refer to themselves or are referred to as "humanistic psychologists," and who in their writings often show themselves to be philosophers *manqué* rather than empirical psychologists, have latched on to this doctrine and have converted it into a quasi-popular cult of "spontaneity," "freedom," "anti-frustration," etc. They propound a "need psychology" that is characterized by an apotheosis of what they call "psychological needs" as objects of imperative moral pursuit and almost religious veneration.

In case my bias is not yet abundantly evident, perhaps it is best that I state my conclusions clearly and categorically now. I believe that a critical analysis of the doctrine inescapably leads to the conclusion that "self-realization" is a morally vacuous concept. The persistence of the illusion that self-realization is an ethical norm, and that acts of self-realization are inherently, by virtue of their being acts of self-actualization, ethically good, or right, or obligatory, is a result of the failure fully to recognize, what even self-realizationists sometimes vaguely recognize, or disclose without being aware of it, namely, that only *certain kinds* of self-actualizing acts are ethically good or right. What is of crucial importance is the fact that the ethical character of these ethically good self-actualizing acts is never contained in the self-actualization of the acts, but rather in other qualities that are judged to be ethically good and that are independent of the self-actualizing character of the acts. It is these other qualities that are discovered in or ascribed to these acts in the independent value judgments about them, that are ethically good and furnish ethical norms for the assessment of particular behavior, and not the character of the acts as acts of self-actualization.

I

We may begin this critical examination by reviewing briefly Stephen C. Pepper's exposition and C. A. Campbell's defense of self-realization. Following that I wish to invite the reader's attention to the humanistic psychologists' version of this doctrine, and also to the contrast between their version on the one hand, and philosophical doctrines of Aristotle and F. H. Bradley on the other. The concluding section of this essay will be devoted to an exposition and vindication of the psychological theory of self-actualization as developed by Kurt Goldstein, whose name is so often taken in vain by the humanistic psychologists under discussion. Pepper's crudely formulated definition of self-realizationism is as follows:

> . . . the ethical ideal of self-realization theory is that a man should to the fullest degree realize his character. . . . The self-realization theory finds its most primitive sense of good in the realization of . . . human capacities.[4]

What is remarkable is that, no sooner has this lucid, unambiguous statement been articulated, than the focus shifts and is blurred. What immediately follows in the exposition is the principle that "a good personality is an integrated one,"[5] that "since the integration of human dispositions is descriptively defined as good, the more of the integration, the better . . . "[6] The ethical norm here has shifted from self-realization to "integration," and it is integration that is the good. Pepper is quite explicit about this: "Self-realization sets up integration as the dominant value in man's life." However, Pepper shifts the focus still further. In the next step the ethical norm becomes "effective functioning in society":

> The ethical ideal for a person is the well-adjusted, well-integrated all-round man effectively functioning in his society . . . the practical ideal for a self-realizationist could hardly be other than the institutional integration of all men into a single harmonious world society.[7]

What has happened to self-realization? The fact is that the ultimate disappearing act of self-realization as ethical norm, in Pepper's exposition, takes place at its very beginning. Pepper says that self-realization theory

> . . . concentrates its attention on the goodness of the person. It maintains that if the person is good he may be relied upon to perform good acts.[8]

To get around this instructive tautology, Pepper says that the theory asks "What constitutes a good personality?" and he answers that

> A good personality is an integrated one . . . and acts are good in so far as they promote integration in persons and their societies.[9]

I have no inclination to quarrel with Pepper's affirmative value judgments on personal and institutional integration and on effective func-

[4]Pepper, op. cit., p. 165.
[5]Ibid.
[6]Ibid., p. 192.
[7]Ibid., pp. 192–93.
[8]Ibid., p. 164.
[9]Ibid., pp. 164–65.

tioning in a harmonious society and world community. But the point here is that these are values independent of and extrinsic to the concept of self-realization. Acts which tend to realize these values are ethically good acts, but they are good not for the reason that they are self-actualizing acts. So much for Professor Pepper's exposition.

C. A. Campbell says that

> According to the most usual interpretation, self-realization as a moral principle implies that the end at which man ought to aim, the ultimate goal of moral aspiration, is a completely satisfying state of the self; all particular obligations deriving their obligatoriness, in the last resort, from conduciveness to the attainment of this egoistic end.[10]

Campbell proceeds to a categorical rejection of the egoistic implications thus generally ascribed to self-realizationism, and says that he would unhesitatingly range himself on the side of the critics of such a doctrine.[11]

However, he develops a lengthy argument in an attempt to show that self-realization as an ethical principle is free of the implication of egoism. Part of this argument is designed to show that though

> . . . the "self" whose realization is for this ethical school the moral norm is a self which is essentially a unity of desires and interests,[12]

it is the good of "the self as a whole" and not of any part of the self that affords true self-realization, and that this removes the element of egoism from the doctrine. The reason for this contention given by Campbell is that

> . . . man has *a natural tendency to wish well to his fellow men*. . . . that man is so framed by nature as to take a sympathetic interest in the well-being of his fellows . . . [13]

Accordingly, Campbell avers, the realization of the self as a whole will assuredly be good, and in harmony with generally accepted moral norms:

> . . . the good of the self as a whole will naturally be, for the ordinary man, predominantly social in character. . . . there is in man a powerful

[10]Campbell, op. cit., p. 122.
[11]Ibid.
[12]Ibid., p. 124.
[13]Ibid., p. 138.

> natural tendency to the formation of social sentiments . . . In short, the ultimate principle of moral obligation proclaimed by self-realization ethics not only need not manifest itself in egoistic content, but in actual fact must strongly tend to manifest itself in content that is predominantly social.[14] [Accordingly,] the self-realization principle . . . is in harmony with the moral judgments of mankind.[15]

Here again, if Campbell's contentions about man's fundamental social nature are true, then man's wishing well or doing well to his fellow men have the quality of ethical goodness, and can serve as ethical guides and norms because we judge them to be ethically good on other grounds, and not because they are acts of self-realization, and independently of this fact.

This is the main thesis of my polemic. If my contentions are right then, at worst, the philosophical doctrine of self-realization as an ethical norm or guide may be dismissed as a harmless aberration that invaded, beguiled, and seduced the minds of some philosophers in the past. However, except for Pepper's exposition, Campbell's defense, and Dewey's views (according to some interpreters) I am not aware of any systematic advocacy of this doctrine among philosophers in recent years.

II

But the popularity that "humanistic psychology" has achieved in American intellectual circles in recent years, and the dangerous vulgarizations that are either present or implicit in the espousal of the doctrine by these psychologists, demand a critical examination of the doctrine as it appears in their writings. Among the group of the so-called humanistic psychologists, the self-realizationist doctrine is most prominently advocated in the work of A. H. Maslow, Erich Fromm, and Carl R. Rogers. In their view, self-realization or self-actualization provides the putative logical nexus between human nature and ethics. Concurring in this view, though less vociferously, are also Gordon W. Allport and Gardner Murphy, among others. However, in the writing of these men the concept of self-actualization functions in two other ways as well. First, it is used *descriptively*, that is, as a short-hand term by which to describe certain aspects of human action. Second, it is also used as an *explanatory* concept, that is to explain aspects of human behavior.

[14]Ibid., p. 141.
[15]Ibid., p. 142.

The concept may be defined or described in Maslow's words:

> A musician must make music, an artist must paint, a poet must write, if he is ultimately to be at peace with himself. What man *can* be, he *must* be. This need we may call self-actualization. . . . This term [was] first coined by Kurt Goldstein. It refers to man's desire for self-fulfillment, namely to the tendency for him to become actualized in what he is potentially.[16] [Emphasis in original]

That there exists, as part of the inner nature of man, a trend, or pressure, or propensity toward self-actualization is maintained by some and hypothesized by others in this group of psychologists. Erich Fromm stated it in his first book as follows:

> . . . there are also certain psychological qualities inherent in man that need to be satisfied and that result in certain reactions if they are frustrated. . . . The most important seems to be the tendency to . . . realize potentialities which man has developed in the course of history.[17]

He restated it in his second book, *Man for Himself*, as

> . . . the principle that the power to act creates a need to use this power and that the failure to use it results in dysfunction and unhappiness.[18]

Carl R. Rogers advances the hypothesis that self-actualization is *the one fundamental human need:*

> The organism has this one basic tendency and striving—to actualize, maintain, and enhance the experiencing organism.
>
> Rather than many needs and motives, it seems entirely possible that all organic and psychological needs may be described as partial aspects of this fundamental need. . . .
>
> This involved self-actualization. . . . The term "self-actualization" is used by Goldstein to describe this one basic striving . . . [19]

Maslow, on the other hand, first proposed the self-actualization tendency as a theoretical postulate:

[16]Maslow, A. H. *Motivation and Personality.* New York: Harper and Bros., 1954, pp. 91–92.

[17]Fromm, Erich. *Escape from Freedom.* New York: Farrar and Rinehart, 1941, pp. 287–88.

[18]Fromm, Erich. *Man for Himself: An Inquiry into the Psychology of Ethics.* New York: Rinehart and Co., 1947, p. 219.

[19]Rogers, Carl R. *Client-Centered Therapy: Its Current Practice, Implications and Theory.* Boston: Houghton, Mifflin Co., 1951, pp. 487, 488, 489.

> . . . various recent developments have shown the theoretical necessity for the postulation of some sort of positive growth or self-actualization tendency within the organism. . . . This kind of tendency to growth and self-actualization, in one or another vague form, has been postulated by thinkers as diverse as Aristotle and Bergson, and by many other philosophers. Among psychiatrists, psychoanalysts, and psychologists it has been found necessary by Goldstein, Rank, Jung, Horney, Fromm, May, and Rogers.[20]

In his next book Maslow again referred to self-actualization as a theoretical, explanatory concept. He made reference to the "evidence that forces us in the direction of a concept of . . . self-actualizing tendencies," and described the evidence as "partly deductive . . . in the sense of pointing out that unless we postulate such a concept, much of human behavior makes no sense."[21] However, on the very next page, Maslow proposed the "tendency" toward self-actualization as a kind of empirical generalization:

> We can certainly now assert that at least a reasonable, theoretical, and empirical case has been made for the presence within the human being of a tendency toward, or need for growing in a direction that can be summarized in general as self-actualization . . . [22]

And again, two pages later, Maslow stated:

> . . . I think these findings can be generalized to most of the human species because it looks to me (and to others) as if most people (perhaps all) tend toward self-actualization . . . [23]

We next look at Gordon W. Allport, and find him asserting that "Human personality . . . is . . . advancing toward the fulfillment of plans and hopes. Self-actualization is the term often employed," a term, he added later, "that covers the main interest systems of adulthood." Relying on Maslow and Kurt Goldstein, Allport categorically stated, in his chapter on "The Development of Motives," that "self-actualization is at the bottom the only motive of men."[24]

In quoting thus at length, care has been taken to show that, whatever other meanings the self-actualization concept may have for these

[20]Maslow, *Motivation and Personality*, p. 124.

[21]Maslow, A. H. *Toward a Psychology of Being*. Princeton, N.J.: D. Van Nostrand Co., 1962, p. 146.

[22]Ibid., p. 147.

[23]Ibid., p. 149.

[24]Allport, Gordon W. *Pattern and Growth in Personality*. New York: Holt, Rinehart and Winston, 1961, pp. 85, 212, 215.

writers, it is proposed by them in the first instance as *a descriptive psychological concept,* the function of which is to describe or to explain aspects of man's behavior. The proposition they propound *in their role of psychologists* is that men *as a matter of fact* tend to actualize themselves. The status of this proposition, therefore, is either that of an empirical generalization based on clinical and other observation, or of an hypothesis advanced as an explanation of men's actual behavior. This is the import of the concept in the work of Kurt Goldstein, to which the psychologists under discussion refer frequently. For Goldstein self-actualization functions exclusively as a *descriptive* concept. His assertion that there is in man's nature a tendency to self-actualization is but a *factual* report of what he had discovered in the course of his extensive research on brain-damaged patients, and of his other psychological investigations. That Fromm, Maslow, and Rogers, and to some extent Allport and Murphy, badly misread and distorted Goldstein's theory of self-actualization will be shown below in the concluding section. For the present it will suffice to emphasize once more that for these psychologists, as for Kurt Goldstein, the proposition that man tends to actualize himself is fundamentally, and irrespective of what other purposes it may be used or misused for, part of the scientific psychological enterprise of describing factually, or explaining, the behavior and nature of human beings. This was underscored by Maslow in his reply to a commentator on his paper entitled "Psychological Data and Human Values":

> I think I have shown that the concepts of psychological health and of self-actualization need not be based on implicit value judgments. When properly defined, they are derived from scientifically observed facts. *They are descriptive concepts.*[25]

III

Logical difficulties therefore arise when we discover Maslow and others employing the concept of self-actualization as a *norm,* as a criterion for distinguishing between good and bad, between right and wrong, between what one ought and what one ought not to do. Using Maslow as our first illustration, we find him innocently making the transition to the *normative* use of self-actualization, and betraying no awareness of any logical problems in this transition:

[25]Maslow, "Reply to Professor Weisskopf," in Maslow, A. H. (ed.). *New Knowledge in Human Values.* New York: Harper and Bros., 1959, p. 246. (Emphasis mine)

> The group of thinkers who have been working with self-actualization . . . have pretty firmly established their case that man has a tendency to realize himself. By implication *he is exhorted* to be true to his own nature, to trust himself, to be authentic, spontaneous, honestly expressive, to look for the sources of his action in his own deep inner nature.[26]

Maslow's own view thus typifies the program which attempts to derive self-actualization *as a norm of conduct* from self-actualization *as an inherent tendency in man:*

> First of all . . . is the strong belief that man has needs, capacities, and tendencies that are genuinely based . . . there is involved the conception that full health and normal and desirable development consist in actualizing this nature, in fulfilling these potentialities. . . . By this conception what is good? Anything that conduces to this desirable development in the direction of actualization of the inner nature of man. What is bad or abnormal? Anything that frustrates or blocks or denies the essential nature of man.[27]

Maslow went further and suggested that there is implicit here a generalized value system. He contended that by taking into account data concerning man's psychological needs,

> . . . we can solve many value problems that philosophers have struggled with ineffectually for centuries. For one thing, it looks as if there were a single ultimate value for mankind, a far goal toward which all men strive. This is called variously by different authors self-actualization, self-realization, integration, psychological health . . . [28]

> All this implies a naturalistic system of values, a by-product of the empirical description of the deepest tendencies of the human species and of specific individuals. The study of the human being by science . . . can discover what is good for him and what is bad for him . . . [29]

I shall limit myself to Maslow as my *bête noire,* though the same reasoning is pursued by Carl Rogers, Gordon Allport, Erich Fromm, and others. But perhaps three brief quotes by Fromm will be helpful in this connection:

> . . . positive freedom . . . is identical with the full realization of the individual's potentialities . . . [30]

[26]Maslow, *Toward a Psychology of Being,* p. 152. (Emphasis mine)
[27]Maslow, *Motivation and Personality,* p. 340.
[28]Maslow, *Toward a Psychology of Being,* p. 145.
[29]Ibid., p. 191.
[30]Fromm, *Escape from Freedom,* p. 270.

> If human freedom is established as *freedom to,* if man can realize his self fully and uncompromisingly, the fundamental cause for his asocial drives will have disappeared . . .[31]
>
> All organisms have an inherent tendency to actualize their specific potentialities. *The aim of man's life, therefore, is to be understood as the unfolding of his powers according to the laws of his nature.*
>
> To sum up, *good in humanistic ethics is . . . the unfolding of man's powers. . . . Evil constitutes the crippling of man's powers . . .*[32]

The logical structure of the argument implicit in the claim of these psychologists that ethical norms can be inferred from self-actualization is approximately as follows:

1. Man has an inner nature, with inherent potentialities and capacities.
2. Part of man's inner nature is the tendency to, the pressure or propensity toward, self-actualization, i.e., toward fulfilling his potentialities and capacities.
3. *Therefore,* self-actualization, the fulfillment of man's potentialities and capacities, is *good,* whereas the denial of self-actualization, i.e., the frustration or denial of the fulfillment of man's capacities, is *bad;* and *therefore,* also, people *ought to* actualize themselves, and *ought to* seek the establishment of a social order in which self-actualization is facilitated and encouraged.

The principal step in the argument, then, is the inference from the alleged fact that the need to self-actualize is a central propensity in man's behavior to the conclusion that self-actualization and its products and consequences are morally good and ought to be pursued and encouraged. The ethical norm, the criterion for ethical judgment, is thus allegedly contained in or built into the phenomenon and pursuit of self-actualization, and the logical guarantee of the correctness of the ethical judgment is allegedly contained within this propensity itself. From the descriptive psychological premise, "Man has a tendency toward self-actualization," is inferred the normative and prescriptive proposition, "All self-actualizing is, *by virtue of its being an instance of self-actualizing,* good, and ought to be encouraged."

Of course, as pointed out earlier, the logic of part of the doctrine of these psychologists is not unfamiliar in philosophical literature, for it appears to resemble the ethical theory found in the writing of some philosophers who appear to offer self-realization as man's highest

[31] Ibid., p. 269.
[32] Fromm, *Man for Himself,* p. 20.

good. To the extent of the resemblance, the position of the humanistic psychologists and the position of the philosophers mentioned are both afflicted with the same fatal difficulties. For invariably, as was shown above in Pepper's exposition and Campbell's defense, the highest good proposed turns out in fact to be *not* self-realization, but something else. Nor do these psychologists ever actually deduce ethical norms from the principle of self-actualization. What they in fact do is advocate or prescribe that *certain aspects* of the self and not the entire self, *certain propensities* of man and not all of his propensities, ought to be actualized, namely, only those aspects of the self or those human propensities that are considered by these psychologists to be "good." That these propensities are "good" is not in fact deduced from the principle that man has a tendency to actualize them; *it could not be,* inasmuch as there are other human propensities that also press to be actualized but are considered undesirable, and their clamoring to be actualized does not transmute these so-called undesirable propensities into so-called "good" ones. The purported "goodness" of some propensities and the "oughtness" that is attached to the idea of their realization are thus not at all intrinsic to the fact that men have an intrinsic tendency to realize them. The claimed goodness or oughtness of these propensities is completely extrinsic to the "need" for their realization, and the justification of the claim that they are good rests upon some other foundation.

IV

This analysis will be pursued further, especially in the work in Fromm and Maslow. But before proceeding with this task, it may be useful to note some salient differences between the self-realizationism of Aristotle and F. H. Bradley and, on the other hand, the self-realizationism of Fromm, Maslow, Rogers, et al. While advocating a position that entails logical problems, it is clear that there was a far greater awareness on the part of Aristotle and Bradley of the difficulties involved in their position than on the part of the psychologists under discussion.

In the first place, unlike the humanistic psychologists, Aristotle and Bradley do not employ self-realization as a descriptive psychological concept. For them the concept (in Aristotle it is implied, whereas Bradley uses the term directly and repeatedly) is *normative* or *prescriptive in the first instance.* But it does not function in isolation. *For these philosophers self-realization is a goal,* but it is a goal only in connection with the normative judgment that *certain aspects* of the self are *aspects worthy of realization.* In the case of Aristotle, it is the function that is unique to man, and is in fact the essence of man, namely, the exercise of reason, that is proposed as worthy of realization.[33] In Bradley's case, the goal of self-realization is to be pursued by that aspect of the self that represents "our function as an organ in the social organism."[34] Thus, neither Aristotle's proposal that it is man's rational self that ought to be realized, nor Bradley's proposal that it is man's social self that should be realized, is inferred solely from the proposition that the part of the self to be realized is a part of human nature. Neither Aristotle nor Bradley proposed that the total, empirically discovered self is the self to be realized. And neither Aristotle nor Bradley proposed that the aspect of the self which is selected for self-realization must be selected *solely because* it is part of human nature.

Both Bradley and Aristotle employ normative criteria in their selection of the part of the self to be realized. For Aristotle, the proposed goal of self-realization for the rational part of man is based on his view that the rational is what is unique to man, and that the fulfillment of the unique capacities of anything is "good." For Bradley, the goal of realizing the social self is based on his view that a person, being a member of society, must transcend himself, and have as his duty the realization of imperatives that go beyond his own particularity and are in some ways universal. Aristotle's and Bradley's employment of avowedly normative criteria for selecting the aspects of the self that are to be realized has of course not prevented these philosophers from leaving important problems unresolved, and to this I shall return in a moment. The point here, however, is that attention to the employment by these philosophers of *normative* criteria by which they determine what aspects of man are to be actualized helps highlight the differences between them and humanistic psychologists, and also helps throw into bold relief the logical failures of the espousal of self-actualization as an ethical norm.

(1) *First*, unlike the psychologists under discussion, who presume to be inferring their proposal of self-actualization as ethically a desideratum from "empirical data about psychic health and psychic illness," Aristotle and Bradley avoid the logical trap of attempting to deduce ethical prescriptions solely from factual data about the nature of man. (2) *Second*, the employment by these two philosophers of normative criteria for selecting the aspects of man to be actualized makes it immediately and abundantly clear that it is *not self-actualization* that is for them the ethical norm or the ethical goal, but rather *the exercise of reason* in the case of Aristotle, and *adherence to the values of the social*

[33]Aristotle, *The Nicomachean Ethics*, Book I, Chapter 7, 1097b 23 - 1098a 18, and Book X, Chapter 7, 1178a.

[34]Bradley, F. H. *Ethical Studies*. Oxford: The Clarendon Press, 1927, p. 163, as well as all of Essay V, entitled, "My Station and My Duties," pp. 160–213.

organism in the case of Bradley, and that neither of these norms is deduced from the facts of human nature, but has other actual or claimed logical foundations. On the other hand, the procedure of Maslow and the other contemporary psychologists blinds them to the fact that what they claim to be ethically desirable is really something other than self-actualization. (3) *Third,* whereas their uncritical step of trying to infer self-actualization as an ethical norm from self-actualization as a descriptive concept prevents our psychologists from seeing the logical difficulties of their position, by contrast, the procedure of the philosophers, such as Aristotle and Bradley, exhibits quite clearly and unmistakably the problems left unresolved by their position.

So far as Aristotle's position is concerned, the obvious questions that it leaves unanswered are:

(a) Is reason, or "man's rational part," really the only unique capacity that distinguishes man from other living things? Conceivably one might find other activities and capacities of man that also are not shared by other animals; would such other unique capacities also be worthy of realization?

(b) Is the element of uniqueness an acceptable criterion of what is "good" and worthy of realization? Is it not possible that some parts or capacities of the self that man shares with some other animals might be judged ethically good, and that some capacities of the self that are unique to man might be judged ethically evil? Specifically, is man's exercise of reason *always* ethically good? The very posing of this question without its sounding self-contradictory or absurd makes it clear that the judgment of any human capacity as good because it is unique to man is not a *necessary* judgment, and that the ethical attribution is likely to be based on some other criteria.

With respect to Bradley's position, it must be said that no one was more keenly aware of the difficulties implicit in it than Bradley himself. Indeed, he proceeded to recite and probe relentlessly and at considerable length the "very serious objections" to his own theory that the self to be realized is the social self. His self-examination led him to the conclusion that morality is "a self-contradiction":

> It is a self-contradiction in this way: it is a demand for what can not be. . . . reality is not wholly good. Neither in me, nor in the world, is what ought to be what is, and what is what ought to be . . . The reason of the contradiction is the fact that man is a contradiction.[35]

Bradley therefore concluded further that "Reflection on morality leads us beyond it. It leads us, in short, to see the necessity of a religious point of view . . . Morality issues in religion."[36]

[35]Ibid., p. 313.
[36]Ibid., p. 314.

It is beyond the scope of this discussion to examine Bradley's proposal to ground morality in religion. However, it may be instructive and helpful in our analysis of self-realizationism to take note of some of the difficulties perceived by Bradley himself with reference to his own self-realizationism. Unlike the humanistic psychologists, Bradley was keenly aware of the fact that his position had not "got rid of the opposition between the 'ought' and the 'is.'" Bradley saw that the "ought" cannot be naively identified with the "is" either so far as the self is concerned or so far as the social organism or the community is concerned. For, as he pointed out:

> (a) . . . The self can not be so seen to be identified with the moral whole that the bad self disappears.
>
> (b) Again, the moral man need not find himself realized in the world. . . . the community in which he is a member may be in a confused or rotten condition, so that in it right and might do not always go together. . . . There are afflictions for which no moral organism has balm or physician . . . [37]

The question "which self is to be realized?" was faced most realistically by Bradley, who saw man as polarized into two selves:

> The existence of two selves in man, a better self which takes pleasure in the good, and a worse self which makes for the bad, is a fact which is too plain to be denied . . . the good and the bad selves exist, and every one knows what they mean. . . . I feel in myself impulses to good in collision with impulses to bad, and I feel myself in each of them.[38]

"What is the content of the bad self?" Bradley asked, and he listed some of the ingredients: "Pride, hate, revenge, passionateness, sulkiness, malice, meanness, cowardice, and recklessness. . . . I please myself and my worse self in all. . . ."[39] "We find ourselves evil," Bradley said further; "the evil is as much a fact as the good, and without our bad self we should hardly know ourselves."[40]

Bradley's question is, of course, fundamental. In any theory of self-realization as a putative logical foundation for ethics, it is *a certain self* that is to be realized. It is never the case that the *total empirically discovered self* is proposed as the self to be realized or actualized, and this includes Aristotle, though for him, of course, reason is the unique essence of man. Rather, it is always the case that selected phases of the

[37]Ibid., pp. 203–04.
[38]Ibid., pp. 276–77.
[39]Ibid., pp. 279–80.
[40]Ibid., p. 308.

total self are the ones to be realized, phases selected *not on the basis of the criterion of their being part of the self,* but on the basis of other criteria, ethical criteria which are not logically entailed by the nature of the self. No prescriptive ethical imperative of self-realization is thus ever deduced *solely* from psychological facts concerning the nature of man.

V

Let us now return to Fromm and Maslow. As shown earlier, at many points they assert that it is the total empirically discovered self, with all its capacities and propensities, that presses for self-actualization, and that such self-actualization is good and should be pursued and encouraged. It is therefore not surprising that further inquiry leads them into hopeless contradictions and circularity, and ultimately in fact, though they do not seem to realize it, to the abandonment of self-actualization as an ethical norm.

Let us again see what it is they are saying. Earlier we quoted Fromm's statement that ". . . the power to act creates a need to use this power and . . . the failure to use it results in dysfunction and unhappiness." According to Fromm, ". . . the only way [man] can succeed in the act of living is to use his powers, to spend that which he has."[41] Fromm places considerable emphasis on the value and importance of "spontaneity" as part of "positive freedom."[42] In other words, Fromm is urging that persons ought to have the courage of their impulses. Maslow's language is even more sweeping in its undifferentiated proposal of the self and the "capacities" to be actualized:

> The muscular person likes to use his muscles, indeed, *has* to use them in order to self-actualize, and to achieve the subjective feeling of harmonious, uninhibited, satisfying functioning which is so important an aspect of psychological health. . . . Capacities clamor to be used. . . . That is to say, capacities are needs, and therefore are intrinsic values as well.[43]

Let us again take note of the logical difficulty here. Using Maslow's example, his argument here may be stated as follows:

[41]Fromm, *Man for Himself,* p. 220.
[42]Fromm, *Escape from Freedom,* pp. 256–76 *et passim.* Also *Man for Himself, passim.*
[43]Maslow, *Toward a Psychology of Being,* p. 144; also p. 187.

> The muscular man's use of his muscles is part of his self-actualization.
> *Therefore:*
> The muscular man's use of his muscles is good.

But obviously one can assert the premise of this argument and at the same time raise doubts about the conclusion, without sounding absurd. It is not nonsensical or self-contradictory to ask: "Granted that the muscular man's use of his muscles is part of his self-actualization, but is his use of his muscles good?" Or one can assert Maslow's premise in conjunction with the proposition that is the contradictory of his conclusion, without contradicting oneself. Thus, it is no logical self-contradiction to say: "The muscular man's use of his muscles is part of his self-actualization, but his use of his muscles is *not* good."

Now, the logical problem arises because it is not at all clear what exactly is meant by Maslow's position. Are *all* cases of a muscular man's use of his muscles ethically "good" in Maslow's view? What about the muscular man who exercises his muscles by frequently provoking fights with people, in which he beats them up? What about the exercise of their muscles by muscular "goons" and "muscle men" in the employ of racketeers, etc.? Such illustrations can be multiplied out of the long annals of human history, and out of the more recent use of muscular men by totalitarian regimes. Clearly Maslow would agree that such use of their muscles by muscular men is not "good." However, since many of these muscle men obviously "feel good," and have "a subjective feeling of . . . successful, uninhibited functioning" in this exercise of their muscles, Maslow's thesis would require him to call this exercise ethically *good.* If he rejects the proposition that *this kind* of use of one's muscles is good, then it follows that he is employing a criterion *other than self-actualization* by which to pass ethical judgment over a case of self-actualizing behavior.

Let us, for a moment, look at Fromm's illustrations:

> Man has the power to walk and move; if he were prevented from using this power severe physical discomfort or illness would result. . . . Freud has called attention to another lack of expenditure as a cause of suffering, that of sexual energy, by recognizing that the blocking of sexual energy can be the cause of neurotic disturbances . . . his [Freud's] theory is a profound symbolic expression of the fact that man's failure to use and to spend what he has is the cause of sickness and unhappiness.[44]

[44]Fromm, *Man for Himself,* p. 219.

Now, the obvious question is again, whether every case of the expenditure of sexual energy is "good," and whether every case of "blocking" of sexual energy is "bad." It is of course true that Freud called attention to the importance of the sex need or propensity in man, and to frustration of the sex need as a source of some neuroses. However, it is a gross misinterpretation of Freud to suggest or imply that he deduced from these factual or descriptive data about man's sex needs an ethical guide to the effect that all gratifications of the sex need are ethically "good" and all inhibitions of the sex need are "bad." This regrettably has been and continues to be a popular vulgarization of Freud's work. Indeed, when Freud steps out of his role as descriptive psychologist and takes on the role of moralist, his emphasis is on the problem of balancing on the one hand need gratification, and on the other hand *controls* over needs, impulses, instincts, etc. The logic of Freud's position is that some expenditure of sexual energy is good, but some blocking of sexual energy is also good; and thus, when some sexual gratification is judged to be good, the criterion for this judgment is not contained solely in the fact that man has a propensity or a need for sexual gratification, but in some other source. The significance of Freud's slogan, "Where id was there shall ego be,"[45] and of much of his book *Civilization and Its Discontents,* is precisely that man's drives require controls for the sake of ethical and social goals which are not in themselves deducible from the facts about human nature.

From the above it should not be concluded that the humanistic psychologists under discussion are altogether oblivious to the fact that any doctrine that proposes self-actualization as an ethical norm must ultimately come up with an answer to the crucial question as to what kind of self is to be realized. When they are aware of it, their awareness is fuzzy, and their attempts to answer this question are either self-contradictory or circular. Consequently they fail to understand that they do not and cannot, on the basis of their own procedure, establish self-realization as an ethical norm, and that they are in fact assuming other ethical norms to justify their advocacy of the pursuit of self-realization.

This is made evident by the fact that they make three kinds of attempts to answer the question as to what kind of self is to be actualized, and thus, in turn to justify (by appealing to other ethical criteria) self-actualization as an ethical norm. They try to argue as follows:

[45]Freud, Sigmund. *New Introductory Lectures on Psychoanalysis.* Translated by W. H. J. Sprott, New York: Norton and Co., 1933, p. 112.

1. *Man is inherently good;* therefore the total self that is to be actualized is good.[46]

2. Self-actualization can be entrusted only to *self-disciplined* people.[47]

3. People who are "self-actualizers" are *good people.*[48]

It is an interesting and instructive exercise to examine with some care each of these three attempts. However, I shall spare the reader this exercise.[49] Suffice it to say (1) that if one espouses the doctrine that man is inherently good and that *therefore* the actualization or realization of the total self is ethically good, then the ethical norm that is assumed is contained in the *assumed goodness of man,* and it is not the fact that a given act is a self-actualizing act which makes the act morally good. (2) If one ends up, as does Maslow, with the principle that self-actualization "can be entrusted only to *self-disciplined* people," then again the ethical character of the self-actualizing acts of such persons is contained in the trait of *self-discipline* which they possess, and not in the fact that these acts are acts of self-actualization. (3) If one propounds Maslow's proposition that "people who are self-actualizers are good people" (Maslow concluded, paradoxically, that there are a very small number of such people), then the obvious question it evokes is: "Are these good people good because they are self-actualizers, or are their ethical goodness and the ethical character of their actions determined by other norms and criteria prior to and independent of the fact that they are self-actualizers?" Manifestly, it is by these prior criteria, independent of and extrinsic to the fact that they are self-actualizers, that they and their actions are adjudged to be ethically good.

It thus seems clear that self-actualization is not an ethical norm. From the proposition that man is in fact a self-actualizer, by itself, one cannot deduce or infer what is ethically good or right. From the fact

[46]Rogers, Carl R. "The Nature of Man," in *The Nature of Man in Theological and Psychological Perspective.* Simon Doniger (ed.). New York: Harper and Bros., 1962, p. 91. Ibid., p. 70, quoted by Rogers from his "A Therapist's View of the Good Life," *The Humanist,* 1957, No. 17; Fromm, *Escape from Freedom,* pp. 22, 269, 288, 290, 294. *The Sane Society,* p. 275; Allport, Gordon W. *Personality and Social Encounter.* Boston: Beacon Press, 1960, pp. 200, 202, 205; Maslow, *Motivation and Personality,* pp. 153, 340. *Toward a Psychology of Being,* pp. 3, 150, 152–53, 181.

[47]Maslow, *Toward a Psychology of Being,* pp. 152–54.

[48]Maslow, *Motivation and Personality,* Chapter 12, pp. 199–234, especially pp. 200–01. *Toward a Psychology of Being,* p. iii, pp. 149–50, 158–59, 181, 233, *et passim.*

[49]Such a detailed examination is provided in my book, *Human Nature in Humanistic Psychology* (unpublished).

that certain behavior is in fact self-actualizing behavior, one cannot infer that it is good behavior. The very need of the self-realizationists to rely on the doctrine of man's inherent goodness, or on the claim that only self-disciplined people can be entrusted with self-actualization, or that self-actualizers are good people, is proof that ethical criteria independent of self-actualization are in fact hidden in their dictum that the pursuit of self-actualization is good.

These and other ethical values and criteria are not based on the purported fact that man is a self-actualizer. Precisely the reverse is the case. The proposition that self-actualization is desirable would make any kind of sense only if it were logically grounded on another and prior proposition to the effect that self-actualization will bring about the realization of ethical goals which have already been espoused as desirable. Without such ethical presuppositions, self-realization vanishes as an ethical desideratum, and is exposed as an ethically barren and vacuous concept.

It seems desirable, before going on to the exposition of Kurt Goldstein's theory of self-actualization, to note a disclaimer with reference to a point of major philosophical importance. In emphasizing, as I have, the fundamental distinction between descriptive and normative propositions, I do not intend to imply that this distinction necessarily entails any claim that normative propositions never do, or cannot, convey *factual* value assertions, i.e., that *value* may not be discoverable as *factually, ontologically existent.* However, if this should be the case, that is, if value is discoverable as existent in the world of fact, the Humean doctrine I have been advocating, namely, that normative or prescriptive propositions cannot be validly inferred or deduced from descriptive propositions, is in no way affected. In other words, if value is factually, ontologically discoverable in nature, then our knowledge of the resulting value assertions is based on such discovery, but is never a product of a *deduction* from other factual propositions.

VI

It now remains only to sketch briefly what has actually been said on the subject of self-actualization by Kurt Goldstein, the man whom the humanistic psychologists repeatedly credit with having introduced into the mainstream of contemporary psychology the proposition that man strives toward self-actualization. In doing this I hope to help make clear Goldstein's use of self-actualization as essentially a descriptive psychological concept, and not an ethical norm. In juxtaposition to Goldstein's use of this concept, the distortion by the humanistic psychologists of the concept of self-actualization will perhaps stand out in bolder relief. Perhaps this will also help us understand more clearly that the transformation of the concept of self-actualization, by the psychologists under discussion, into a putative ethical norm and guideline for conduct, is in part motivated by their moralistic but misguided desire to provide, for the ethical and social ideals which they espouse, a logical justification in descriptive facts concerning the psychological nature of man.

Goldstein advanced the proposition that man has the need for self-actualization, as an empirical generalization, and as an explanatory principle. His simple statement of the proposition is repeated in two of his books:

> The organism has definite potentialities, and because it has them it has the need to actualize or realize them. The fulfillment of these needs represents the self-actualization of the organism.[50]

Indeed, it was Goldstein's belief that the "drive" of self-actualization is the one basic drive. He stated this several times:

> The tendency to actualize itself is the motive which sets the organism going; it is the *drive* by which the organism is moved.
>
> Since the tendency to actualize itself as fully as possible is the basic drive, the only drive by which the sick organism is moved, and since the life of the normal organism is determined in the same way, it is clear . . . that we have to assume only one drive, the drive of self-actualization.
>
> We assume only one drive, the drive of self-actualization . . . [51]

The purely descriptive character of the principle is made clear by the evidence and the illustrations adduced by Goldstein for the presence of the drive. Let us limit ourselves to two examples. The first concerns the completion of incomplete actions:

> A special form of self-actualization is the need to complete incomplete actions, a tendency which explains many of the activities of the child. In the innumerable repetitions of children we are . . . dealing with . . . the tendency toward completion and perfection . . . the goal is the fulfillment of the task. The nearer we are to perfection, the stronger is the need to perform. This is valid for children as well as for adults.[52]

[50]Goldstein, Kurt. *The Organism*. New York: American Book Co., 1939, p. 204. Also *Human Nature in the Light of Psychopathology*. New York: Schocken Books, 1963 (originally Harvard University Press, 1940), p. 146; cf. also pp. 172, 194.

[51]Goldstein, *Human Nature in the Light of Psychopathology*, pp. 140, 142, 145.

[52]Ibid., pp. 146–47.

The second example comes from Goldstein's studies of brain-damaged people, and of patients with severe bodily diseases such as severe heart failure. He reported that, following the acute state with its experiences of extreme anxiety and fear of catastrophe, these patients undergo an adjustment to their new condition, abnormal though it is, and endeavor to actualize themselves, "even if in an imperfect way."

> Innumerable instances teach us that it is the basic tendency of the sick organism to utilize what capacities it has in the best possible way (considered, of course, in relation to the normal nature of the organism concerned).[53]

The range of self-actualization of these patients is diminished by their injury or severe illness, and they accordingly either do not react to situations with which their now limited capacity cannot cope, or, if such overdemanding situations are forced upon them, their reaction is catastrophic. The brain-damaged or severely sick person

> can exist—that is, actualize his capacities—only if he finds a new milieu that is appropriate to his capacities. Only then can he act in an orderly way . . . [54]

Unlike brain-damaged patients, those with severe heart failure

> are aware of the restrictions in their activities and of the shrinkage of their world by the conditions of a regained order, and with that they are aware of their diminished self-realization. . . . They tend, as all mentally normal individuals do, to achieve a self-realization that corresponds to their unchanged personality, their intrinsic nature. They can achieve a higher self-realization only if they can endure suffering. They are in a dilemma that demands a choice between accepting and enduring suffering and getting fuller self-realizations, or the simultaneous diminution of suffering and of self-realization. . . . it is not the task of therapy merely to reduce mental and physical suffering . . . health is not an objective condition that can be understood by methods of natural science alone. It is, rather, a condition related to a mental attitude by which the individual has to value what is essential for his life.[55]

Self-realization, then, is a tendency, a need, a propensity, and whether one chooses more self-realization at the price of enduring pain, or

[53]Ibid., p. 141.

[54]Ibid., p. 194.

[55]Goldstein, "Health as Value," in *New Knowledge in Human Values*, ed. A. H. Maslow, pp. 182–83.

less self-realization in order to reduce pain, is a matter of attitude or decision. Such decision is not guided by any normative or ethical directives that are inherent in or deducible from the factual data that are summarized under the term "self-realization." Now, to conclude Goldstein's report, what is true about his patients is true about people in general:

> A comparison of the behavior of our patients with that of normal persons leaves us no doubt that the life of the normal organism is also governed by this rule. We may say, then, that an organism is governed by the tendency to actualize its individual capacities as fully as possible.[56]

From the above alone it should be abundantly clear that for Goldstein the concept of self-actualization is, to repeat, a *descriptive,* factual concept, and that it is a gratuitous distortion and misinterpretation to ascribe to him any of the notions of our psychologists, such as that self-actualization is in itself a desideratum; that it can serve as an ethical norm or guideline; that self-realization is good and what blocks it is bad; that man should be exhorted to self-actualize; that self-actualization provides a single ultimate value or goal for mankind; that maturity and psychic health consist in self-actualization and that the denial of self-actualization constitutes psychic illness; that the society which facilitates and encourages self-actualization is the good society and the social order which frustrates or inhibits self-actualization is bad, etc. However, the distortion and misinterpretation become even more glaringly evident if we pay attention to Goldstein's treatment of the concept of self-actualization when he departed from his role as descriptive scientist to the extent of being concerned with the problem of the relationships of the individual to others, and with the problems of "norms" of "freedom," or of "the adequate social organization of mankind." In such normative contexts, where the purpose of Goldstein's discussion was to outline the conditions for a good and just society, he concluded that social life "implies the *incomplete realization* of every individual's nature,"[57] and that *renunciation* and *self-restriction* are imperatives that must counterbalance self-actualization.[58]

First, let us note that, unlike Fromm, Maslow, and Rogers, who identify self-actualization with maturity, Goldstein, in his discussion of the development of the child, identified self-actualization with the child's *immature* state.

[56]Goldstein, *Human Nature in the Light of Psychopathology,* p. 141.
[57]Ibid., p. 203. (Emphasis mine)
[58]Ibid., pp. 202–23 *passim,* and p. 238.

> [The child's] tendencies, feelings, attitudes, come into conflict with what is demanded of him; there is a clash between *his tendency to self-realization, which corresponds to his immature state,* and what is forbidden.[59]

Secondly, unlike Maslow's uncritical and unqualified assertion that a person's self-actualization *will* be "good for him and good for others," Goldstein asserted that self-actualization *can* take place without harm, *only* under proper social organization.

> It can not be said often enough that individuals, peoples, races, can actualize themselves without harming each other, that this can be accomplished only by an adequate organization of group life. . . . [60]

Moreover, it is the concept of *self-restriction,* which Goldstein advanced as necessary for sound social relationships and social justice, that for Goldstein "corresponds to what we call the ethical, to the norms," in man.[61]

Goldstein outlined his social theory in a chapter entitled "The Individual and Others." This social theory may be summarized as follows:

1. The individual human being does not exist alone. "The existence of one man presupposes another man." Human life entails "connection with and dependence upon others . . . "
2. The self-actualization of the individual can take place "only by his encroaching on another's freedom, by claiming something from another, by imposing upon another to a certain degree."
3. Man's social existence and his drive for self-actualization thus "entail impact, antagonism, conflict, and competition with others."
4. This "necessarily implies the incomplete realization of every individual's nature." "Self-actualization on the part of one individual can be attained only by some renunciation on the part of another, and each must ask from others that renunciation."
5. "There is no pre-established harmony between human beings." Man has to "seek" harmony with others "in an active way."
6. Man is free to make his own decisions and choices. Man's being free "implies the necessity of encroaching upon the freedom of others. . . . Therefore, we may say that the activity of encroaching also belongs to the nature of man."
7. Social life therefore requires "self-restriction in the interest of

[59]Ibid, p. 157. (Emphasis mine)
[60]Ibid., p. 197.
[61]Ibid., p. 208.

another." "Self-restricting behavior . . . is [thus also] due to an underlying tendency which belongs to human nature."

8. Self-restriction and encroachment are thus two major and interrelated types of behavior. "Man is neither aggressive nor submissive by nature. He is driven to actualize himself and to come to terms with his environment. . . . Whenever either form of behavior achieves dominance . . . then something has gone wrong . . ." "Normally behavior fluctuates in adequate proportions between self-restriction and encroachment upon the freedom of others."

9. "*Self-restriction* is experienced as inherent in human nature; it *corresponds to what we call the ethical, the norms.*" [Emphasis mine]

10. Freedom "does not mean the arbitrary right of each individual to do what he likes . . . it . . . presupposes the possibility of actualization on the part of all other individuals." Freedom therefore presupposes "freedom for all others—equality . . . equal rights and equal duties."

11. "Self-restriction and encroachment upon the freedom of others," when properly balanced, "are the avenues for the best possible self-actualization of all individuals forming . . . society, and by virtue of this they are the instruments for the creation of the best possible society."

12. A society based on this maximum of self-actualization possible within the necessary limits of the self-restriction required by social life would be successful because it would be "in accordance with the essence of human nature."[62]

Goldstein's views raise important problems, and are worthy of careful analysis. However, this is outside the scope of the present essay. The purpose of the summary of this part of Goldstein's social theory is to show the fundamental differences between his use of the concept of self-actualization and its use by our humanistic psychologists. Its purpose is also to point out that the errors made by Maslow, Fromm, Rogers, *et al.*, in their use of the concept of self-actualization, are completely their own, and are in no way chargeable to Goldstein. For Goldstein never proposed to transform the fact of man's drive for self-actualization into an ethical norm or a guide for conduct. He identified self-actualization with "encroachment upon the freedom of others," and with "antagonism, conflict, and competition with others." For him *it is self-restriction that corresponds to the ethical,* and the ethical norm or guide for conduct that he proposed is that of a proper balance between self-actualization (or encroachment) and self-restriction.

To be sure, Goldstein argued that a social order based on this norm

[62]Ibid., Chapter VIII, pp. 201–23 *passim*.

will be a successful social order, because it would be in accordance with the nature of man. In other words, he made a judgment as to *feasibility,* or *workability.* He was saying that a society based on this norm is likely to *work out,* because it would make possible a certain amount of satisfaction of the drive for self-actualization, and at the same time would not impose upon men demands for self-restriction or renunciation of a magnitude greater than they are *able* to carry out. A society based on norms that would "oppose human nature" would not work out; it "would be bound to fail." The *ethically desirable* social order proposed by Goldstein thus turns out to be a *feasible, practicable, workable* social order as well.

Needless to say, there are value assumptions hidden in Goldstein's value-free notion of the "success" or feasibility of a social order. The decisions as to which social order is a success, and as to what constitutes a failure in the organization of society, are themselves value decisions entailing prior value judgments. These value judgments cannot be deduced from the facts concerning human nature, or from predictions about the consequences of establishing a social order based on one kind or other kinds of ethical norms. These value judgments have other foundations. These prior value judgments are brought to bear upon the facts concerning the nature of man, or upon the predicted consequences of this or that kind of social order, and are used as ethical yardsticks by which to judge the facts or the predictions; they are not deduced from these facts or consequences.

But there is no confusion in Goldstein's writings on the subject of self-actualization. From the fact that man has a drive for self-actualization Goldstein did not infer the ethical proposition that self-actualization is good or that it is bad. Neither did he infer, from the fact that social life entails self-restriction, the proposition that self-restriction is good or that it is bad. His ethical judgment that a proper balance between self-actualization and self-restriction is good, has packed within it a large number of assumptions as to what is good or evil, right or wrong. But these assumptions, Goldstein recognized, are not deducible from the facts of self-actualization and "encroachment." Thus, a reading of Goldstein, while it tends to show him to have believed that there is some kind of relationship between ethical norms and the kind of being man is, also leads to two other conclusions: first, that Goldstein was not any more successful than others in establishing the nature of this relationship; and second that, whatever this relationship may be, it is not possible to *deduce* ethical norms from factual, descriptive information about the nature of man.

11. *A Philosophy of Jewish Ritual*

One of the recurring and persistent motifs in the history of Judaism is its perennial preoccupation with the phenomenon of ritual in human experience. From earliest days to our own, in the unfolding of thirty-five centuries of Jewish life and thought, this almost incessant concern has manifested itself repeatedly and variously either in the form of imperative prescriptions of certain rituals, or in stern, rigid prohibitions of certain other rituals, or in thunderous prophetic denunciations of ritualism, or in painstaking, critical analysis of the meaning and purpose of rituals and observances. The subject is unavoidable even in the most perfunctory perusal of any period in the vast body of both the sophisticated theological and philosophical Jewish literature, and the expository or popular writings in Judaism, from the first books of the Hebrew Bible to the most recent textbook in Judaism for teen-agers in religious schools. An underlying assumption seems to be discernible in Judaism's millennial attention to this phenomenon, namely, the assumption that ritual is apparently an inescapable element in human behavior; that man, the social animal, is also a ritualistic animal and necessarily engages in the activity we call ritual.

It is therefore not surprising that part of the energy expended in the course of historic Judaism, with its preoccupation with ritual, is directed toward forging the important distinction between "good" ritual and "evil" ritual, between ennobling ritual and corrupting ritual, between ritual that elevates and enriches the human spirit and ritual that

Presented on September 21, 1979, as the third lecture in a series on "The Functions of Ritual," held at the School of Philosophy, The Catholic University of America, Washington, D.C.

Dr. Franck gave the lecture on the basis of a rough draft, some parts of which he read verbatim. A few adjustments have been made in the draft, for incorporation of the lecture in the present volume.

debases the human spirit through self-deception, auto-intoxication, and diversion of humans from the pursuit and fulfillment of their ethical and spiritual responsibilities. Indeed, the repeated and ever-renewed hammering out of this differentiation within Judaism, between these two exemplifications of ritual, is an extension of its early revolt against the rituals, observances, and ceremonies of ancient paganism, the temptations of which beckoned so seductively from the tribes and nations in the midst of which Israel dwelled in its infancy as a people.

The cults of Baal, and Moloch, and K'mosh, with their rituals of human sacrifices and of sacred prostitution, were the extremes in a broad spectrum of pagan rituals and observances in which the dominant elements were magic and both group and individual self-hypnosis. One need only recall the worship of the golden calf at the foot of Mount Sinai, and the broken tablets of the law that were among the consequences of that shattering root-experience, that almost suicidal episode, in the spiritual life of the Jewish people in its early, formative stage, to understand the generalization that Judaism has been characterized by an ongoing dialectical tension between the revolutionary rejection and condemnation of ritual as idolatry, and the prescription and warm affirmation of ritual as the gateway to morality and sanctification.

A point of no minor philosophical significance may be distilled out of this characteristic of Judaism. Ritual, as was stated above, appears to be an inescapable ingredient in human behavior. Prayer is part of ritual. "The reason we pray," said William James, "is simply that we cannot help praying." When Cardinal John Henry Newman, in *The Grammar of Assent,* explained "Natural Religion" as a *universal* phenomenon, he pointed to prayer as part of it, and gave as illustrations the activities of the priests of Baal and of the dancing dervishes of Mohammedanism, without, Cardinal Newman continued, thereby "including in *our* notions of prayer" either "the frantic excesses of the worship of Baal or the artistic spinning of the Dervishes," and without "sanctioning their respective objects of belief, Baal or Mahomet."

Ritual and prayer, like any other innate propensities or inclinations in human nature, like any other universal tendencies or ingredients in human behavior, are *in themselves* neither good nor evil, neither moral nor immoral. It is on *the actions* engendered by these propensities that moral judgment can be passed. Judaism's doctrine of human nature portrays man as a creature in a state of constant tension between two inclinations: the inclination toward good and the inclination toward evil (the *yetzer tov* et al. and the *yetzer ra*). But, the ancient rabbis of the Talmudic period tell us, man's good inclination may produce evil. Consider excessive, over-protective mother-love, which can smother a child and thus destroy its capacity to lead an autonomous life. By the same token, the rabbis tell us, without the evil inclination, that is, without temptation, "a man would not build a home, take a wife, or procreate children."

So it is with ritual. In the perspective of Judaism, the question "What are the functions of ritual?," standing by itself, is a misplaced question, because it appears to contain the implicit assumption that all functions of ritual are inherently good. But not all are. Rituals are not religiously, ethically, socially self-validating *because they are rituals.* The question that must be asked in Judaism about ritual is threefold: 1) What are the proper, the good functions of ritual? This is the normative question. 2) How do we go about analyzing and differentiating between the good functions of ritual, and the multitudinous delusive, treacherous, corrosive, corrupting functions of innocent-looking and even beneficent-looking rituals? This is the analytico-descriptive question, and it is the most difficult, because the differences are often so subtle, so tricky, so conducive to self-deception. 3) How do we go about prescribing and maximizing the implementation of those functions of ritual that meet the normative criteria?

These are the questions asked in Judaism. The moral teaching of the Bible and the Hebrew prophets, as well as the religious law evolved by the rabbis, answered by condemning rituals unaccompanied by virtuous deeds and moral behavior. They eliminated from Jewish ritual all vestiges of magic, and all traces of the pagan notion that rituals not only have an hypnotic effect on God that moves Him to fulfill the entreaties of prayer, but also contain an automatic guarantee of God's favorable response.

The Torah consigns cults and rituals to a secondary place, and proclaims the primacy of moral action. Isaiah, in his stern first chapter, condemns rituals, prayers, and sacrifices that are detached from moral responsibility.

> To what purpose is the multitude of your sacrifices unto me? says the Lord. . . . And when you come to appear before me, who has required this of you, to trample my sanctuary? Bring no more vain oblations; it is an offering of abomination unto me. New Moon and Sabbath, your solemn assembly . . . they are a burden unto me. . . . When you spread forth your hands, I will hide my eyes from you; and when you make many prayers, I will not hear. . . . Cease to do evil; learn to do good. Seek justice, relieve the oppressed, judge the fatherless, plead for the widow.

And on Yom Kippur, the solemn Day of Atonement, a day of complete fast and reflection, the prophetic selection that is read in the synagogue is from Isaiah, chapters 57 and 58, in which the prophet denounces those who go through the ritual of fasting without corresponding ethical commitment, and by contrast he proclaims God's solemn admonition:

> *This* is the fast I have chosen, to loose the fetters of wickedness, to undo the bands of the yoke, and to let the oppressed go free. . . . To deal thy bread to the hungry, and that thou bring the homeless to thy house. When thou seest the naked, that thou cover him, and that thou hide not thyself from thy fellow man. Then shall thy light break forth as the morning . . .

Isaiah, Jeremiah, Ezekiel, Hosea, Amos, and the other prophets denounce cults and rituals that are detached from moral action. The rituals of fasting and praying can regrettably be made ends in themselves, and become deceptive substitutes for the goals or objectives they were intended to achieve, namely, justice, righteousness, spirituality, and sanctification. One can easily delude oneself into thinking that, having fasted and prayed, one has fulfilled one's religious and moral responsibilities.

The warning here is not just against conscious, deliberate hypocrisy in the exercise of the ritual, important as this is. The admonition is against self-delusion, self-deception, against the fantasy that in just performing the ritual one is doing something good. Ritual may serve as a delusive diversion from *true* fulfillment of the commandments. Ritual and prayer, with their esthetic components of symbolism, poetry, music, ceremonial objects, ceremonial attire, architectural design, can easily induce a comforting, soothing self-hypnosis in the worshipper or participant that comes close to a kind of idolatry, and that results in a delusive diversion from the true contemplation of God and of our relationship to God.

Having dwelt upon these dangers and pitfalls built into ritual, prayer, and observance, dangers to which authentic Judaism has been deeply sensitive, I must address what is an obvious question and also what is a puzzling paradox for anyone who is familiar with traditional Judaism and its practices. The obvious question is: "How does Judaism attempt to cope with the ever-lurking dangers and pitfalls and self-delusional possibilities in ritual?" I shall try to suggest some answers to this question shortly. But I want first to draw your attention to what I just referred to as a puzzling paradox.

If indeed there are these seductive dangers and pitfalls in ritual and observance, and if indeed Judaism always was and continues to be sensitive to them, isn't it surpassingly strange that traditional Judaism has prescribed so large a number of ritual commandments and observances? For the fact is that, according to rabbinic tradition, Biblical religious law prescribes a total of 613 basic commandments, 248 of which are affirmative prescriptions, and 365 are prohibitions. A large number of the 613 are ethical or moral laws, but also many are laws of ritual and observance. Moreover, to these latter laws, rabbinic interpretation has added numerous supplementary prescriptions, and thus the life of the traditional, observant Jew is regulated and governed every day in the week, and almost every hour of the day, from the time he rises in the morning to the time he retires at night, by a regimen of prayers, blessings, observances, and rituals connected with every conceivable human activity.

I once explained this fact to one of my classes at Georgetown University, and added the observation that, if a person meticulously observed all the prescribed commandments, he couldn't possibly do any evil. One of the members of the class made the wry comment: "Of course not. He wouldn't have any time left to do evil."

This was a shrewd observation, and, given the arithmetic of time, it is probably true; except that I never cease being amazed with what ingenuity we manage to find time for thinking and doing evil, even the most righteous among us. No wonder the Book of Ecclesiastes, in its realism, tells us in one of its verses that "There is no righteous man on earth who does good and who does not sin." Which is all by way of providing commentary and interpretation to the truth of that student's remark, and explicating the paradox about the plurality of ritual commandments.

There is no gainsaying the dangers inherent in ritual, as there are dangers inherent in all human life and activity. However, at the same time, Judaism teaches that it is precisely through ritual and observance and prayer—properly enacted—that man can be led to a sanctified, ethical, and spiritually meaningful life. The many commandments, properly practiced, are directed to such goals as the steadfast and continuous stimulus to good deeds and moral actions; the lifting of human life above the biological level of animality; and the awareness of man's finitude and limitedness in relation to God and to the infinity of His creation, and thereby the avoidance of arrogance and self-worship.

Indeed, my student was right. One of the ways of trying to avoid the pitfall of ritual is not *less* ritual, but rather *more* ritual—properly practiced. This is the traditional design for Jewish living: to fill the lives of human beings with the fulfillment of the ethical and ritual commandments. In the liturgy of monthly prayers at the time of the new moon, there is a plea for a life of "reverence for God and dread of sin," or avoidance of sin. On the other hand, in one of the most moving prayers in the daily morning liturgy, it is important to note what it is that Jewish ritual habituates the observing Jew to petition for every morning, as he addresses his Father in heaven:

> With abounding love Thou hast loved us, O Lord our God; great and overflowing tenderness Thou hast shown us. O, our Father, our King, for our forefathers' sake, who trusted in Thee, and whom Thou didst teach the laws of life, be also gracious unto us and teach us. O our Father, compassionate Father, have mercy upon us, and put it into our hearts to

> understand, to discern, to hearken, and to learn, to teach and to obey, to practice, and to fulfill in love all the teachings of Thy Torah. Enlighten our eyes in Thy Torah, and make our hearts cleave to Thy commandments, and unite our hearts to love and revere Thy name.

The petition addressed to the loving and merciful God is that people be granted understanding, and that they be imbued with the will to learn, to teach, to obey, to practice, and to fulfill the teachings and the commandments. Praying and observing alone will not do. These must be the vestibules, the entrance halls, to understanding, to goal-directed guidance, and finally to *doing*, as the instrumentality of sanctification.

And here it is appropriate to return to the question asked earlier, namely, how does Judaism try to cope with the dangers and pitfalls of ritual, and the possible self-deceptions and delusions which are involved therein? I believe that part of the answer is contained, though paradoxically, in the *multiplicity* of rituals and observances, though, of course, it can hardly be claimed that this multiplicity has succeeded in banning enough of either hypocrisy or self-deception. However, another and perhaps more important answer is contained in a concept that recurs repeatedly in the literature and thought concerning Jewish ritual, a concept that constitutes in fact a prescriptive principle for the practice of ritual, and that is imbedded in the long prayer just quoted. The Hebrew term for this concept is *kavanah,* and a precise translation of it into English is quite impossible.

The meaning of *kavanah* is approximated by all of the following words taken together, in combination: "intent," "intention," "intentionality," "purposiveness," "earnestness," "devoutness," "serious and knowledgeable intent." For shorthand purposes I shall occasionally use in what follows the English word "intent," where the English locution seems to be natural. But I shall resort to the use of the Hebrew word, *kavanah,* where it seems important to convey the precise and untranslatable concept. Part of the philosophy of Jewish ritual, as I interpret it, is that one ought to perform rituals with *kavanah.* One ought to understand or try to understand what one is doing or saying in the performance of ritual or in the recitation or chanting of a prayer or blessing; one ought consciously to aim at the fulfillment of the commandment's purpose; and there should be an intentional continuity between the ritual performed and other elements in one's past and future experience.

In performing the ritual, one ought to include in one's *kavanah* the awareness that one is *commanded* to perform the ritual; that this is a purposive, not a hurried, perfunctory, or purely self-gratifying act; that it is an act of self-transcendence and sanctification. Indeed, many of the ritual blessings begin with the words: "Praised be Thou, O Lord,

Sovereign of the universe, *who has sanctified us with His commandments, and has commanded us to . . .* "

One could use numerous illustrations from the prescribed observances of everyday life, and note their sanctifying intent, and effect if they are enacted with *kavanah*. Instead, I cite two books about the fabric of life in the small Jewish town in Eastern Europe known as the *shtetl*. The first is an anthropological study first directed by the late Ruth Benedict, and later completed under the direction of the late Margaret Mead: *Life Is With People: The Culture of the Shtetl*, by Mark Zborowski and Elizabeth Herzog.[1] The other is an historico-poetic reconstruction of that life of the spirit in the *shtetl* by the late Rabbi Abraham Joshua Heschel, of blessed memory. The book is entitled *The Earth Is the Lord's: The Inner World of the Jew in East Europe*.[2] In addition to these two books, a pale and feeble reflection of some of the moral and spiritual fabric of that society is given in the popular musical, "Fiddler on the Roof."

The philosophy of Jewish ritual expounded in the present paper, in this discursive manner, is, I believe, repeatedly advanced by many of the outstanding thinkers, theologians, and philosophers in the mainstream of Jewish religious thought and literature. The generic question to which they respond is, to state it again, "What are the reasons for the commandments?" "What are the purposes of the prescribed rituals, observances, and prayers?" A medieval Jewish thinker, Abraham ibn Ezra (1089–1164), answered succinctly: "The essence of all commandments is to make the human heart upright." The towering figure in medieval Jewish thought—the twelfth-century Rabbi Moses ben Maimon, popularly known as Moses Maimonides—similarly explained, in his seminal work, *The Guide of the Perplexed*, that rituals and observances are essentially pedagogic devices for the cultivation and disciplining of the masses, the true end being the knowledge of the divine through the study of the Torah.

You must remember, says Maimonides, that "all the practices of the worship, such as reading the Torah, prayer, and the performance of the other commandments, have only the end of training you to occupy yourself with His commandments, . . . rather than with matters pertaining to this world . . . If, however, you pray merely by moving your lips while facing a wall . . . or if you read the Torah with your tongue while your heart is set upon" other matters, "without reflecting either upon the meaning of that action or upon Him from whom the commandment proceeds or upon the end of the action, you should not think that you have achieved the end."

Maimonides pursues this matter to the following conclusion:

[1]Introduction by Margaret Mead. New York: Schocken Books, 1962.
[2]New York: Henry Schuman, 1950.

> Every commandment, be it a prescription or a prohibition, has as its purpose the abolition of reciprocal wrongdoing, or urging to a noble moral quality leading to good societal relationships, or communicating a correct opinion that ought to be believed either on account of itself, or because it is necessary for the abolition of injustice or for the acquisition of noble moral qualities.

This conclusion arises out of Maimonides' doctrine of two kinds of beliefs: First, beliefs which are true in themselves, not in relation to any other purpose, that is, theological and metaphysical beliefs about the nature of God, His unknowability, creation *ex nihilo*, etc. Second, what Maimonides calls "necessary beliefs." He explains this second kind of belief as follows:

> Sometimes a belief is necessary for the abolition of reciprocal wrongdoing, or for the acquisition of good moral qualities, as, for example, the belief that God has a violent anger against those who do injustice, as it is written in *Exodus* 22:25, "And my wrath shall be kindled, etc.," and as the belief that God responds instantaneously to the prayer of someone wronged or deceived.

This kind of belief is necessary for the moral welfare of mankind and for its spiritual life, but it distorts the nature of God. It ascribes to God human qualities, and anthropomorphizes Him. God is imperturbable, He does not get angry, He is not moved by ritual or prayer. As the prophet Malachi said, "For I the Lord change not." It is philosophically and theologically presumptuous, and borders upon a primitive kind of religion, to espouse the belief that we ought to perform the commandments because, if we do not, God will be angry at us, but if we do, *we can change God*. Immanuel Kant makes the same point in his *Religion Within the Limits of Reason Alone:* "It is . . . not only a preposterous but also a presumptuous illusion to try to divine whether, through the persistent importunity of one's request, God cannot be diverted (to our present advantage) from the plan of his wisdom." However, this belief is necessary for the masses of the people, in order to make possible a Torah-society characterized by justice and tranquility.

Some commentators attacked this doctrine of Maimonides as heretical. Others understood it, as was the case of a contemporary of Maimonides, Shem Tov Falaquera, whose commentary on the Maimonidean texts quoted above reads as follows:

> . . . it is necessary that the mass-man should believe that God is moved by human petitions and rituals of propitiation. Though this belief is false, strictly speaking, it is necessary for the existence of society. Therefore these beliefs are called necessary. The wise man will understand that

> these beliefs are said in accord with the principle: "The Torah spoke in the language of human beings."

The nature of ritual, therefore, has to be understood not in terms of propitiating God, or pleasing God, or extracting rewards or forgiveness from God. God does not need our rituals, but our rituals need God. Without the awareness of God, ritual could not raise man to levels of spiritual nobility, or to heights of moral aspiration and performance. Ritual, performed with *kavanah,* "inculcates in our hearts useful lessons," says Maimonides. It is prescribed he says, "with a view to purifying the people."

With respect to the ritual slaughter of animals for food, Maimonides asks, "What does it matter to God how the animal is slaughtered?" Well, first of all, hunting, killing animals for sport, is strictly prohibited by the law. But, since man must eat, and the meat of animals is one kind of food, then the act of killing for food must be transformed from the insensitive act of brute killing into the ritual act to be performed with the least possible pain to the animal. The person who is authorized to perform this act is a special person; he must be trained for the performance of the act; the knife must be flawlessly sharpened, without the slightest imperfection; and the cut must be made expertly, only at the neck, with one swift motion, severing the carotid artery, so that there is an instantaneous evacuation of the blood from the brain of the animal, thus reducing pain to a minimum.

To quote Rabbi Moses ben Maimon again, "As necessity occasions the eating of animals, the commandment (of ritual slaughter) was intended to bring about the easiest death in the easiest manner." It is a contribution to the purification of the people if they know that cruelty to animals is forbidden, and that the act of ritual slaughter may not be practiced by just anyone, in just any manner. Indeed, it must be a religious act, performed in a context of religious observance.

Let me now turn to the subject of prayer, since prayer may perhaps be considered paradigmatic of ritual. In the course of developing the theory of prayer, I want to accentuate the three functions of ritual, that should have become clear, I trust, out of what has already been said; the three functions being the cognitive, the behavioral, and the esthetic as part of the behavioral. It would be interesting and instructive to present and analyze a typology of prayer, dwelling on the significance of each type. Suffice it here simply to list a number of the types of prayer. There are prayers of contemplation, prayers of adoration and praise, prayers of thanksgiving, prayers of affirmation, prayers of resignation, prayers of confession, prayers of penitence, prayers of protest, prayers of quest, prayers of intercession, prayers of petition.

As we said above, God does not need our rituals, or prayers of praise or thanksgiving. Neither can we, in our arrogance, presume that we can affect or change God with our prayers of praise, penitence, or confession. But even petitionary prayer cannot properly be interpreted as primitive, conditional prayer. Petitionary prayer is not an attempt to make a deal with God, saying: "If you, God, grant my petition, I will worship and adore you, but if you do not grant my petition I will rebel against you." The Talmud says: "Man must bless God in his affliction as well as in his joy." Rabbi Akiba, the great and saintly sage of the Talmudic period in the second century, said:

> Be not like one of the idolators: when all goes well with him, he honors his gods, but if misfortune overcomes him, he curses them. Not so with the Israelites. If God sends them happiness, they bless Him, and if God afflicts them with sorrow, they bless Him.

This was said by a man who knew suffering. He was tortured horribly by the Romans during the Roman persecution of the second century, and was put to death in a most barbaric way.

Rabbi Abraham Isaac Kook, the chief rabbi of the Jewish community in Palestine before World War II, a profound scholar, philosopher, mystic, and poet, said: "Prayer does not desire to change anything in the divine, which is the source of eternity, and hence without alteration." Prayer, done with serious intent, with *kavanah,* endeavors to change man.

Why do Jews pray on the High Holy Days for forgiveness of sins? Why do they engage in the public confessional: "Our Father, our King, we have sinned, we have transgressed, etc."? Is it because if we pray, and if we fast, and if we repent, these actions will affect God and He will forgive us? The answer, contrary to popular religion and popular belief by the masses who accept literally the human and anthropomorphic language of scripture, is *no!*

Judaism commands the Jew to do it because if the person does this earnestly, with *kavanah,* if in praying he attends to what he is doing, if he contemplates the significance of his prayers and fasting, then he will truly recognize that he has indeed sinned, that he has helped bring evil into this world, and having thus led himself to this recognition, he will be more likely to repent truly—not just to say he is sorry for what he has done, but to repent in the sense of the Hebrew word, *teshuvah,* return, turn around, change his ways, and resolve to refrain from doing evil, and resolve to do good. This is the efficacy of prayer, this is the function of prayer. To quote Maimonides again:

> . . . all that is involved in prayer is not for the purpose of changing God, but rather in order that the prayers may be an opening for the soul to confess its sins and to abandon all its sins; this way the soul rises from impurity to purity, and finds itself closer to God, but God does not change. . . .

> . . . the essence of prayer depends upon him who prays—for prayer does not help, except for purity of the soul. . . . You have thus learned that God has no desire for this matter of prayers and entreaties and crying out, but all depends on him who prays—when it purifies his soul and turns him away from his iniquity, his soul comes nearer to his Creator.

There is an interesting problem in the philosophy of Jewish prayer, and that is the tension between two kinds of prayer: a) spontaneous prayer, and b) prescribed prayer with received traditional texts. The question is asked, which of these two kinds of prayer is more important? Furthermore, how can one achieve *kavanah,* intentionality, earnest devoutness, in the recitation of ready-made prayer texts? The consensus is that there is room for both kinds of prayer; each can help fulfill the proper function of prayer.

Here again, dangers must be recognized and avoided. The ecstasy of private, purely spontaneous prayer may be self-intoxicating, an eruption of emotion for its own sake, an eruption which is self-terminating because it does not lead to cognition of the human state in relation to God and one's fellow man, and does not lead to purification and moral action. The danger in prescribed, ready-made prayer texts is, of course, that they may become, as they so often do, mechanical recitations by rote. But it is precisely here that the prescription of *kavanah* becomes so important. The prescribed prayers contain moral and theological instruction, exalting and inspiring poetry, exhortations and admonitions. Many of the moral and spiritual heights reached for and touched in the texts of the prayer book could not possibly be expected out of the limited range of the mass of worshippers on their own. Therefore, though there are repeated admonitions in the rabbinic literature against making one's prayers fixed and mechanical, it is nevertheless emphasized that, with *kavanah,* the prescribed prayers can on the one hand become worship as study for instruction and moral direction, and on the other hand provide goal-directed, lyrical and emotional exaltation as a dimension in the religious experience.

But part of the intentionality of prayer is the requirement that prayer not be detached from the rest of life. This is explained in a charming and inspiring commentary by the late Rabbi Abraham Isaac Kook. He explicates what sounds like a puzzling statement by one of the ancient rabbis in the Talmud, who said: "A person should pray only in a house that has windows." Rabbi Kook's twentieth-century *explication de texte* is as follows:

> Prayer, to be sure, is private worship in the soul of the worshipper, but a necessary condition for its perfection is his recognition of the importance of the outside world around him. But if the privacy of his worship

> in his heart leads him to become separated from any relationship to the outside world, he will not attain the ultimate perfection of prayer, which should make man alive and awaken him with the divine spirit to be prepared to act in and be affected by justice and righteousness. Therefore a person should pray only in a building that has windows, where the ability to look outside will awaken him to his duty and to his relationship to the whole world in which he lives.
>
> The fear of sin also must be tied to daily and social life, in order that the fear of sin be intermingled with life. Thus the comment of our sages: "I shall walk before God in the land of the living." This refers to marketplaces. That is, the walking before God should be in the marketplaces, among activities, and transactions.
>
> Even prayer, which is distinctly a religious, spiritual activity, must not be constricted to the realm of the spirit alone, but must influence all of man's paths of life. And this explains Rabbi Joshua ben Levi's saying that he who prays should tarry an hour following his prayers. The function of this hour following prayer is to tie together the exaltation of his soul and the elevation of his spirit during prayer with his way of life and his material transactions during the entire day. Through the uplifting of the soul and its sanctification in prayer, all the paths of life become sanctified, so that they may be made holy and may advance toward the goal of truth and justice.
>
> This end can be served by tarrying for an hour after prayer, to tie the ideas one has learned, and one's exalted feelings of the period of prayer, with all the paths of one's material life. And this is the proper level of a person's life, that he does not separate himself from the affairs of this world, but rather occupies himself with them, broadens them, and strengthens them in order to attain successfully a true end. (My translation)

Not unexpectedly, I have had to omit a number of other aspects of Jewish ritual, consideration of which would be essential for even a superficial understanding of the subject, and for insight into and *Einfühlung* for the place and significance of ritual and observance in traditional Judaism. Some degree of the phenomenology of ritual as experience manages to be communicated, I believe, in the two books referred to above, and the reference to them will have to suffice.

One cannot, however, omit at least mention of the rituals connected with the sanctification of periods of time. Judaism does not dichotomize the world and existence into the sacred and the profane. The distinctions made are between the sacred, the secular or worldly, and the profane. 1) There are sacred times, such as times of prayer, holy days, and festivals, which are discussed below. 2) The secular, the worldly, the ordinary, the everyday—this realm of life is not anti-sacred. The secular, the everyday, is that which is to be sanctified to the greatest extent possible, because it is capable of sanctification. Part of the function of the commandments and the rituals is to achieve such sanctification. 3) Only the profane, the contumacious, the deliberately and defiantly evil is anti-sacred.

Time is a dimension of life that can be sanctified. The time one engages in study of Torah, the time one engages in prayer, the time one devotes to performing good deeds, are examples. But some portions of time are perceived as almost inherently, ontologically sacred: the Sabbath, the Holy Days, and the Festivals. Some rituals have the function of ushering in sacred time, and in turn of marking the conclusion or departure of sacred time. The *Kiddush,* or *ceremony of sanctification* on the eve of the Sabbath or of Holy Days or Festivals, is the ceremony that invokes the commandment to do this, and that signalizes the resolve that the day or days now being embarked upon are different. It is to accentuate the spiritual in man, and to remind him that in his pursuits on this earth he must remember the enslavement in Egypt and his duties to his fellow humans, including the stranger, and also to the animals that serve him. It is a reminder of creation and of man's creatureliness. The ceremony of *Havdalah*—of distinguishing between the sacred time and the everyday time at the conclusion of the holy day—is full of the almost mystical reluctance to give up the spiritual joy of the sacred time, and the yearning desire to extend the Sabbath or Holy Day as much as possible, and to carry over some of the sanctity into one's workaday life.

In conclusion, it should be observed that ritual and prayer have an important esthetic function. The perspicacious remark of my student, that if a person observed all the commandments he would have no time left for doing evil, may leave a wrong impression. In our contemporary culture, this sounds as if he who fulfilled all the commandments would have no time left to have fun in life, to enjoy life. The vocabulary of Judaism indeed often speaks of the "burden of the commandments," and it all sounds like a stern, bleak doctrine, unrelieved by beauty and joy and mirth and laughter. But such an impression is terribly, misleadingly wrong.

The vocabulary of Judaism also includes the phrase "the joy of the commandments," "the adornment of the commandments." It is a good deed to add beauty to the observances, and to make and choose beautiful ritual objects, to rejoice on the Sabbath and Festivals and Holy Days, and to enrich them with melodious chants, good, savory foods, with dancing and celebrations. Have you ever been to a traditional Jewish wedding? Have you ever attended the festival of the Rejoicing of the Law in a traditional synagogue? Do you know of the joys of family observances and rituals, and indeed of traditional Jewish family life within the framework of tradition?

Rabbi Leo Baeck, the late sainted Chief Rabbi of Berlin, Germany, who managed to survive in one of Hitler's concentration camps, says in his book, *The Essence of Judaism,* that actually the burden of the commandments seldom weighed upon Judaism. He continues:

> . . . An examination of Judaism's history shows that all of the ritual and ceremonial statutes were an element in the community's joy of life. The term, "the joy in fulfilling a commandment," was applied to them and the experience of each generation has confirmed anew the validity of that description. Only those who do not possess or know these joys, have spoken so much about the "burden of the law." But no matter how much Jewish piety stressed the idea of commandment and service, it always emphasized this joyful element. . . . All obedience to a commandment which man imposes upon himself carries and elevates him. This was equally true with regard to the ritual and ceremonial statutes, for through them was discovered a spiritual world, full of devoutness and duty, full of life-giving joy.
>
> . . . With ever fresh symbols they seek to keep man above all that is low and common, to indicate to him the divine will, and to awaken in him that earnest and yet joyful consciousness that he always stands before God. These statutes . . . leave him to his work and his home where they connect him with God. . . . Each morning, noon and evening, each beginning and each ending, has its prayers and worship. The atmosphere of the house of God, the halo of religious devotion, is spread over the whole of existence; each day has its lesson and consecration; the Law has prevented Judaism from becoming a mere religion for the Sabbath. And similarly it has overcome sacraments, with their separation of holiness from life, by its introduction of holiness into life.
>
> This was especially true of home life. . . . every home is a miniature community and all the customs meant to preserve the community also guard the home. . . . They sanctify the earthly, consecrating the workaday and prosaic character of the home. This is done through an abundance of symbols—the language of religious ideas. From them Sabbaths and festivals received their poetic charm and atmosphere. . . . The Law gave purity to leisure and distinction to the evening in both of which the character and freedom of man are most distinctly revealed. . . . Although these statutes were established only to protect the religion, they ultimately enriched it.

The liturgy of each of the three daily prayer services—morning, afternoon, and evening, every day and on Sabbaths and Festivals, concludes with the prayer for the establishment of God's kingdom on earth:

> We therefore hope in Thee, O Lord our God, that we may soon behold thy majestic glory, when the abominations will be removed from the earth and when all idolatry will be abolished; when the world will be perfected under the kingdom of the Almighty, and all mankind will call upon thy name; when Thou wilt turn unto thyself all the wicked of the

> earth. . . . May they all accept the yoke of thy kingdom and do Thou rule over them speedily and forevermore. . . .

But it is *doing* that will build God's kingdom, not prayer. That fulfillment requires a partnership between man and God. Prayer and ritual, in themselves, at best produce nothing and at worst become an idolatrous self-deception that delays the coming of God's kingdom. Ritual and prayer lead to the kingdom only if they are aids to the fulfillment of God's commandments, only if they are prolegomena to moral action under God.

Biographical Sketch of Isaac Franck

By Pearl C. Franck

Isaac Franck made notable contributions to two widely disparate fields of human activity. He combined a distinguished career as a leader in *Jewish community service* with dedicated scholarship and dynamic teaching in *philosophy*. His wholehearted devotion to both roles, the activist and the academic, arose from a personality characterized by conceptual acuity, love of literature, motivation toward service, compassion, humor, and affability.

Early Years

Isaac was born on March 17, 1909, in Zozov, Russia, a village in the Ukraine where about fifty Jewish families lived. He was a sixth-generation direct descendant of Rabbi Levi Isaac ben Meir of Berdichev (c. 1740–1810). Isaac's ancestor was the founder of Hasidism in central Poland and a pillar of the Hasidic movement in Lithuania and the Ukraine. In the middle of the nineteenth century, Rabbi Levi Isaac became a popular hero among European Jewry, and his life and teachings were often celebrated in poetry, fiction, and drama, not only in Yiddish but also in Hebrew. Isaac Franck took pride in the learning and wisdom of his famous forebear.

Isaac's father, George, earned his livelihood as a storekeeper, but he was also a zealous student of the Talmud, who was lovingly remembered by Isaac as the possessor of a keen analytical mind.

When Isaac was three years old, he began to study Hebrew with his father and a maternal uncle. At the age of seven and one-half, he was admitted to a Russian gymnasium to pursue secular studies.

Shortly thereafter, when Isaac was about eight, the peaceful, albeit restricted existence of the Franck family was demolished by the Russian Revolution and its aftermath. It was due to the insistence of Isaac's mother, a true woman of valor, that the family, consisting of his parents, Isaac, and his two younger brothers, fled from Russia to Rumania. They lived in Rumania for two years, accumulating funds for a steamer trip to America, by steerage.

When a sufficient amount had been saved, they set out for America, arriving in New York in October 1923. Isaac was then fourteen and one-half. His English was limited to three words: boy, girl, door.

His promise of later achievement, however, was evidenced upon his graduation from Public School 109 in Brooklyn a few years later, when he was awarded a prize for English composition and also received the Isidore and Ida Strauss medal for loyalty to the school's ideals.

During 1926–1928, Isaac continued his Hebrew studies in New York at the Herzliah Hebrew Academy and the Tarbuth Teacher's Seminary. In 1929, he taught Hebrew literature and Jewish history in the high school department of the Herzliah Hebrew Academy, serving at the same time as the school's librarian.

He continued to pursue a livelihood in the field of Jewish education. This work enabled him to finance his undergraduate studies at Washington Square College, New York University, where he majored in philosophy. In June 1934, at the age of twenty-five, he received a B.S. with honors in philosophy. He was also awarded the Augusta Lundin Prize for the best undergraduate essay in philosophy.

At New York University, Isaac met Pearl Crystal, a fellow student. They were married in October 1934. In 1985, they celebrated their fiftieth wedding anniversary, along with their son Walter, their daughter Phyllis, and their son-in-law Paul Tauber.

Career in Jewish Community Service

From 1934 to 1949, Isaac served the Jewish communities of Portchester (New York), Manchester (New Hampshire), Detroit (Michigan), and Brooklyn (New York), as educator, social worker, and community relations executive. Although these were full-time posts, he managed to engage in graduate studies in philosophy at Columbia University in 1934–1937, Harvard University in 1937–1939, the University of Michigan in 1940–1942, and again at Columbia University in 1947–1949; and also was a part-time instructor in political science at Wayne State University in 1943–1946.

In 1949, Isaac was appointed executive director of the Jewish Community Council of Greater Washington. He later became executive vice president of the Council. He served the organization for almost twenty-five years, until October 1973. During Isaac's association with the Council, it grew from a small, struggling body representing fifty-seven organizations and enjoying little public recognition into a widely respected confederation with 173 member organizations, accepted not only as the voice of the organized Jewish community but also as a focus of influence and authority in the general community and its educational, political, and religious institutions.

This period encompassed the struggle for civil rights, on both the local and the national scene. In that struggle, Isaac was among Washington's outstanding pioneers. For example, he assisted in the establishment of the Interreligious Committee on Race Relations and of the Metropolitan Urban Coalition, and served as secretary of both bodies for many years. Residents of the capital city remember with special pride his significant help in transforming Washington from a segregated to an integrated city.

Recognizing Isaac's astuteness in strategies for replacing strife with cooperation, the Department of State utilized his services as a consultant in its international information programs in 1951–1954. In 1962, in specific recognition of his contributions to lessening tensions between religious and ethnic groups, the National Capital Chapter of the American Jewish Congress awarded him the Stephen S. Wise Medallion, inscribed "For His Dedicated and Distinguished Leadership in Furthering the High Ethical Values and Humanitarian Traditions of the Jewish People."

During these crisis-laden years, Isaac also engaged in teaching on a part-time basis, continued doing graduate work until he completed his work for the Ph.D., and served as editor of a community service periodical, as follows:

—From 1956 to 1973, he taught philosophy and social psychology at American University, attaining the rank of adjunct professor in 1972.

—In 1966, he received a Ph.D. in philosophy from the University of Maryland, with a major in philosophy and a minor in sociology. His dissertation was entitled *The Concept of Human Nature: A Philosophical Analysis of the Concept of Human Nature in the Writings of G. W. Allport, S. E. Asch, Erich Fromm, A. H. Maslow, and C. R. Rogers.*

—From 1971 to 1973, he served as editor of a periodical, *Under-Cover,* issued by the Soviet Jewry Committee of the Jewish Community Council. The periodical publicized the difficult situation of Soviet Jewish dissidents and the harsh punishment meted out to them when they applied for emigration visas.

Full-Time Teaching

A second stage in Isaac's career began in 1973, when he retired from professional Jewish community service. In the next six years, he taught at a number of universities, as follows:

—From 1973 to 1977, Isaac was a full-time lecturer in philosophy at Howard University. In the middle of that period, in the spring of 1975, he was visiting professor at Baltimore Hebrew College, teaching contemporary Jewish philosophy.

—In 1977, after leaving Howard University, he served twice as visiting professor—in the summer, at the Catholic University of America, teaching a graduate course in Spinoza's *Ethics;* and, in the fall, at the University of Maryland, teaching twentieth century Jewish philosophy.

—In the spring of 1978, Isaac was professorial lecturer at Georgetown University, teaching philosophy and philosophical poetry. At the same university, in 1978–1979, he was the Hymen Goldman distinguished lecturer in Jewish studies.

Concentration on Ethical Issues

At this point, Isaac entered the final stage of his career, in which he was active and productive mainly in research and teaching on medical ethics and ethics in general. Thus, from 1979 until his death on May 14, 1985, he was senior research scholar at the Kennedy Institute of Ethics, Georgetown University, where academicians and concerned practitioners investigate ethical issues arising not only from biomedical advances that have occurred in our century but also developments in a broad range of aspects of contemporary society, including business, government, the press, social work, and interreligious relations.

Among the problems with which Isaac and his colleagues at the Kennedy Institute were concerned are ethical perplexities relating to pre-natal diagnosis, abortion, prolongation of life, and allocation of medical resources. Isaac brought to bear on the analysis of these problems the perspective of Jewish teaching.

Equally challenging was Isaac's service in the Georgetown University School of Medicine's department of community and family medicine, where he was appointed adjunct associate professor in 1979 and adjunct professor in 1981. In that department, he participated in the faculty team teaching the course in bioethics to second-year medical students and also was a member of a team of three professionals who conducted a weekly psychosomatic conference for fourth-year medical students.

In addition, during the late 1970's and early 1980's Isaac was associated with the Forum on Psychiatry and the Humanities, Washington School of Psychiatry, in its seminar program; taught contemporary Jewish ethics at Georgetown University's School of Continuing Education during the spring semester of 1983; and taught Jewish ethics and values in the master's program conducted jointly by the College of Jewish Studies of Greater Washington and American University during the fall semesters of 1983 and 1984.

Besides the research, teaching, and lecturing which occupied his later years, Isaac continued to engage in other public service activities. For example, he was a founding member of the ethics committee of the Hebrew Home of Greater Washington (which was among the first ethics committees in the country serving in old-age facilities), and he was a member of that committee from 1979 to 1985. He served on the board of trustees of the College of Jewish Studies of Greater Washington from 1971 to 1985 and was chairman of the board in 1979. He also served as a member of the board of directors of the Philosophy Education Society, 1971–1985, and as president of the Washington Philosophy Club, 1975–1976.

Isaac's final years were marked by two major health problems. In 1981, he underwent open heart surgery, from which he made a successful recovery, and within three weeks he resumed his professional activities. Four years later, early in 1985, his health again declined, but he continued with his work. For example:

—In January, he lectured to the medical staff of the Saint Francis Hospital, Miami Beach, Florida, on "Ethical Problems in Death and Dying" and, later on the same day, participated in an interreligious dialogue in the city of Miami on "Bioethical Problems Relating to the Beginning of Life."

—In February, he lectured to the psychiatric staff at the Veterans' Administration Medical Center in Washington, D.C., on "Psychotherapy and Ethics."

—In April, despite a substantial deterioration in his health, he flew to Louisville, Kentucky, to participate in an interreligious symposium held at Bellarmine College on "Religious Ethics and Medical Experimentation."

A few days after his return from Louisville, tests revealed that he had cancer of the pancreas. Shortly thereafter, he underwent an eight-hour operation for removal of the tumor. In conformity with Jewish beliefs, heroic life-sustaining measures were administered, but this man of almost boundless energy and perennially youthful outlook did not respond, and he passed away nineteen days after the operation.

Isaac Franck had a many-faceted career—activist, scholar, teacher, ethicist. In each of these areas, as testified by many who worked with him or studied under him, Isaac always excelled, guided by the maxim which he first heard as an immigrant boy from his teacher at Public School 109 in Brooklyn decades ago, "Whatever is worth doing is worth doing well."

List of Isaac Franck's Writings

Compiled by Pearl C. Franck

Note.—This list *supplements* (i.e., *it does not include*) the essays published in the present volume.

1935

Reviews of exhibit of work by Saul Raskin and other artists, and paintings by Lionel Reiss, at the Jewish Center, Portchester, New York, in the Portchester *Daily Item,* January 16 and March 28, 1935.

1936

Review of Ludwig Lewisohn (ed.), *Rebirth: A Book of Modern Jewish Thought* (New York: Harper and Brothers, 1935), in *The Jewish Pioneer,* March 1936, pp. 13–14.

Review of Marquis Childs, *Sweden: The Middle Way* (New Haven: Yale University Press, 1936), in *The Jewish Pioneer,* March 1936, p. 14.

Review of Otto Klineberg, *Race Differences* (New York: Harper and Brothers, 1936), and Julian S. Huxley and others, *We Europeans* (New York: Harper and Brothers, 1936), in *Jewish Frontier,* Vol. 3, May 1936, p. 34.

Review of Duncan B. MacDonald, *The Hebrew Philosophical Genius: A Vindication* (Princeton: Princeton University Press, 1936), in *Jewish Frontier,* Vol. 3, June 1936, p. 29.

Review of Shoshana Harris Sankowsky, *Short History of Zionism* (New York: Avukah, 1936), in *Jewish Frontier,* Vol. 3, July 1936, p. 25.

1937

Review of John Lewis and others (eds.), *Christianity and the Social Revolution* (New York: Charles Scribner and Sons, 1935), in *Jewish Frontier*, Vol. 4, March 1937, p. 30.

Review of S. Y. Agnon, *The Bridal Canopy* (Garden City, N.Y.: Doubleday, Doran and Co., 1937), in *Jewish Frontier*, Vol. 4, June 1937, p. 28. Reprinted in *The Jewish Week* (Washington, D.C.), November 24, 1966, p. 4.

1938

Review of I. J. Singer, *The River Breaks Up* (New York: Alfred A. Knopf, 1938), in *Jewish Frontier*, Vol. 5, October 1938, p. 30.

1939

Review of Sidney Meller, *Roots in the Sky* (New York: Macmillan and Co., 1938), in *Jewish Frontier*, Vol. 6, February 1939, pp. 26–27.

Review of I. J. Singer, *East of Eden* (New York: Alfred A. Knopf, 1939), and Sholom Asch, *Song of the Valley* (New York: G. P. Putnam's Sons, 1939), in *Jewish Frontier*, Vol. 6, June 1939, pp. 53–55.

1940

Review of Nettie P. McGill, *The Youth of New York City* (New York: Macmillan and Co., 1940), in *Jewish Frontier*, Vol. 7, November 1940, p. 28.

1941

Review of June P. and Arthur A. Guild, *Social Work Engineering* (New York: Harper and Brothers, 1940), in *The Jewish Social Service Quarterly* (name changed in 1956 to *Journal of Jewish Communal Service*), Vol. 17, March 1941, pp. 317–318.

"C.I.O.'s Detroit Dilemma," *Jewish Frontier*, Vol. 8, December 1941, pp. 14–16.

1942

Reviews in issues of *The Detroit Free Press,* as follows: combined review of John Stirling (ed.), *The Bible for Today* (New York: Oxford University Press, 1941), and Louis M. Notkin (ed.), *The Quotable Bible* (New York: Samuel Curl, 1941); and a separate review of Edgar Johnson (ed.), *A Treasury of Biography* (New York: Howell, Soskin, 1941).

1944

Review of Judah Pilch, *Jewish Life in Our Times* (New York: Behrman's Jewish Book House, 1943), in *The Jewish Social Service Quarterly* (name changed in 1956 to *Journal of Jewish Communal Service*), Vol. 20, June 1944, pp. 157–159.

"The Jewish Community Council Idea," *The Jewish Social Service Quarterly* (name changed in 1956 to *Journal of Jewish Communal Service*), Vol. 20, June 1944, pp. 191–200. Reprinted in slightly shortened form in *Intermountain Jewish News* (Denver, Colorado), Vol. 28, July 12, 1945, p. 8 (full newspaper page), and in Robert Morris and Michael Freund (eds.), *Trends and Issues in Jewish Social Welfare in the United States, 1899–1958* (Philadelphia: Jewish Publication Society of America, 1966), pp. 425–437.

1951

Das Religiöse Leben der Juden in Amerika. New York: American Jewish Committee, 1951. Translated into English and published as *Jewish Religious Life in the United States* (New York: American Jewish Committee, 1953).

Review of Solomon M. Schwartz, *The Jews in the Soviet Union* (Syracuse: Syracuse University Press, 1951), in *The Washington Post,* August 19, 1951, p. B6.

1953

Review of Peter Mayer and others, *The Jews in the Soviet Satellites* (Syracuse: Syracuse University Press, 1953), in *The Washington Post,* November 1, 1953, p. B7.

"Three Hundred Years of Jewish Community Organization," *The Reconstructionist,* Vol. 19, October 23, 1953, pp. 8–22. Reprinted, under the title "The Changing American Jewish Community," in Eugene

Cohen (ed.), *American Jewry: The Tercentenary and After* (New York: The Reconstructionist Press, 1955), pp. 18–45.

1954

Review of Maurice Samuel, *Level Sunlight* (New York: Alfred A. Knopf, 1953), in *The Washington Post,* March 21, 1954, p. B7.

Review of Alfred Lilienthal, *What Price Israel* (Chicago: Henry Regnery, 1953), in *The Washington Post,* May 16, 1954, p. B7. Reprinted in *Congress Weekly* (American Jewish Congress), Vol. 21, July 19, 1954, pp. 17–18.

1955

Review of Bernard Postal and Lionel Koppman, *A Jewish Tourist's Guide to the United States* (Philadelphia: Jewish Publication Society of America, 1954), in *The Washington Post,* February 13, 1955, p. E6.

"The Scope of Jewish Community Relations," *The Jewish Social Service Quarterly* (name changed in 1956 to *Journal of Jewish Communal Service*), Vol. 31, Spring 1955, pp. 304–315. Excerpted in Ann G. Wolfe (ed.), *A Reader in Jewish Community Relations* (New York: Ktav, 1975), p. 3.

"Maimonides' Philosophy Today," *Judaism,* Vol. 4, Spring 1955, pp. 99–109.

"Maimonides' Legacy Endures 750 Years," *The Washington Post,* April 3, 1955, p. E7. Reprinted in *The National Jewish Monthly,* Vol. 69, June 1955, pp. 6, 26–27.

"Oversimplification of Motivations," *Jewish Social Studies,* Vol. 17, July 1955, pp. 195–199. (Comment on an article in the same issue by Norman Miller entitled "Changing Patterns of Leadership in the Jewish Community.")

1956

Review of Moshe Davis (ed.), *Israel: Its Role in Civilization* (New York: Harper and Row, 1956), in *The Middle East Journal,* Vol. 10, Spring 1956, pp. 328–329.

1957

Review of Maurice Samuel, *The Professor and the Fossil* (New York: Alfred A. Knopf, 1956), in *The Washington Post,* January 13, 1957, p. E6.

Review of Nathan Glazer, *American Judaism* (Chicago: University of Chicago Press, 1957), in *The Washington Post*, December 22, 1957, p. E6.

1958

"Jews and Judaism in the New Germany," *Jewish Heritage,* Vol. 1, Spring 1958, pp. 23–28.

Review of Moses Hess, *Rome and Jerusalem* (New York: Philosophical Library, 1958), in *The Middle East Journal,* Vol. 12, Spring 1958, pp. 220–221. (Hess's book was published in German in 1862; the first English version was published in 1918.)

"Racial Integration in the Nation's Capital," *Community Organization; Papers Presented at the National Conference on Social Work* (New York: Columbia University Press, 1958), pp. 92–100. Reprinted in adapted form, under the title "Integration in Washington," in *The Commonweal,* Vol. 68, August 15, 1958, pp. 493–496; also reprinted, with verbal changes and updating of statistics, in the *Journal of Intergroup Relations,* Vol. 1, September 1959, pp. 1–12.

Review of Jacob B. Minkin, *The World of Moses Maimonides, With Selections from His Writings* (New York: Thomas Yoseloff, 1957), in *Judaism,* Vol. 7, Fall 1958, pp. 374–376.

1959

"Toward Authentic Zionism," *The American Zionist,* Vol. 49, February 1959, p. 5.

"Rabbis and Jewish Community Relations Workers—Serving the Jewish Community," *Journal of Jewish Communal Service,* Vol. 36, Fall 1959, pp. 73–78. Reprinted with minor omissions in Graenum Berger (ed.), *The Turbulent Decades: Jewish Communal Services in America, 1958–78* (New York: Conference of Jewish Communal Service, 1980), pp. 1330–1337.

1960

"The Layman in Judaism—Yesterday and Tomorrow," *The Torch* (Philadelphia), Vol. 19, Spring 1960, pp. 3–10.

1961

"The Case for the Eichmann Trial: Its Legal and Moral Implications," *The Sunday Star* (Washington, D.C.), April 23, 1961, pp. B4–B5.

"The Legacy of Maimonides," *Judaica Post* (Detroit), September 1961, pp. 161–164.

1964

"Teaching the Tragic Events of Jewish History," *Jewish Education*, Vol. 34, Spring 1964, pp. 173–180.

Review of Erwin R. Goodenough, *Jewish Symbols in the Greco-Roman Period*, Vols. 9 to 11 of a 12-volume work (New York: Pantheon Books, 1964), in *The Middle East Journal*, Vol. 18, Autumn 1964, pp. 512–514.

1966

The Concept of Human Nature: A Philosophical Analysis of the Concept of Human Nature in the Writings of G. W. Allport, S. E. Asch, Erich Fromm, A. H. Maslow, and C. R. Rogers. Doctoral dissertation, unpublished. 613 typewritten pages.

1967

S. Y. Agnon, "The Tale of the Scribe," translated from the Hebrew by Isaac Franck, in *Midstream*, Vol. 13, February 1967, pp. 3–11. Reprinted in Nachum Glatzer (ed.), *Twenty-One Stories* (New York: Schocken Books, 1976), pp. 7–25.

1968

"Hymen Goldman: A Personal Tribute," *The Record* (Jewish Historical Society of Greater Washington), Vol. 3, March 1968, pp. 3–4.

"The Validity of Other Religions from the Point of View of Judaism," in *The Validity Which Each of the World Religions Accords to Other Religions* (Washington: First Conference on Interreligious Understanding, 1968), pp. 32–39.

"The Challenge to Jewish Purposes of Communal Agencies in the Light of Evolving Public Policies and Trends," *Journal of Jewish Communal Service*, Vol. 45, Fall 1968, pp. 17–25. Reprinted with minor changes in Graenum Berger (ed.), *The Turbulent Decades: Jewish Communal Servic-*

es in America, 1958–78 (New York: Conference of Jewish Communal Service, 1980), pp. 572–586; and excerpted in Ann G. Wolfe (ed.), *A Reader in Jewish Community Relations* (New York: Ktav, 1975), p. 232.

1969

"Anti-Semitism Now," *Jewish Spectator*, Vol. 34, December 1969, pp. 12–14. Summarized, under the title "American Jewry Rediscovers Anti-Semitism," in *Jewish Digest*, Vol. 16, November 1970, pp. 71–74.

1970

Review of Frank Riessman, *Strategies Against Poverty* (New York: Random House, 1969), in *Journal of Jewish Communal Service*, Vol. 47, Fall 1970, pp. 97–99.

1971–1973

Editor of *Under-Cover*, March 31, 1971–February 2, 1973 (29 issues), published by the Soviet Jewry Committee of the Jewish Community Council of Greater Washington.

1973

The Concept of Freedom in Jewish Tradition (Philadelphia: Gratz College, 1973; Annual Sol Feinstone Lecture). Reprinted with minor changes in *Jewish Spectator*, Vol. 40, Summer 1975, pp. 26–32.

1974

"What Is New in the 'New Anti-Semitism'?," an essay review of Arnold Forster and Benjamin R. Epstein, *The New Anti-Semitism* (New York: McGraw-Hill, 1974), in *Journal of Jewish Communal Service*, Vol. 51, Fall 1974, pp. 102–108.

1975

Five Critics of the Freudian Theory of Human Nature. Unpublished. 295 typewritten pages.

1976

"The American Jewish Experience," *Judaism*, Vol. 22, March 1976, pp. 7–18.

"American Jewry Today," *Midstream*, Vol. 22, March 1976, pp. 7–18. Translated into Hebrew and published in *Tsefutsot Israel* (Jerusalem), Vol. 14, April–June 1976, pp. 11–28. Summarized, under the title "The Jewish Influence in American Culture," in *Jewish Digest*, Vol. 22, October 1976, pp. 62–68.

1979

"Can Diaspora Judaism Survive?," *Conservative Judaism*, Vol. 32, Winter 1979, pp. 58–64.

1980

"Foreword" and "Jewish Biomedical Ethics in a Non-Jewish World: Reflections on the Conference," in Isaac Franck (ed.), *Biomedical Ethics in Perspective of Jewish Teaching and Tradition: Proceedings of an Academic Conference, November 13, 1977* (Washington: College of Jewish Studies of Greater Washington, 1980; reprinted 1982), pp. i and 50–57.

1982

"Moral Dilemmas Which Are Acute Within a Religious Tradition," in *Proceedings of a Conference on Genetic Decision Making and Pastoral Care* (Washington: Georgetown University School of Medicine, 1982), pp. 44–45. Reprinted with minor changes in *Hospital Practice*, Vol. 18, July 1983, pp. 192–196.

1983

"Understanding Jewish Biomedical Ethics: Reflections on the Papers," in Isaac Franck (guest editor), *The Journal of Medicine and Philosophy* (issue on medical ethics from the Jewish perspective), Vol. 8, August 1983, pp. 207–215.

"Jewish Religious Law as a Model of the Patient-Physician Relationship: Comment on Professor Brody's Essay," in Earl Shelp (ed.), *The Clinical Encounter* (Dordrecht/Boston: Reidel Publishing Co., 1983), pp. 141–146.

1984

Freud on Human Nature: Attacked and Defended. Unpublished. 229 typewritten pages.

1987

Comment on David M. Hartman and Elliott Yagood, "God, Philosophy and Halakhah in Maimonides' Approach to Judaism," in George F. McLean and Hugo Meynell (eds.), *Person and God* (Lanham, Maryland: University Press of America, scheduled for publication in 1988), pp. 181–189.